AUGMENTED REALITY

DEVELOPMENT WITH UNITY

AUGMENTED REALITY
DEVELOPMENT WITH UNITY

INDIKA WIJESOORIYA

MERCURY LEARNING AND INFORMATION
Boston, Massachusetts

Publisher: David Pallai
MERCURY LEARNING AND INFORMATION
121 High Street, 3rd Floor
Boston, MA 02110
info@merclearning.com
www.merclearning.com
800-232-0223

I. Wijesooriya. *Augmented Reality Development with Unity.*
ISBN: 978-1-50152-258-1

Library of Congress Control Number: 2024938179

242526321 This book is printed on acid-free paper in the United States of America.

To

My beloved wife, Thilini

&

My mother, Swarna

CONTENTS

PREFACE

Augmented Reality (AR) has been a key component of immersive technologies in the past decade. With the entrance of web3 and related technologies, AR has become a key player in providing extended user experiences for people around the world. Whether it is education, training, manufacturing, healthcare or military, AR can help people augment and enhance the core components related to them. One of the major challenges for an enthusiast to begin development of AR applications is the knowledge of the many tools available in the current context.

This book will introduce AR, its user cases and history to better understand its power and utility. The second part of this book will focus on the available tools and technologies for developing AR applications. Later, the book will introduce the Unity 3D engine, fundamentals of C# programming with Unity, vector mathematics, implementing AR applications with Unity, followed by best practices in creating AR applications.

Using this book, readers will have a comprehensive knowledge for bringing an idea into an augmented reality application, and for using C# and the Unity 3D engine to design and develop a prototype, or a finished application.

Chapter 1: Getting Started with Augmented Reality

In this chapter, we will learn about the key concepts of AR including the technology behind AR applications and the principles of content recognition. It is important to review the underlying technology to better understand AR's behavior. It also provides a brief history of AR and the existing and future use cases of the technology.

Chapter 2: Visualizing the AR Environment and Its Components

In this chapter, we will discuss the placement of objects in a virtual world and how these are mapped in order to generate the illusion of an augmented reality. We show how various Augmented Reality setups perform and, to better understand these principles, basic mathematical theories are discussed.

Chapter 3: Exploring Tools and Development Platforms

This chapter provides an in-depth introduction to the tools and technologies available for building AR applications and experiences, along with their respective platforms. We compare the pros and cons of each tool and discuss various use cases to determine which platform and tools are best suited for each scenario.

Chapter 4: Up and Running with Unity 3D

In this chapter, we utilize the Unity3D engine as our primary development tool for the remainder of the book. We cover the steps for installing the necessary tools and setting up your computer for development. Additionally, we will build a 3D scene in Unity3D, providing an overview of the Unity engine, its tools, and an introduction to 3D concepts essential for creating AR applications in future chapters. We also delve into the key components of Unity, exploring the structure of GameObjects, their components, and the main elements within Unity

Chapter 5: Creating Your First Custom Component

Here, we introduce C# with Unity by creating our first custom component. We guide you through the process of creating a base script, understanding the basic components of a C# script, and how C# script execution works. By the end of the chapter, we will have created a simple clock using the concepts learned.

Chapter 6: Refreshing C# Concepts with Unity

In this chapter, we explore C# programming to build functionality within Unity. We will develop an endless top-down shooting game targeted at mobile devices, learning C# concepts, and utilizing key Unity components relevant to building interactive applications.

Chapter 7: Trying Out First 3D Mobile App Development

During this chapter, we continue developing the top-down shooter game and install the application on mobile devices. We cover the requirements for both Android and iOS platforms, detailing how to set up project settings accordingly. Additionally, we explore various debugging methods for running your app on a device.

Chapter 8: Building Marker-based AR Apps with Vuforia

This chapter focuses on building an Augmented Reality treasure hunt game using the Vuforia AR SDK. We introduce marker-based tracking with Vuforia, its key capabilities, and its use of marker-based tracking. We walk through creating a Vuforia account, registering the application, configuring project trackers via the Vuforia portal, downloading, and installing the SDK in Unity, and testing with a PC webcam.

Chapter 9: Developing Marker-based Dynamic AR Apps

In this chapter, we extend the use of marker-based AR to dynamic application design. We will build two AR applications: a sample AR machine inspection tool and a dynamic AR billboard that changes without app updates. For the inspection tool, we use a marker system to identify different objects without significantly altering the marker graphic. For the dynamic billboard, we host files in the cloud to create a dynamic AR app that can update content and markers without needing app updates.

Chapter 10: Marker-less AR Apps with ARKit and ARCore

We will build multiple mini-projects covering the AR detection modes provided by ARKit and ARCore, compatible with iPhones, iPads, and Android devices. We will learn the similarities between both platforms and use AR Foundation as a cross-platform method for building AR apps.

Chapter 11: World Scale AR App with Niantic Lightship

This chapter focuses on developing mini-projects using the Niantic Lightship SDK to create world-scale AR applications that interact with environmental obstacles, including collision and occlusion. The first project involves building a simple AR throwing experience, while the second project covers scanning an environment to create custom area-based AR applications.

Chapter 12: Best Practices in Augmented Reality Application Design

We discuss various best practices in AR application design and development, categorized into design-based practices, development practices, and provide sample project snippets illustrating these best practices.

Chapter 13: AR App Performance Optimization

In this chapter, we learn about key performance metrics and optimization techniques to enhance AR applications, reducing resource requirements. We identify essential actions to address performance-related challenges in your app.

Companion files with code samples and color figures from the book are available for downloading by writing to info@merclearning.com.

ACKNOWLEDGMENTS

I would like to express my deepest gratitude to my wife, Thilini, whose unwavering encouragement and unconditional support have been instrumental in bringing this book to fruition. Her belief in me and constant motivation were an invaluable source of inspiration throughout this journey. I extend my heartfelt thanks to Chamira Jayasinghe, CEO of Arimac, for opening my eyes to the vast world of immersive technology. His guidance and mentorship have played a pivotal role in shaping my career and fueling my passion for AR development.

I would like to extend my appreciation to Lou, Mike, and Jerry from Circuit Stream. Their support and guidance have helped me discover my passion for teaching and sharing knowledge with others. Their expertise and collaboration have been instrumental in shaping the content of this book. I would also like to acknowledge Dejan, my dear friend, for his unwavering motivation and continuous support. His belief in my abilities has been a driving force throughout this writing process. I am grateful to Mana Saei and Leena Prasad for their insightful reviews and valuable comments on the manuscript. Their expertise and constructive feedback have immensely contributed to the quality of this book.

Finally, I would like to express my sincere appreciation to all the readers and supporters of this book. Your interest and enthusiasm for augmented reality development have been the driving force behind my commitment to sharing knowledge and empowering others in this exciting field. Thank you for joining me on this journey.

1

GETTING STARTED WITH AUGMENTED REALITY

INTRODUCTION

Before building *augmented reality* (AR) applications, it is important to understand what AR is and how hardware and software technology are combined to present an AR application to the end user. The second decade of the 21st century can be seen as a pivotal period for immersive technology, mainly AR and virtual reality. One of the main reasons for the exponential growth in the AR field can be the escalated CPU power of mobile smartphones. The processing power required to perform real-time image processing calculations while estimating virtual element poses was previously unavailable in mobile devices. Therefore, technology did not have a greater reach toward the masses.

A practical definition for AR can be as follows: "AR is a view of the real physical world in which some elements are computer generated and graphically enhanced, allowing extended capabilities in terms of input and output."

The definition seems unrealistic, but the motivation for AR has been there for decades through science fiction stories. Almost a century ago, the golden age of comics introduced many superheroes and characters with superhuman and augmented abilities, who were placed in scenarios where they used AR technologies as in science fiction. *Holograms* have been one of the key elements to demonstrate advanced technologies within the stories. These holograms and augmented elements in the physical world had many things in common, such as interactivity with hands or voice, feedback from the elements with animations, showing information with text or sound effects, and the flexibility to spawn them anywhere, regardless of the context. Even though humans are not as advanced as predicted in the movies, there is still rapid development in research and development to invent such concepts.

STRUCTURE

This chapter covers the following topics:

- AR implementation and application
- History of AR
- AR across the world
- AR enabling technologies
- Machine learning and artificial intelligence

OBJECTIVES

By the end of this chapter, it will be clear that AR was not invented during the last decade but is a topic with a history of many decades. The chapter will also explain the fundamental technologies used to create AR applications and the use cases of AR in different industries.

AR IMPLEMENTATION AND APPLICATION

Consider a holographic AR implementation that may be implemented in the future. The technology behind the implementation must first capture and identify the context. There may be a hardware component with built-in sensors to recognize people, objects, and planes, as well as the world around them.

Once the context has been captured, the collected data must be converted into a virtual environment so that a virtual object can be placed on top of it. This conversion may be done using computer algorithms placed within the holographic device. This process can also be identified as the transformation layer.

The final steps of the implementation may include a presentation layer, which consists of all the audio and visual feedback, interactions, logic, and so on. The users of the holographic device may use this presentation layer to generate AR content. The final layer would be the output layer, which generates the accumulated set of components so that the user can see the final implementation. In a hologram, this is the final holographic output. In 2023, there is still a long way to go and years of research and development to implement a nonblocking output layer for a real hologram. Figure 1.1 represents the conceptual representation of a holographic AR implementation:

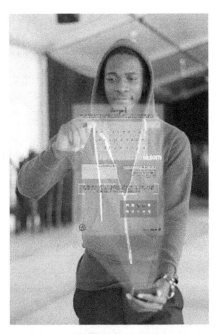

FIGURE 1.1 Conceptual representation of a hologram.
Source: *https://pixabay.com/photos/science-hologram-artificial-fiction-4642115/.*

Currently, existing AR systems are very advanced but not yet able to visualize the AR content without another screen or a wearable in between the actual and virtual worlds. Consider a wearable AR device as an example. Such a device contains a camera and other sensors at the front to capture the world around it and uses software to recognize the context. Like the hologram example in Figure 1.1, objects can be placed in the virtual environment generated within the presentation layer. Finally, the generated 3D content will render on the wearable screen, mapping to the physical world that can be seen through the glass.

A smartphone-based AR application would be the same, except that the final output layer would be through the mobile screen, having the camera input as the background. In these AR applications, the camera input must be captured and rendered inside the 3D space behind the 3D models, giving an illusion of how the 3D models are placed in the real-world context. Figure 1.2 illustrates the structure of an AR application:

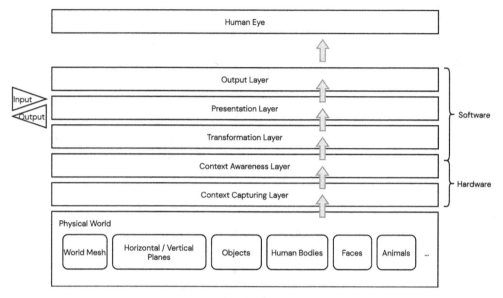

FIGURE 1.2 Structure of an AR application.

HISTORY OF AR

In order to understand current AR development, it is better to know the brief history of AR and where everything started.

1968—The Sword of Damocles

The first implementation of AR that can be found in the history books is not through a computer screen but a prototype head-mounted display. Ivan Sutherland, an American computer scientist and a widely known computer graphics expert, created the first head-mounted display in 1968, known as *The Sword of Damocles*. The fundamental nature of such a device was to create an illusion on a transparent display, depending on a concept known as the *kinetic depth effect*.

The display was fixed to the ceiling of a room and could be worn by the user. The linkage in the ceiling measured the pose of the head and transferred that data to the computer program. A miniature cathode ray tube attached to the side of the display projected the image onto the eyeglass display optics, changing the orientation of the image based on the movement of the head. The research paper on this implementation can be obtained within the chapter titled "A Head-Mounted Three-Dimensional Display" of the *Fall Joint Computer Conference Journal* in 1968. Figure 1.3 features the display:

FIGURE 1.3 The first head-mounted display and how a 3D object can be seen through it.
Source: *Fall Joint Computer Conference Journal*, 1968.

1975—Videoplace by Myron Krueger

Another implementation of artificial reality, even though it is not directly an example of AR, can be seen through one of the first augmented interactive applications, known as *Videoplace*. The idea behind the application is to use external sensors and capture context and interactivity without the use of goggles, buttons, gloves, or anything attached to the user.

The application used a camera to capture the user in front of a projector screen in front of the person. The captured video is transmitted to a computer, which performs image processing to generate a silhouette of the person with an additional interactive element as a separate layer. The layers are generated in different flat colors to differentiate each. The processed final image is then projected to the same projection screen using a back projector. This does not completely fulfill the requirements of AR, but it can be recognized as a step toward artificial reality and contained image-recognition algorithms. Figure 1.4 is an illustration of the Videoplace system:

FIGURE 1.4 Structure of the Videoplace system.

1999—AR Toolkit

Ever since the first AR implementations, technology has improved to move away from hardware-only solutions to programmable software solutions. One of the major implementations of such solutions is the AR Toolkit, which is a library that was developed in 1999 by Hirokazu Kato of the Nara Institute of Science and Technology.

AR Toolkit was known as the world's first mobile AR software development toolkit was incorporated after it, and a version was released to the public. The library was used in early OS-based smartphone devices such as Symbian around 2005, all the way to iOS and Android during the 2010 era.

Early versions of the AR Toolkit focused on predefined physical AR trackers (also known as *fiducial markers*) to recognize the planes and visualize virtual 3D objects following the orientation of the trackers. Later versions of the AR Toolkit introduced *natural feature tracking*, which allowed developers to train natural features of colorful images rather than using predefined AR trackers.

Figure 1.5 illustrates an AR Toolkit fiducial tracker, which is an example of an AR target:

FIGURE 1.5 Example of an AR target (AR Toolkit fiducial tracker).

More information on AR Toolkit can be found at the following link:

http://www.hitl.washington.edu/artoolkit.html

AR over the Years

Ever since the development of the AR Toolkit, many developers and organizations have stepped into the field of research and development of AR software development kits and supportive hardware. This was followed by the development of smartphone devices and their easy accessibility, which encouraged engineers and developers to focus more on handheld devices. Early software-based AR applications leveraged the power of desktop computers and attached Web cameras to generate 3D models using magazine covers as image targets. A magazine advertisement done for *Mini* in 2008 is an example of one of the first AR implementations as a commercial use case. See the following link:

https://www.youtube.com/watch?v=HTYeuo6pIjY

Esquire magazine worked with Hollywood actor Robert Downey Jr. to color their magazine with AR. See the following link:

https://www.youtube.com/watch?v=wp2z36kKn0s

The introduction of Google Glass in 2014 has become one of the key events in the history of AR. It was the first AR-inspired wearable device targeted at consumers. From 2010 to 2015, many software-based development kits and libraries were developed, targeting mainly mobile operating systems. Qualcomm Vuforia, AR Toolkit open source, MetaIO (acquired by Apple to develop its current AR software development kit, ARKit), Wikitude, and ARMedia are some of the early adaptors of AR in the domain of smart hand-held devices.

In 2016, Microsoft joined the AR market by introducing the HoloLens, which is the world's first wearable AR tracking and meshing device, as can be seen in Figure 1.6:

FIGURE 1.6 Microsoft HoloLens.
Source: Kai Kowalewski Creative Commons BY-SA 4.0,
https://creativecommons.org/licenses/by-sa/4.0, via Wikimedia Commons.

Apple released its native AR software development kit (SDK), known as ARKit, and Google started working on a hardware–software implementation known as Google Tango. The project was discontinued and later announced again as a complete software-based implementation known as ARCore. Google also invested in a wearable AR device, Magic Leap, an alternative to Microsoft HoloLens.

The later chapters of this book will dive into some of the most popular AR development tools currently available to develop AR applications in cross-platform devices.

AR ACROSS THE WORLD

In order to build AR applications, it is better to research and understand the use cases of AR in various disciplines. Emerging technologies during the last couple of decades have been used in various applications outside the field of computer science. This section explores some of the use cases of AR currently.

AR in Entertainment

Many use cases of AR that are consumer-based circle around entertainment. In 2016, Niantic released its widely popular location-based game Pokémon Go. Niantic had been working with location-based games such as Ingress before stepping into AR.

Pokémon Go innovatively implemented the *catching a Pokémon using a pokéball* interaction using an AR interface within the game. This was a major boost for AR technology as more people could experience AR for the first time.

With the release of Pokémon Go and smartphones having native AR capabilities, many games were developed that used AR as the backbone. Minecraft World, Harry Potter Wizards Unite, and Jurassic World Alive are some of the popular games that have been released since then. Stepping out of the mass outreach of AR games, the technology has also been used in various physical activations and live events. Video-based AR technologies such as Vizrt and Wtvision have taken over the world, offering real-time AR over broadcast. Various augmented content is appearing on news programs, sports events, and other live shows to make the shows more interesting through television. Vizrt technologies have been used in thousands of TV events around the world, mainly covering sports events and news. Some of their customers include Eurovision, ausbiz, Mediacorp in Singapore, CNN-NEWS18, Al-Jazeera documentaries, and many more.

Figure 1.7 features the use of AR in a museum:

FIGURE 1.7 AR at Museu de Mataró linking to Catalan.
Source: Kippelboy, CC BY-SA 3.0, *https://creativecommons.org/licenses/by-sa/3.0>, via Wikimedia Commons*.

AR has been used in art galleries and museums around the world. In 2021, the Muséum National d'Histoire Naturelle in Paris launched an AR experience. The experience was called REVIRE and allowed visitors to hire a Microsoft HoloLens and interact with digital animals throughout the museum. The National Museum of Singapore has an AR installation called *Story of the Forest*. An AR installation known as ReBlink is available at the Art Gallery of Ontario, Toronto, enhancing the art experience of the artwork within the gallery. Google has a virtual museum with AR capabilities, allowing users to visit an AR gallery virtually. It can be found at *https://artsandculture.google. com/project/ar*. These are just a fraction of the thousands of AR installations all around the world.

Having explored some of the existing AR-related use cases in the world and thinking of the future, it is apparent that AR can replace many entertainment channels such as television, billboards, and live events. Think of an AR wearable device that can turn a living room into a stadium with live matches running on the coffee table. Imagine how a wall can be converted to a large cinema screen where one can watch the latest movies without stepping out of the room. The possibilities of AR in the entertainment world are endless, provided the correct tools and technologies.

AR in Manufacturing and Logistics

Google Glass has had many challenges in reaching the consumer market, even though it is the first ever widely announced wearable display device. The device has a camera mounted in front, and there is no indication to the outside world whether the user is capturing the surroundings and streaming a video to a third party. This caused many conflicts with regard to security and privacy. Ultimately, Google discontinued the product to the public as a consumer device and revived it to be used in enterprise applications, mainly focusing on manufacturing, logistics, and anything that requires hands-free work but with access to additional information. Currently, Google Glass provides real-time collaboration, access to training visualizations, and voice input, enhancing the capabilities of factory workers. Even though it is not a completely AR-enabled device, it has been used by many larger organizations across the world, including DHL, Schenker, Samsung, and Volkswagen.

Mainly, AR has been used in factories for maintenance assistance, machine operation training, and data visualization in real time for machinery data retrieval and preventive maintenance. Dynamic arrangement of manufacturing facilities leverages AR for navigation within the factories. Imagine a logistics facility that rearranges the inside of the facility rapidly based on dynamic adaptations. This may allow the facility to change the navigation system along with any rearrangements needed. This can be easily realized by setting up navigation in AR that can instantly replace the data points. Imagine a wearable within a factory that allows machine supervisors to just look at the machine and visualize its sensory and machinery data in real time next to the machine itself. This reduces the overhead time the teams spend searching through data logs through a separate interface matching the data to the machines. Imagine a 3D machine or vehicle construction that can be previewed through AR in a collaborative environment. This allows the designers and engineers working together to visualize the elements on a real-life scale and thus reduces the time required to make foam models of the machine. There are limitless possibilities where AR can be beneficial in manufacturing.

Real Estate

In 2020, Unity, a leading 3D development engine, teamed up with Autodesk Revit, a specialist in building information modeling (BIM), to create a tool known as Unity Reflect. This allowed creators to link BIM model data to a 3D environment in real time. Unity, known for AR, used the same links to visualize 3D models of buildings and architecture in real time in an AR environment. A great use case of this turned out to allow the client to visualize their building design exactly on the building site as a 1:1 scale in AR while the architects change the model data in real time according to the client's needs.

Similarly, many real estate agencies use AR to enhance the customer experience in buying real estate by providing AR virtual tours. Imagine an application allowing people to go to real estate locations and visualize the price charts and how different buildings appear without spending for concept creators. Imagine, as a real estate agency, customers being able to freely walk around within any available houses with the AR app providing additional information based on their needs. Using AR technologies, the realtors get a competitive advantage in providing more unique personalized experiences to their customers.

Health

Imagine visualizing a 3D reconstruction of the bone structure of a patient while walking around the subject instead of taking multiple X-ray images. AR can allow that to happen, provided the hardware and software required to obtain scan data of a patient are available. AR is a great alternative to current healthcare imaging solutions. Many of the imaging output channels can be replaced by a simple AR wearable that can use its surroundings to import as many 3D visualizations of the environment as possible. Imagine a surgeon performing surgery and being able to visualize a patient's vital data on top of the patient's body parts. The surgery can be done faster, reducing the time required for the professionals to look away from the patient. Also, such use cases reduce surgeon errors due to misreading information.

AR can also be used in medical training. Instead of using custom-made physical dummies for health-related simulations, AR glasses can be used to quickly change training scenarios for the trainees to perform interactions and get trained more efficiently.

Education

As suggested in the previous subsections, training can be offered in any competency. It can be the health industry, manufacturing, logistics, or a common school classroom. Schools invest heavily in chemical and physics laboratories, not only by building new labs but also by maintaining them. Imagine an enhanced school physics laboratory where the students can create AR-based tabletop physical simulations while changing the parameters of the objects dynamically. This allows the students to learn the activities by trying out limitless scenarios without changing any physical object in the lab. Imagine a wearable AR headset that can convert a living room into a classroom. Microsoft HoloLens provides shared experiences with the help of *spatial anchors* allowing people to connect, share, and learn the same experience. Science books make use of marker-based AR to allow the experiments to be viewed outside the book by using a mobile application. The ability to move around freely to observe 3D constructions enables student engagement to learn by doing rather than by memorizing.

Marketing and Retail

One widely used AR application can be found within marketing and retail use cases of AR. IKEA Place is a great initiative done by the company to allow people to add furniture to their own space to visualize whether the piece of furniture fits properly. Dulux has built an AR app to scan any wall and immediately change the color to any available color it offers. There are many marketing-enabling AR apps currently available, such as Blippar, 8th Wall (acquired by Niantic), Zappar, and Augment, which allow companies to use their platforms as authoring tools to build content for their marketing campaigns. Children's cereal producers use AR apps to extend their cereal boxes for children to collect and play custom-made games for rewards. E-commerce sites make use of AR product viewers to spawn 3D models of products into a user's space for visualizing them on a real-life scale. Companies like Nike and Adidas use the power of AI and AR and have built apps such as Wannakicks and Wyking AR to visualize shoes directly attached to a customer's feet. Product visualization, product configurators, and marketing engagement activities have become key entry points for AR in retail. Unlike decades ago, the spectrum of possibilities has expanded with the introduction of AR. It not only provides the *wow factor* to customers but also creates unforgettable memories in their minds about the products and services that have been marketed with AR. Many businesses have been leveraging the use of AR, providing marketing and retail solutions around AR to bigger companies around the world. Leading service-oriented companies, such as Accenture and Volume Global, have already filled their portfolios with AR case studies, and there is more to come.

Any readers of this book who hope to provide services with AR solutions can think of the problems that are faced in different disciplines across the world and evaluate how those problems can be solved using AR. However, there are many AR use cases that create problems rather than offering solutions. Therefore, it is vital to understand the requirements and measure the importance of AR in replacing existing workflows. Considering the costs, maintainability, and usefulness of AR technology, any industry can leverage it for greater savings, higher profits, and increased engagement.

AR ENABLING TECHNOLOGIES

AR relies heavily on computer vision. The use of additional data, such as depth sensing for meshing, catalyzes the accuracy of the trackers. Ever since the use of machine learning and AI, the accuracy of target detection and tracking and the extended capabilities of AR have expanded. The following section explores some of the computer vision techniques that enable AR.

Image Recognition and Tracking

In order to enable AR in a predefined target image (for example, a poster, magazine cover, photo, QR code, and so on), the features of the image must be matched and recognized. This process is known as *feature detection and matching*. Once the image has been detected, the data can be used to track the image with its movement with respect to the position of the camera. These algorithms are used not only for AR but in many applications. Robot navigation systems, image retrieval, object tracking, motion detection, and segmentation are some of the other applications of feature detection and matching. A feature of an image can be recognized as a piece of information in the image that can be used by the computer program to recognize the image. As an example, the points and edges of an image can be used as features of the image. The challenge of image detection is to detect and capture the features, collect information about the appearance around the feature point, and match similar features with a known feature distribution set. These feature points are identified by various algorithms based on either the brightness of the image or the boundary/edge details of the image.

A feature recognition algorithm gets an image as an input and outputs a series of vectors. The output of an image would be a series of encoded data points in a machine-understandable format. This is known as a *feature descriptor*. The information that is generated from an image is supposed to be independent of the orientation and the transformation of the image. Therefore, the output data remains the same regardless of the movement of the image. This provides one of the fundamental abilities of AR, which is the ability to track a detected image based on the image features by recognizing and tracking the image detected. Figure 1.8 illustrates a colored poster and how its transformed feature points are aligned together:

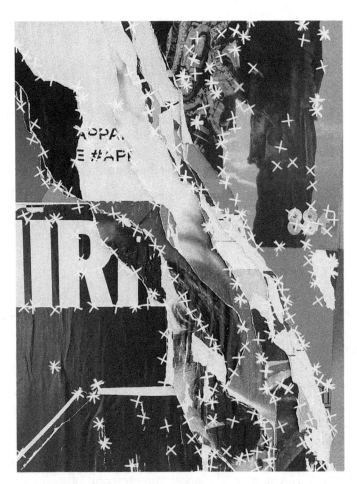

FIGURE 1.8 Features of an image (features are marked with x).

The neighborhood around a feature point is known as a local *descriptor*, which resembles the appearance of an area around its feature point. The basic flow of feature detection and matching can be listed as follows:

- Use image processing methods to detect certain points. They can be based on the contrast of the image, edge detection, and so on.
- Capture the information around the detected feature point.
- Generate a local descriptor, an encoded vector that describes the region around the feature point.
- Match the local descriptors based on another factor, such as the time, predefined descriptor, and so on.

Following are the image processing algorithms that support feature detection and tracking:

- Harris corner detector
- Scale invariant feature transform (SIFT)
- Speeded-up robust feature (SURF)
- Binary robust independent elementary features (BRIEF)
- Features from accelerated segment test (FAST)
- Oriented FAST and rotated BRIEF (ORB)
- Binary robust invariant scalable key points (BRISK)

OpenCV is a library of computer vision algorithms that is under Apache open-source license. In-depth details of all the listed algorithms can be read via OpenCV documentation at *https://docs.opencv.org/*.

Simultaneous Localization and Mapping

Simultaneous localization and mapping (SLAM) has been an integral part of not only AR but of many research areas in the engineering field, such as robotics. The basic idea of SLAM is to use the cameras and other sensors of the computational device to generate a virtual map of the surroundings. Once the map has been generated, the information is then fed into its own movement system, where it can localize itself within the virtual map.

SLAM can be achieved in many ways depending on the device. For robots, it uses cameras, LiDAR sensors, motion, and other sensors to map the virtual world. Some systems use beacons placed around the world to help the device map the environment more accurately. For mobile AR, however, it is only the camera, the gyroscope, the accelerometer, and other movement-based sensors that can be used to map the environment.

For example, consider a mobile AR solution that works on top of a SLAM integration. The ultimate goal is to capture the outside world and convert it into a map. The flow of the process can be listed as follows:

- Use the camera of the device to capture the image and the gyroscope and the accelerometer to capture the pose and the movement vectors of the device.
- Extract the features based on the input data. As described in the image processing section, a feature descriptor is used to convert the image data to vector data, such as key points and neighborhood data.
- Association of data is done to neglect the features that have been captured before. This is a repetitive process. Therefore, the features that were captured in one frame (in one iteration) should be passed to the other frame. Instead of duplication, similar data points must be recognized. This is also known as a *loop closure*.
- The captured data are used to determine the movement of all the feature points and transferred to map construction. Based on the algorithm, the generated map will be a point cloud or a sparse reconstruction based on the distribution of the feature points. Figure 1.9 illustrates how feature detection and tracking is done:

FIGURE 1.9 Feature detection and tracking.

▥ The mapped data are used again with the pose of the capturing device to map its position with respect to the generated virtual space. This is known as a *SLAM estimate*, as can be seen in Figure 1.10:

FIGURE 1.10 Example of a SLAM estimate.
Source: Martin Holzkothen, Michael Korn, CC BY 3.0,
https://creativecommons.org/licenses/by/3.0, via Wikimedia Commons)

In AR, SLAM is mainly used for environment detection where there are no predefined trackers, such as in images, posters, or QR codes to enable tracking. The first frames captured through the camera are used to generate the feature vectors in real time, and the same are used over time to convert the mapped point data to planes and obstacles.

Recent AR frameworks not only capture still images or an unknown environment but also faces, body parts, barcode data, textual data on billboards, and many more. Based on the processing power required just for SLAM and feature descriptors, heading for more traditional image processing may result in unnecessary processing overhead. Therefore, machine learning and artificial intelligence are used to enhance the capabilities of AR.

MACHINE LEARNING AND ARTIFICIAL INTELLIGENCE

Machine learning has become one of the key factors in the growth of artificial intelligence throughout recent years. Machine learning algorithms have been used in many use cases, such as object recognition, natural language processing, predictive analytics, and automated processing of many tasks that span across multiple disciplines.

AR too has seen an enhancement with the integration of machine learning. The concept of machine learning for computer vision is as follows:

- Collection of data samples
- Training data using the collected samples
- Generation of the machine learning model
- Testing the generated model
- Use in implementation

Consider an AR solution that tracks the change in color of human hair while showing 3D sunglasses over the eyes. Machine learning models can be used to detect the face and the pose of the face, generating a face feature model to be modified in a 3D environment. At the same time, another machine learning algorithm will be extracting the image features to detect only the hair portion changing color.

There are multiple machine learning algorithms that are available within OpenCV. An in-depth analysis of these algorithms can be learned through the following link: *https://docs.opencv.org/4.x/dc/dd6/ml_intro.html.*

Deep learning is a type of machine learning that works by mimicking a human brain solving problems. Unlike standard machine learning algorithms, deep learning uses artificial neural networks for representation learning and predictive modeling.

Deep learning algorithms in computer vision can be used not just for recognition but for image generation as well. *Generative adversarial networks (GANs)* are widely used in generating images based on training data and a generator. There are AR applications that can capture a human face for direct conversion to an animated character in real time. These algorithms use modified versions of GANs to generate a new image based on the training set and a generator and replace the content from the original camera.

Currently, most of the AR development kit providers make use of the technologies discussed in this chapter. Image descriptors are used for marker training for later recognition and can be used directly in AR applications that can track predefined targets. SLAM, or at least modified or enhanced versions, has been used by many marker-less AR SDK developers such as Apple, Android, and Microsoft. The use of machine learning and AI works as a catalyst to provide unique and enhanced AR experiences to the user.

In the next chapter of this book, the difference between marker-based and marker-less AR will be discussed.

CONCLUSION

This chapter discussed how people looked at AR from a technical point of view and the research done around the technologies related to AR, such as image processing and machine learning–related recognition technologies. Even after decades, technology is still in its early stages despite increasing exponentially due to the growth of supporting technologies. The chapter also looked at the history of AR, use cases, and potential use cases of AR in different industries that sum up the objectives of AR.

From the next chapter onward, the aim is to dive deeper into the principles behind AR applications, the tools available for building AR apps, and the steps of building and deploying AR apps with different interaction methods.

KEY POINTS

- AR technologies are built on top of image recognition.
- Image recognition uses different mathematical algorithms to extract images to data that computers can process, which are known as *descriptors*.
- Real-time area recognition technologies use cameras and other sensors to capture and determine position with respect to the environment. This is known as SLAM.
- Machine learning technologies are used to extend tracking accuracy and implement additional features.

QUESTIONS

1. What was The Sword of Damocles in the context of AR?

    a. A famous sword used in an AR-based video game

    b. The first-ever AR headset prototype developed by Ivan Sutherland

c. A mythical weapon depicted in an AR-themed movie

d. An AR app used to teach sword-fighting techniques

2. Who developed the AR Toolkit, a popular open-source software library for creating AR applications?

a. Richard Feynman

b. Hirokazu Kato

c. Alan Turing

d. Grace Hopper

3. What does SLAM stand for in the context of AR and robotics?

a. Simultaneous localization and mapping

b. Sensory light and motion

c. Spatial localization and measurement

d. Systematic learning and management

4. Which of the following is an example of how AI is used in AR applications?

a. Creating 3D models from physical objects in real time

b. Enabling seamless integration of AR content on mobile devices

c. Providing AR glasses with extended battery life

d. Generating holographic displays without the need for any hardware

Answers appear in the appendix.

VISUALIZING THE AR ENVIRONMENT AND COMPONENTS

INTRODUCTION

The previous chapter discussed what makes augmented reality (AR) a reality and how AR is being used in different industries. This chapter will step a bit further into the concepts of 3D and the basics of the mathematics that are required for building applications that make use of 3D virtual spaces. This chapter can be considered the basic building block of any computer graphics application. The intention is a better understanding of how a virtual world is generated, how virtual objects are placed in such a world, and how real input is converted into a virtual interaction.

In order to understand some of the concepts discussed during this chapter, it is first necessary to take a step back and go through the basics of the mathematics involved, as the related terminology will be helpful in the long run.

STRUCTURE

This chapter covers the following topics:

- Basics of mathematics for 3D visualization
- Understanding the 3D environment
- Vector mathematics
- Basic trigonometry
- Understanding different spaces

- Context recognition concepts
- Placement of virtual objects on physical worlds
- Converting physical input to virtual interactions

OBJECTIVES

Completing this chapter will help lead to a basic knowledge of mathematics relevant to 3D application development, a sound understanding of 2D and 3D spaces, and how the AR components are placed in a virtual environment mapping a real physical space.

BASICS OF MATHEMATICS FOR 3D VISUALIZATION

Beginning in the first grade, students learn about numbers. Growing older, students learn different types of numbers. Even if this book assumes basic mathematical skills, understanding the underlying concepts will be beneficial for 3D interaction development.

Start with the number zero (0). Anything that is not a zero can be either positive or negative. A minus sign (−) in front of a number denotes a negative number. Consider the following examples:

Zero: 0

Positives: 1, 6, 89, 1.98, 2.37384723, 98.1823

Negatives: −1, −5, −0.1212, −0.6, −10.1829, −124.123632

Any number, regardless of being positive or negative, can also be a whole number without a fractional component. These whole numbers are known as *integers*. Between two integers, there exists an infinite number of nonintegers. These numbers contain a fractional component or a part of an integer component to represent a fraction of the proceeding integer with respect to the ending integer. In computing, these fraction numerals are known as *floating-point arithmetic*. Any number that is not an integer is represented as a *float*, and it is written with a decimal point dividing the whole number and the fractional component. These floating points can either be rational or irrational. A simple fraction can express rational numbers, while irrational numbers cannot be expressed easily. Here are a few examples:

Integers: −2, −23, −1, 3, 6, 34, 1234346

Floats: −43.234, −1.234234, −0.55, 21.001, 45.23507, 23.56

Rational: 2.5 or 5/2, −4.5 or −9/2, 2.34 or 117/50

Irrational: √8, √11, √50—numbers that cannot be expressed as fractions

Computers use numbers for mathematical processing. Even though the underlying process uses binary calculations, computers can perform various mathematical calculations on numbers. In computer languages such as C#, the following symbols are used to denote mathematical calculations:

- *Addition*: Plus, sign (+)
  1 + 2 = 3
- *Subtraction*: Minus sign (−)
  10 − 2 = 8
- *Multiplication*: Star sign (∗)
  3 ∗ 3 = 69
- *Division*: Backslash (/)
  10/2 = 5
- *Modulus* (remainder after division): Percentage sign (%)
  10 % 3 = 1

When building 3D applications, one of the many areas of mathematics that cannot be left out is algebra, a branch of mathematics that represents problems in mathematical expressions. This is where the term *variable* comes into play. In programming, there are different types of variables. When it comes to mathematical calculations, numbers can be considered as integers and floats. Variables can be defined based on the type, and mathematical expressions can be written using combined numbers, variables, and mathematical operations:

$$Area = diameter * \pi$$

Area is a variable that represents the final value. The *diameter* is a variable that can hold any value. π is just a constant that represents a floating-point value of approximately 3.14. In programming, these are combined in order to calculate the properties of objects. Imagine a scenario of an AR experience that captures the diameter of a circular object and provides the area of that object. Developers can use a similar calculation to simply represent the area to the user.

Now that the basic steps of mathematics have been covered, it is time to step into the 3D world. Before jumping into 3D, however, two more steps are needed, the first of which is understanding the Cartesian coordinate system with 1D and 2D mathematics.

UNDERSTANDING THE 3D ENVIRONMENT

If one draws a line on a sheet and divides the line into ten similar sections, numbering the section breaks from 0 to 10, the result would look like Figure 2.1:

FIGURE 2.1 Number line.

Now, represent a number on this line by adding a dot. The dot can be moved based on various mathematical calculations. As an example, check Figure 2.2 (for $9 - 5 + 3 - 4$):

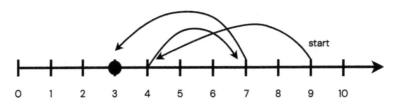

FIGURE 2.2 Representing a calculation on a number line.

In mathematics, this can be considered as a one-dimensional space. Any variable or number can be represented as a point on the line. In a situation where a floating number has to be presented on the line, it can be represented within two integer sections as a proportion. Figure 2.3 represents the real number π on a one-dimensional line:

FIGURE 2.3 Representing a number on a number line.

Now, go a bit further. With a line, it is possible to represent a position of just one number. By combining two lines, two numbers can be represented. By keeping the lines perpendicular to each other, the two numbers can represent a position on a plane. This can now be identified as a two-dimensional Cartesian plane. A checkerboard is a great example for this, as can be seen in Figure 2.4:

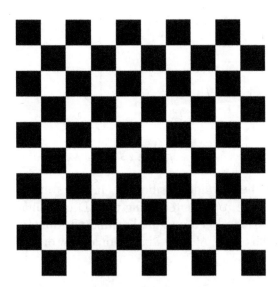

FIGURE 2.4 A checkerboard.

A checkerboard uses numbers to represent square shapes. Numbering the horizontal and the vertical plane, any square in the checkerboard can be represented using two numbers. In chess, one line is numbered, and the other line is represented using the alphabet. Similarly, a position on a plane can be represented using two lines. The combination of the two lines is called the *coordinate system.* These lines are known as *axes*. As a practice, a horizontal axis is labeled as the *x-axis* and the vertical line as the *y-axis*. A mathematical representation of a point on a plane will be given as *(x,y)*. In considering where the two lines should be merged perpendicularly, there can be many depending on the use case. In general, two lines representing negative to positive merge on 0, respectively. The point is the center of the coordinate system and is known as the *origin.*

For example, (5,3) represents a point in the 2D space where the *x* value is 5 and the *y* value is 3. This can be used to specify many mathematical representations. As an example, a position on a given plane that can be visually represented is shown in Figure 2.5:

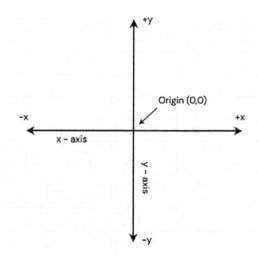

FIGURE 2.5 2D Cartesian plane.

Similar to the 1D line positioning, integers and any positive or negative number can be represented using the 2D coordinate system. Imagine a 2D Cartesian plane placed on a table while positioning a pencil vertically, right on top of the origin. A three-dimensional view of it is illustrated in Figure 2.6:

FIGURE 2.6 Placing a pencil on a 2D Cartesian plane.
Source: "Pencil" (*https://skfb.ly/6TAAV*) by Akshat, licensed under Creative Commons Attribution (*http://creativecommons.org/licenses/by/4.0/*).

Visualizing the three-dimensional space is a bit difficult to describe. Nevertheless, imagining a real-world example helps one understand how the three dimensions are placed with respect to each axis.

Now, convert the pencil to another virtual line, giving it the label z. Imagine a point placed on the x-y plane. Lifting it directly parallel to the pencil, or the z-axis, produces a floating dot in the air. The position of the point can now be represented with respect to the origin point of the plane by using x, y, and z numbers. The orientation of the x-, y-, and z-axis may change, but three values can now give the position of any point. A visual representation of a position in the 3D space and a 3D Cartesian space is shown in Figure 2.7:

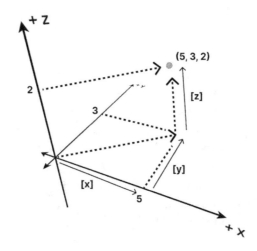

FIGURE 2.7 A point in a 3D Cartesian space.

Now that one knows how a 3D space is represented, imagine flipping one of the axes. As an example, change the z-axis's minus to plus and plus to minus. Now one may realize that both coordinate systems can never be aligned on top of each other. This is because all the 3D coordinate spaces are not equal. There are two different 3D coordinate spaces regardless of the change of axis direction, called the left-handed coordinate space and the right-handed coordinate space. Any similar-handed coordinate system can be rotated and aligned on each other, while the opposite is impossible.

Try to align both hands, as shown in Figure 2.8, and see whether they can be aligned together in any way. It becomes clear that any two fingers can be aligned, while the other can never be:

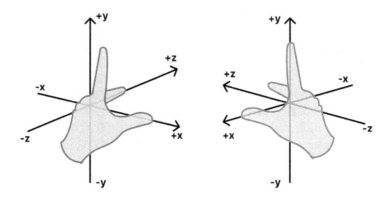

FIGURE 2.8 Left- and right-handedness of 3D coordinate space.

In 3D application development, the user will manipulate objects using transform values, mainly on position, rotation, and scale. The transformations use the coordinate spaces of the 3D system to perform these calculations. Considering the rotation of any point with respect to the origin, it can be defined by the handedness of the coordinate space.

A positive rotation can be clockwise or counterclockwise based on the coordinate space. This is known as the left-hand rule or the right-hand rule. In rotating anything around a given axis, consider making a fist of either hand. By pointing the thumb up toward the positive direction of the axis, the rest of the fingers will be curved and rotated toward the positive direction of the rotation. This is illustrated in Figure 2.9:

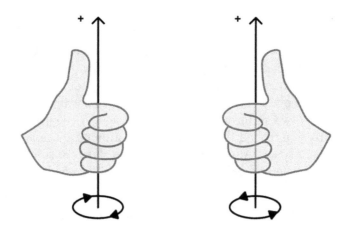

FIGURE 2.9 Left-hand and right-hand rule for positive rotation.

This book will be using the left-hand rule and the left-hand-based coordinate system, mainly because the Unity 3D engine uses the left as its three-dimensional space. Simply put, any rotation performed with a positive amount will result in a clockwise rotation.

VECTOR MATHEMATICS

In mathematics, a vector is a collection of numbers. It can be just one number or a list of numbers within a single entity. The number of elements in a vector can define the number of dimensions of the vector. As an example, check the following set of vectors:

- Vector1: (34.45), (−12.4), (0.0)
- Vector2: (12.3, 3.45), (1,5), (−1, −4)
- Vector3: (45.6, 22.2, 6.2), (−1, −4, 6), (0, 0, 0)

In physics, a vector is known as an entity with a magnitude and a direction. Usually, this applies to 2D and 3D modes since a single number cannot define a direction, and more than three values cause complexity in defining directions. Imagine placing a ring at the center of a board and pulling it toward a given direction using a thread. The pull applied can be known as the *force*. The force and direction are variables, and each can change, keeping the other constant. This allows the force to be applied in various different ways in this 2D plane. Hence, it has characteristics that can be defined mathematically. The same force can be applied using two forces that are perpendicular to each other, as shown in Figure 2.10:

(2, 3)

FIGURE 2.10 Pulling a ring using a string with (2, 3) force.

Instead of pulling the ring with just one thread, one can get the same move-ment with two threads that pull the ring horizontally and vertically. The result will be the ring moving diagonally based on the forces by the two threads. The two forces can now be determined with just two numbers, or termed differ-ently, a 2D vector. This can be seen in Figure 2.11:

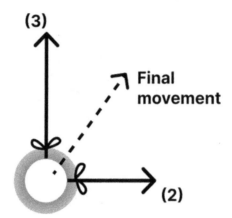

FIGURE 2.11 Pulling a ring with two perpendicular strings.

The representation of a 2D vector can be done on a Cartesian plane, as shown in Figure 2.12:

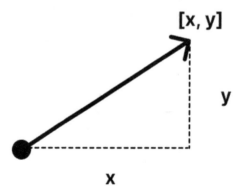

FIGURE 2.12 Representation of a vector in 2D space.

Similarly, a 3D vector can be represented on a 3D Cartesian plane. Imagine the ring is being pulled out by another force upwards; the result can be a movement in the 3D space. This can be seen in Figure 2.13:

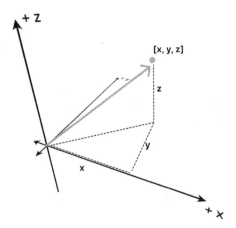

FIGURE 2.13 Representation of a vector in 3D space.

TERMINOLOGY OF VECTORS

- *Magnitude:* This is the size or length of the vector. The magnitude is always positive.
- For example, the magnitude of [3,4] vector is 5.
- *Direction:* This is the direction that the vector is pointing toward.
- For example, the direction of the [4,4] vector is 45° clockwise from north.
- *Negating a vector:* Changing the direction of the vector to the opposite direction. This way, all the numbers representing the vector will be multiplied by −1.
- For example, the negation of [4, −6] is [−4, 6].
- *Unit vector:* The vector with the same direction but a magnitude of 1.
- For example, the unit vector of [3,3], [5,5], [6,6], and so on, is [1,1].
- *Dot product:* Given two vectors, the dot product is the multiplication of both magnitudes and the cosine of the angle between the two vectors. Generally, this determines if another vector is perpendicular to a given vector.
- *Cross product:* Given two vectors, this gives another vector perpendicular to both. The direction of the resultant vector depends on the angle between the given two vectors.

The vectors represent both scalar and directional components; they are used in physics-based calculations to represent transform values, forces, and velocities in 3D development tools.

BASIC TRIGONOMETRY

The vectors generate virtual triangles in 3D and 2D spaces, involving transformations, rotations, angles, and so on. Therefore, having a basic knowledge of the fundamentals of trigonometry helps build 3D applications. Consider a circle divided into 360 pieces. One of these pieces is known as 1 degree (1°). The total circle is 360°, and half of it is 180°. This is illustrated in Figure 2.14:

FIGURE 2.14 A circle has 360 divisions, each called a degree.

Consider a circle of radius R. Place a dot on the circumference of the circle and move it on the circle such that the distance traveled is exactly R. Given that, the total rotation covered by the dot with respect to the center of the circle is known as a *radian*, as shown in Figure 2.15:

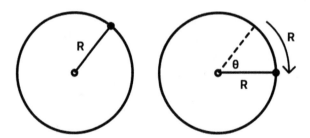

FIGURE 2.15 Defining a radian angle.

The dot should travel roughly 6.2831... radians to complete a full circle. This amount is an *irrational* number, and half of it is generally known as the constant π. 2π radians are equal to 360 degrees. Any angle can be represented using either degrees or radians. If one takes a right triangle with one angle being θ, the edges of the triangle can be used to determine the trigonometric functions, as shown in Figure 2.16:

$$Sin(\theta) = \frac{a}{c} \quad Cos(\theta) = \frac{b}{c} \quad Tan(\theta) = \frac{a}{b}$$

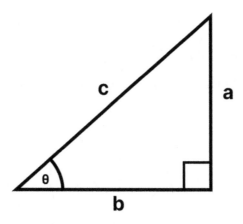

FIGURE 2.16 A right triangle.

Representing rotations in 3D space can be tricky. One can use vectors and angles to present the orientation of the x, y, and z components of a vector, or one can use the number of degrees with respect to each axis, known as *Euler angles*. This can be harder than it seems, however, when one wants to rotate something around a given axis.

Imagine looking at something above and immediately turning to look at something below. This whole rotation path should be calculated and presented in a 3D environment. A straightforward way is to use a 3D vector representing the degrees; however, the rotation needs to be done in a sequence. Rotate x, then y, and then z by changing the values separately. This flow of the change of values ends when it meets the loss of the degree of freedom, known as the *gimbal lock*. Therefore, instead of vectors or Euler angles for rotations, *quaternions* determine rotations in the 3D space.

Quaternions are based on complex numbers. Many 3D programs, like Unity, use quaternions for rotation-based calculations, and they can be converted to Euler angles and vice versa. Therefore, developers are not required to provide quaternion inputs directly for rotation-based interpolations.

UNDERSTANDING DIFFERENT SPACES

Imagine the world as a three-dimensional cubic space. Assuming a house's front door to be the origin point of that 3D Cartesian space, one may visualize one's position with respect to that origin. Standing at the door, one's position will be exactly $(0, 0, 0)$. Moving away to the house next door, one's position has changed toward the horizontal plane. After climbing a tree, one's position now has a third-dimensional value. When one considers a 3D world a Cartesian plane, one can define everything in the world with respect to a given origin point. This is known as the *world space*.

Now, imagine holding a large wooden box, with another wooden ball fixed inside that box. Because the ball is fixed inside the box, there is no movement inside. Now consider the position of the ball with respect to the center of the wooden box. Does it change if one moves the wooden box around the neighborhood? The answer is no, because the ball's position is fixed with respect to the center of the box. Now consider the position of the ball with respect to the front door. When one moves around with the box, the position of the ball changes only with respect to the origin. If one releases the ball inside the box, now the ball can be freely moved within the box; hence, the position with respect to the center of the box is changed. The box can be identified as a *local space*, and this is illustrated in Figure 2.17:

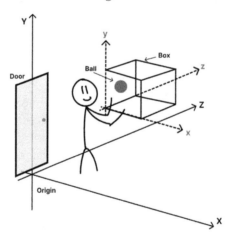

FIGURE 2.17 World space and local space.

If one considers the ball having its own virtual space, this is also a local space. Sometimes it can be considered as *object space* as well. In 3D spatial applications, space is important to determine the poses of objects with respect to either the world or a given local space. Using different coordinate spaces is more convenient and thus easy to manipulate in different situations.

CONTEXT RECOGNITION CONCEPTS

There are two main types of AR discussed here. Considering the workflow of AR recognition, identifying the space to generate 3D content is the first step. This identification can either be based on a predefined environment or an environment that is created in real time. Under this, the two types of AR can be described as follows:

- Marker-based
- Marker-less

As discussed in Chapter 1, "Getting Started with Augmented Reality," marker-based recognition requires a predefined context. This is known as a tracker that has been converted to a mathematical model, in which a comparison is made to build the virtual world. Now consider a scenario where a marker has been recognized in the 3D world. Once such a predefined target is detected, a virtual space is created in the 3D world with respect to the marker. The marker can then be in any position of the 3D world space, but any object that is placed on the marker will consider the marker as its space. Therefore, the marker's local space is considered the space of the AR content. In multitarget tracking, there can be multiple image targets placed around the world. Any 3D content that tracks these image targets is placed in the world space, but the positioning will take place according to the orientation and the position of the target image. Refer to Figure 2.18 for an illustration:

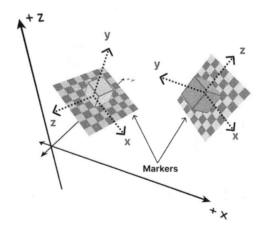

FIGURE 2.18 AR markers use their own local space within the world space.

In a marker-less environment, the starting point of the experience can be considered as the world origin. Scanning the world around will keep generating virtual planes inside the 3D world, which are placed with respect to world space. These virtual planes cannot be moved once tracked. If moved, the scan has to be restarted to recalculate the planes/targets. Similar to marker-based tracking, objects that are placed on the planes will be located with respect to those planes. Depending on the tracking algorithm, the targets can be moved or placed constantly. In marker-less tracking environments, a concept known as *device tracking* is used; that is, based on the movement of the capturing device, the pose of the virtual camera within the virtual world also moves at a 1:1 proportion.

PLACEMENT OF VIRTUAL OBJECTS ON PHYSICAL WORLDS

In AR, virtual objects are placed on physical objects, and that illusion is presented to the user. In a virtual 3D space, a virtual camera can capture 3D objects. The movement of this virtual camera maps to the movement of the capturing device. Both the movements are aligned, and both virtual and physical environments are aligned to provide the final output to the user. Consider a mobile AR use case, as shown in Figure 2.19:

FIGURE 2.19 Alignment of 3D objects in a marker-less AR application.

In Figure 2.19, the user is scanning a tabletop. Based on the scans, a virtual plane is generated in the 3D space, and the movement of the device is mapped with the virtual camera in the 3D space. The final output is the combination of the 3D space and the physical camera input. The placement of the objects can be presented as seen in Figure 2.20:

Mobile Screen   3D Objects   Camera Input

FIGURE 2.20 How the final output is aligned on the phone screen.

The algorithms are used to track and place the 3D objects, determine the pose of the 3D models, and map the physical object properties with the virtual planes.

CONVERTING PHYSICAL INPUT TO VIRTUAL INTERACTIONS

In AR applications, input is one major component to consider, regardless of the channel. It can be a wearable, a mobile AR app, or a fixed AR display; input must be captured and transferred to the application, and feedback must be provided based on the input.

Starting with a mobile AR application, the user can see a 3D object placed on a table. The user is supposed to tap on the object and manipulate it based on touch input. It can be just a button press or a swipe to rotate, pinch to scale, or touch and hold to move. Even if the world being interacted with is 3D, the touch input is captured through a 2D screen, which is the mobile screen. Therefore, the 2D screen tap details must be converted into 3D. One of the methods of identifying such interaction is known as *ray casting*. Imagine this as a laser that is sent from the mobile screen to the 3D world. A visual representation is shown in Figure 2.21:

FIGURE 2.21 Converting a touch input to a ray cast input in 3D space.

In ray casting, the screen point details are converted to the world space coordinates to determine a world space origin point for the interaction. Then a virtual ray (more like a laser) is sent parallel to the camera direction. If the ray hits a 3D object, the result will be returned to the application logic. Any interaction can then be continued based on the 2D positional differences of the touch input. An in-depth look into such input will be discussed in Chapter 5, "Creating a First Custom Component."

In wearable devices, handheld controllers use the same methods to interact with objects. In these use cases, the controller or hand-tracking algorithms generate a virtual representation of the controller within the 3D world. There will be a 3D model with the other 3D models that tracked the controllers to perform interactions in the 3D environment. Devices like *HoloLens* and *Magic Leap* have hand tracking, which provides native support to integrate a 3D model that tracks hands. Collision-based triggers and ray casts are generally used to interact with virtual content.

CONCLUSION

This chapter covered the fundamental mathematical concepts for understanding the 3D environment and how objects can be placed in a 3D environment when building AR applications. The placement and implementation methods on different platforms will differ, but the fundamental structure remains the same.

The next chapter explores some popular development tools and frameworks available to build and distribute AR applications.

KEY POINTS

- Numbers can be represented in single-dimension number lines.
- 2D Cartesian planes are used to represent 2D positions, and 3D spaces are used to represent positions in 3D.
- Vectors are used to represent positions, rotations, and other physical properties of objects in 3D spaces.
- A 3D space can be global or local to an object with respect to its orientation.
- AR applications match real-world poses with virtual world poses and provide a combination of both to the end user.

QUESTIONS

1. Which of the following is a negative floating point irrational number?

   a. 1.23

   b. −2.44542324562364323…

   c. −2.56

   d. −5

2. In the Unity 3D engine, the right is the x-axis, up is the y-axis, and forward is the z-axis. What is the handedness of the 3D space?

   a. Up

   b. Right

   c. Left

   d. Down

3. A museum is requesting an AR app that allows one to scan paintings and show animating views in 3D. Which method is the most suitable?

   a. Marker-based AR

   b. Marker-less AR

   c. Location-based AR

   d. Device tracking

4. An AR app is being built to scan the ceiling and place virtual chandeliers. What will be the most suitable method from the following?

    a. Marker-based AR

    b. Marker-less AR

    c. Location-based AR

    d. Device tracking

5. An AR application uses two different images to spawn 3D characters on top of them. When one gets closer to the other, both characters start to fight. Which of the following is true regarding this application?

    a. Both characters and the markers are in the world space.

    b. One character is in world space, and the other is in the marker's local space.

    c. Both the markers are in local space, and the character is in world space on top of the markers.

    d. Both the markers move in world space, while the characters use the local space of the markers individually.

Answers appear in the appendix.

3

EXPLORING TOOLS AND DEVELOPMENT PLATFORMS

INTRODUCTION

Now that the augmented reality (AR) principles and the underlying concepts behind AR applications have been explained, this chapter will look at available AR platforms and tools to build AR applications. Going beyond the scope of the book, the image recognition algorithms and 3D tools can be used to create one's own AR framework. There has been an exponential growth in available tools to build AR apps that can be evaluated and chosen based on the use case, the target audience, the target platform, and the complexity of the application.

Currently, there are two main ways to build AR applications. It can be for an AR-based wearable such as Microsoft *HoloLens, Magic Leap*, or *Epson Moverio*. One can also build mobile app-based AR experiences that merely use mobile phones as the platform. This chapter provides an overview of all the platforms, understands their pros and cons based on the use case, and evaluates the available technologies for each platform development.

STRUCTURE

This chapter will cover the following topics:

- AR platforms
  - Smartphones (Android, iOS)
  - Microsoft HoloLens

- Magic Leap
- Snapchat spectacles
- Other wearables
- WebXR (AR)
- Social AR
- AR development tools
  - Native
  - Social AR—Spark AR, Snapchat Lens Studio, TikTok
  - Unity 3D
  - Apple Reality Composer
  - 8th Wall
- AR software development kits (SDKs)
  - Microsoft Mixed Reality Toolkit (MRTK)
  - Wikitude
  - Easy AR
  - Vuforia
  - ARCore
  - ARKit
  - AR Toolkit
  - AR Foundation
  - Niantic Lightship

OBJECTIVES

After completing this chapter, the reader will be able to understand a requirement, evaluate all the available platforms, and choose the platform that meets the requirement. It will also be possible to evaluate available AR frameworks and SDKs for the selected platform and choose one to start the development.

AR PLATFORMS

The end user of any AR application will employ an AR-enabled platform to get the experience. Currently, handheld and wearable devices provide AR experiences. This section covers the most popular AR platforms available in the world to build and run AR experiences.

Smartphones Android, iOS

Smartphones are the earliest adaptors of AR applications in the consumer space. Of course, AR experiences have been made for desktop computers with webcams, early camera phones, and smartphones such as Nokia Symbian devices throughout the decade. With developer-friendly operating systems such as iOS (Apple) and Android, however, software development has grown exponentially, focusing on image processing and AR. This has resulted in smartphones being the most used platform to experience AR applications today.

Based on the previous chapters, it was learned that just camera input may not be enough to recognize context; however, smartphones have already come up with sensors that can help any AR-based algorithms work. Sensors like the accelerometer to measure the movement and the gyroscope to measure the alignment of the device with respect to the world have been catalysts for AR algorithms. Early smartphone AR applications were limited to what third-party developers could offer. AR Toolkit, the first-ever AR SDK, was initially ported to Symbian operating system devices and then into Android devices. It was able to track fiducial markers and black and white predefined planes to view AR content. SDKs such as *Wikitude* and *Vuforia* enabled natural feature tracking, which allowed developers to use any image target for marker-based AR. With the introduction of ARKit by Apple and ARCore by Android, the AR development field developed exponentially, allowing developers to build marker-less and marker-based AR without third-party tool involvement.

Apple iPhones use an operating system known as iOS, built by Apple Inc. The Android operating system is open source and can be used by any hardware manufacturer, given it has the licenses. Therefore, Android devices cannot be limited to one electronics manufacturer, as any company can make them. Leading Android device manufacturers include Samsung, Sony, Huawei, and Xiaomi. The features of all of these devices, including AR capabilities, depend on the hardware capabilities and the performance of the device. Figure 3.1 features an Apple iPhone running iOS:

FIGURE 3.1 Apple iPhone running iOS.

The following figure illustrates a Google Pixel device running Android OS HoloLens:

FIGURE 3.2 Google Pixel device running Android OS Microsoft HoloLens.

Developed in 2016, Microsoft HoloLens is the first-ever consumer-targeted AR wearable device in the world. Even though it was available in the market, their target audience used to be professionals and corporations participating in the preproduction of the device. The HoloLens device still does not target the everyday consumer and relies mainly on corporate implementations in that the cost of one device goes over $3,000 in 2022.

Microsoft HoloLens is a head-mounted wearable device that consists of a front tinted visor, a pair of transparent combiner lenses, and an array of sensors at the top of the device, which is mounted to a cushioned head strap. The array of sensors includes an accelerometer, gyroscope, and magnetometer to capture the device's orientation and position, an energy-efficient depth camera, a 2.4-megapixel photographic video camera, a four-microphone array, and an ambient light sensor. The sensor technology is said to be a successor of Microsoft's depth sensor technology, *Kinect*, which used to be an add-on camera for Xbox 360. HoloLens runs a modified spatial version of the Windows 10 operating system.

The operating system runs on a custom-made holographic processing unit designed and developed by Microsoft especially for the device. Using the cameras and the sensors, it has capabilities for spatial mapping, hand gesture recognition, and voice and speech recognition. The device works by projecting augmented content onto the inner pair of sensors that aligns with the physical objects around it. The core system does not provide recognition technologies such as image tracking and anchoring. Still, spatial mapping can be extended, and additional tracking tools can be used to augment its capabilities. Figure 3.3 shows a Microsoft HoloLens 2 device:

FIGURE 3.3 Microsoft HoloLens 2.

Microsoft has released two versions of the HoloLens so far. The second version, HoloLens 2, has a longer battery life, increased field of view, higher processing power, and additional features such as improved voice and gesture recognition and eye tracking. Developing applications on HoloLens requires a Windows SKD and only supports Microsoft Windows development environments. The Unity 3D engine can also be used to develop 3D applications that can run on HoloLens, and Microsoft has released official Unity developer kits to get started easily. Their operating system can be downloaded separately as an emulator, so developers can develop and test applications without having a HoloLens. Figure 3.4 shows a HoloLens emulator:

FIGURE 3.4 HoloLens emulator.

More information on the Microsoft HoloLens and available developer tools can be found at *https://www.microsoft.com/en-us/hololens/developers*.

Magic Leap

Magic Leap is a wearable AR headset designed and developed by Magic Leap Inc. The company was founded in 2010 and until 2015 focused mainly on AR and computer vision research. Between 2010 and 2015, Magic Leap raised over $2 billion from investors including Google and Alibaba. Based on their investor portfolio, industry enthusiasts have had a high interest in their technology.

After 8 years of research and development, they released their first version of the Magic Leap device in July 2018. At the time of writing this chapter, the Magic Leap 2 had been revealed but was not going to be available in the market until the end of 2022. The Magic Leap device is a wearable compact headset that rests on the nose, wrapping around the face and distributing its weight similarly to eyeglasses. The latest version of the device has a depth camera, 12.6-megapixel color camera, ambient light sensor, 4× eye-tracking cameras, positional sensors (gyro, magnetometer, accelerometer), and an altimeter. The device has 16GB of RAM for a stand-alone device with a storage capacity of 256 GB. The device's battery can provide over 3 hours of continuous use with a 7-hour sleep mode. Unlike the HoloLens device, the Magic Leap package has a controller for precise input and a separate compute pack, which moves the processing components out of the wearable. The release version of the Magic Leap 2 costs $3,299 and the enterprise version is valued at $5,000. Figure 3.5 shows a Magic Leap 2 device:

FIGURE 3.5 Magic Leap 2.

The device originally used an operating system known as Lumin OS; however, the second version of the device runs an *Android Open-Source Project (AOSP)*—based operating system, which supports WebXR and OpenXR, allowing developers to create applications targeting multiple platforms without the hassle of platform dependencies.

Snapchat spectacles

Snap Inc. is one of the leading AR-based companies in the world, offering AR face filters through their mobile social media app, Snapchat. Their initial spectacles implementation was a simple wearable with a camera attached for quick photo and video capturing in order to support people creating content easily. Since then, their research has focused more on AR. Snap Inc released its AR filter authoring tool, Snapchat Lens Studio. Lens Studio allowed developers to create and integrate AR applications within the Snapchat application. Along with the research and development effort put into the Snapchat lenses and Lens Studio, the company released a developer version of the spectacles, which leverages the power of Snapchat lenses to run AR applications. Figure 3.6 features a pair of Snapchat spectacles:

FIGURE 3.6 Snapchat AR spectacles.

Although a consumer device with just a front camera and no AR view through the lenses is available for purchase, the Snapchat AR spectacles are not available in a consumer version and are only offered for aspiring creators, AR development companies, and individuals heavily involved in AR development. Developing AR apps on this device cannot be done directly. Since it uses the same AR effect backend, developers must design and build AR filters using Snapchat's authoring tool, Lens Studio.

Other wearables

While the HoloLens and Magic Leap are the most expensive but most precise AR headsets available in the market, other players are developing their own hardware, mainly for enterprise use cases. Vuzix is one of the oldest virtual reality (VR) hardware companies in the world. They currently design and produce an AR wearable known as Vuzix Blade. This device primarily focuses on being a heads-up display, but marker-based AR applications can be developed and run using additional software. Figure 3.7 features a Vuzix Blade device:

FIGURE 3.7 Vuzix Blade.

Nreal is another company that specializes in building AR smart glasses. They have multiple AR wearable devices. Their implementation uses a standard

Android smartphone as the processing device, and the wearable becomes a display while using the real world as the background. This has a 6-degree-of-freedom space recognition capability, hand tracking, and plane detection capabilities. Therefore, apps can be developed that allow wearers to use the existing space as an AR world. Figure 3.8 shows an Nreal Air device:

FIGURE 3.8 Nreal Air.

Epson Moverio is a similar device developed by Seiko Epson Corp and uses Android as its operating system. Their device capability is similar to Nreal devices. Their development kits provide direct access to pose-tracking sensors for custom AR application development, leveraging plane tracking, device tracking, object and image tracking, and so on. Figure 3.9 features the Epson Moverio device:

FIGURE 3.9 Epson Moverio.

Revealed in mid-2023, Apple's Vision Pro is a device discussed by many spatial computing enthusiasts over the world. It is not an AR device with a transparent front surface but consists of 12 cameras that capture the world and project an image into the eye through stereo lenses. Additionally, it has cameras within the device that capture one's face and projects outside. The concept of using a camera to work as a channel between the human eye and the world is known as *passthrough*. This is the first device to operate both ways so that observers outside can see the user's eye movement. At the time of writing this book, it is not yet released to the public as a consumer device. Note that the first device is priced at $3,499, which is one of the expensive examples of wearable immersive technology. Refer to Figure 3.10:

FIGURE 3.10 Apple Vision Pro with external battery.

WebXR AR

WebXR AR cannot be considered hardware but a platform for which AR applications can be built. Based on heavy research by companies such as Google, Niantic, OpenXR, and Mozilla, sensory data have successfully been accessed through Web browsers to generate AR content on the Web. Imagine an AR application that can run on a mobile device. By default, the application has to be installed on a smartphone and then launched. WebXR allows anyone to view an AR experience through a mobile browser without needing to install different applications. This is game-changing since it allows any device with the necessary processing power and hardware to view AR content, regardless of the device or the operating system, and allows developers to build just for WebXR and deploy their creations to any operating system that can open a Web link. WebXR currently supports desktop computers with VR hardware, stand-alone AR/VR headsets, as well as smartphone devices. WebXR uses WebGL 3D technology to view 3D content within the browser windows. More information on WebXR can be found at *https://immersiveweb.dev/*.

Social AR

Social AR is an emerging topic. One of the difficulties in building smartphone-based AR applications is that they have to be deployed to app stores, and users must download them separately to experience the AR content, requiring the building of different applications for different AR experiences. Smartphone app stores have enforced restrictions on building similar applications and blocked apps with minimal functionality, such as viewing AR content, filters, and so on.

People using social media apps like Facebook, Instagram, Snapchat, and TikTok can use their internal features to open AR filter cameras. With the native capabilities of smartphones, AR filters or social media AR applications have allowed many content creators to build AR experiences using their authoring tools. Social media can also be considered a nonhardware platform to build AR applications on.

Building AR filters on these platforms can be challenging, however. The content is limited to what the platform offers. There are limitations on resource usage, languages, review processes, and so on that can make a developer spend additional time optimizing and following these processes before sharing content. Considering the target market, people who do not use social media cannot be targeted through social AR filters and apps. Marketing-wise and engagement-wise, however, these platforms nevertheless provide improved capabilities and authoring tools for people to build content.

AR DEVELOPMENT TOOLS

Now that different platforms that can run AR applications have been described, this section will explore the tools that are available to build AR applications on the different devices and platforms discussed in the previous section.

Native

Native depends on the platform that runs AR applications. Android uses the Java programming language and requires integrated development environments (IDEs, software used to code and build apps) such as Android Studio to develop AR applications. Conversely, iOS (iPhone/iPad) applications are developed using IDE software, Xcode (which runs only on Apple Mac OS devices) with the Swift programming language. Both Android and iOS native

AR application developments are time-consuming and require additional tools to visualize the behaviors and simulate AR content in 3D. The application performance will however be enhanced since the apps developed directly use native *application programming interfaces (APIs)*. The interface for starting native AR development with Xcode is shown in Figure 3.11:

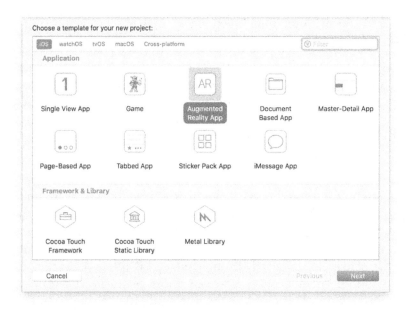

FIGURE 3.11 Choosing an AR app to start native development with Xcode.

Microsoft HoloLens requires the Windows SDK, while many other AR wearables depend on the Android operating system. WebXR applications require HTML, JavaScript, and additional frameworks such as WebGL for 3D content rendering and visualization, WebXR to enable AR features, and other APIs for platform capabilities.

Social AR—Spark AR, Snapchat Lens Studio, TikTok

As described in the previous section, social media uses their applications to distribute AR content among users, allowing developers and creators to design and develop AR applications with their authoring tools.

The first-ever AR tool and capability were built by Snap Inc. when they released front-cam face filters for the first time through their application.

They added the ability to author AR content via their Snapchat Lens Studio application. Anybody with a Snapchat account can download Lens Studio, develop AR content, and share with friends using a Snap code (QR code specific for the AR content created). Lens Studio provides features such as face tracking, plane tracking, image tracking, body tracking, AR occlusion, wrist tracking, foot tracking, cloth simulations, and voice recognition. Figure 3.12 features AR filter development with Lens Studio:

FIGURE 3.12 AR filter development with Lens Studio.

Facebook followed and integrated AR filters into their Facebook and Instagram applications. They also released an authoring tool known as Spark AR, which provides similar capabilities to Snapchat. TikTok released their own version of the development tool, Effect House, and at the time of writing this book, their version is still in beta. The tool is as powerful as Spark AR and Lens Studio and provides similar capabilities through their platform.

Apple Reality Composer

iOS released its version of Web/native ARKit integration known as AR Quick View. This allows developers to upload 3D content using the USDZ (Universal Scene Description) format to Web links and load them to Apple devices to view them in AR mode. This is a comparatively easy tool for anybody to develop AR content without writing logic using coding languages. With this tool, designers can upload 3D models, animations, sound effects, music, and images to design an AR experience and convert everything to USDZ format. USDZ format can contain a 3D scene, including images and audio that can be used by Apple devices to load and render in an AR world. Reality Composer supports horizontal and vertical planes, image, and face tracking. Figure 3.13 shows the Apple Reality Composer window:

FIGURE 3.13 Apple Reality Composer.

Reality Composer experiences come with limitations. Developing such an experience requires Apple MacOS devices. The experiences can only be viewed using Apple iPhones and iPads. Apart from trigger behaviors and action sequences, developing custom behaviors is limited compared to other AR development tools; however, this can be a good tool for a beginner to learn AR, provided the necessary hardware is available.

8th Wall

8th Wall is a Web-based AR development tool recently acquired by the AR research and development game development company Niantic, currently the largest Web-based AR tool provider in the world, supporting many capabilities for Web AR projects. The platform provides building AR content that uses plane tracking, image tracking, face tracking, light estimation, and many other features. 8th Wall contains a scripting environment and a developing environment within their platform, and projects are saved under their tenants. The platform also provides hosting for the developed AR content, and depending on the license, customizations can be made. This is a very straightforward tool for building Web-based AR content, and it also has an internal IDE to script custom logic and behaviors. Figure 3.14 shows some sample projects from 8th Wall:

FIGURE 3.14 Sample projects from 8th Wall.

8th Wall provides a platform to build AR content for the Web without the hassle of implementing WebXR and other 3D frameworks. Companies currently use this for their engagement campaigns since it allows users to quickly open the link and experience the AR content.

Unity 3D

Unity 3D is recognized as one of the leading 3D game engines in the world. Not only can it build 3D games but Unity has also been employed in many use cases ranging from simple mobile apps to high-end 3D emulations in many industries around the world. Unity is cross-platform, meaning that its one project base can be used to build applications for many platforms, including Android, iOS, Windows, Magic Leap, WegGL, and all the available gaming consoles. Because of its ability to provide support for many platforms and it being primarily a 3D engine, Unity has become the leading candidate to build VR and AR applications for many platforms.

Unity applications can be developed using the C# programming language, and many AR and VR hardware manufacturers provide support for the Unity engine through their SDKs. Unity supports available headsets and smartphone devices for extended reality (XR) application development through their XR plug-in management capability. Installing additional packages and modules extends the engine's capabilities for XR development.

Since AR is a cross-platform use case, as noted in previous sections, the Unity 3D engine will be used in the next chapters of the book to build AR applications. In going through the steps of understanding the tool, polishing C# skills with Unity, and diving into AR development, the primary focus will be to develop applications for broad use. Therefore, the focus will be on AR application development for iOS and Android smartphone devices.

AR sdks

As mentioned in the previous section, the Unity 3D engine will be used as the AR app development tool; however, Unity alone cannot build AR applications on the provided platforms. Many SDKs support Unity for building AR apps. The following are the most popular and widely used AR SDKs in app development for AR hardware and smartphones.

Microsoft mixed reality toolkit

MRTK provides easy AR application development for Microsoft HoloLens, offering a set of components and features that can be used to accelerate cross-platform mixed-reality application development with Unity. It runs on top of Microsoft Mixed Reality, Open XR, or Oculus XR frameworks. MRTK is incapable of AR meshing and tracking since it relies on the hardware capabilities of the wearable device. The kit provides many features, such as hand tracking, eye tracking, user interface (UI) controls, spatial awareness, boundary system, speech recognition, and many more. The toolkit is built and maintained by Microsoft, and currently, the latest version of it, MRTK 3, is in public preview at the time of writing this book.

ARToolkit

ARToolkit is the oldest SDK available for AR development. Built in the 1990s, it has seen many iterations, thus providing capabilities for cross-platform development. After being made open source in 2001, it was available for Android and iOS app development around 2015. ARToolkit was then developed further, and Unity SDK was released to the public by Daqri, an AR helmet manufacturer that took over the software rights. ARToolkit uses marker-based recognition mainly on fiducial markers with extended natural feature-tracking capabilities; however, after Daqri went out of business and with many other reliable AR SDKs available for developers, ARToolkit's popularity declined over time. The open-source version of the kit is still available through a university Web site page: *http://www.hitl.washington.edu/artoolkit/*.

The Unity SDK for ARToolkit is currently available through ARToolkitX, supported by Realmax Inc., a Chinese-based AR company (*https://github.com/artoolkitx*).

Wikitude

Wikitude is an AR SDK that supports Android, iOS, and Windows platforms and provides a Unity SDK for cross-platform development. The first version of the SDK released in 2012 utilized image recognition and tracking. In 2021, the company was acquired by Qualcomm. The SDK supports location-based AR, image recognition, simultaneous localization and mapping (SLAM), and object and scene recognition. It also supports cloud AR detection, a system to update image targets through the cloud, which allows developers to provide AR content without app updates through app stores. Wikitude is primarily a commercial SDK and comes with a yearly subscription fee.

Easy AR

Easy AR is an emerging AR SDK developed by VisionStar Information Technology (Shanghai) Co. Ltd. This is also primarily a commercial SDK, but they have provided a free version with almost all the AR-related features included. Their SDK provides image tracking, SLAM, spatial mapping, motion tracking, cloud tracking, and multiplayer modes. They also have a city-scale AR framework to detect and identify large objects for world-scale AR app development. Easy AR is a powerful SDK that uses its own algorithms and supports native frameworks such as ARKit and ARCore.

Vuforia

Vuforia is one of the earliest AR SDKs in the world. It was owned by Qualcomm in the beginning and was sold to an IoT company PTC in 2015. Since then,

Vuforia has been leading the marker-based tracking AR world and has partnered with Unity to provide its SDK as a part of Unity modules. The latest versions of Vuforia feature plane tracking, world-scale AR through cloud recognition and area targets, and object and 3D model detection. Among many commercial AR SDKs, Vuforia provides the most reliable tracking technology and has a stable version that supports native Android and iOS as well as the Unity 3D engine. This book uses Vuforia to build marker-based AR applications and a dynamic AR app with the Vuforia Cloud recognition service.

ARCore

ARCore is a module built by Google for Android devices. The technology is in-built into any Android smartphone, providing marker-less AR through plane tracking, image recognition, and face recognition. ARCore SDK is natively available for Android and iOS, as well as through the Unity Engine and Unreal Engine. ARCore uses positional tracking sensors for device tracking and light estimation to illuminate 3D models to match the environment lighting.

ARKit

ARKit is Apple's AR SDK and was released in 2018. The technology is built on top of the work of Meta IO, an AR company acquired by Apple years before. ARKit primarily focuses on marker-less AR, and the latest version of the SDK provides face recognition, body tracking, marker-based recognition, and plane detection and tracking. The SDK is used natively for Apple's measurement application, AR Quick Look, to visualize 3D models in physical space. The devices with Apple LiDAR sensors allow the SDK to generate mesh data, increasing its tracking capabilities' accuracy. The SDK only supports iOS and can be used within their Xcode development environment and Unity.

AR Foundation

Both ARCore and ARKit have released their versions for Unity. In addition to that, AR headset manufacturers such as HoloLens and Magic Leap have their own AR SDKs. This allows developers to freely use any SDK to develop apps that run on each platform; however, the development flow using each SDK is different, making developers use different methods to maintain a single project base. To overcome this issue, Unity released AR Foundation, a plug-in that manages all the AR SDKs underneath and provides a single interface for developers. This has allowed developers to use just one project code for all the platforms provided with the native SDK support. Figure 3.15 provides a feature comparison of what AR Foundation offers through the native SDKs:

Unity's AR Foundation
Supported Features

Functionality	ARCore	ARKit	Magic Leap	HoloLens
Device tracking	✓	✓	✓	✓
Plane tracking	✓	✓	✓	
Point clouds	✓	✓		
Anchors	✓	✓	✓	✓
Light estimation	✓	✓		
Environment probes	✓	✓		
Face tracking	✓	✓		
Meshing			✓	✓
2D Image tracking	✓	✓		
Raycast	✓	✓	✓	
Pass-through video	✓	✓		
Session management	✓	✓	✓	✓

FIGURE 3.15 AR Foundation feature comparison.

Unity also released a commercial no-code AR framework, Unity MARS, allowing designers to leverage AR Foundation and build AR applications without coding. AR Foundation will be used to build a marker-less AR application in the coming chapters.

Niantic Lightship

AR became widely popular due to the location-based smartphone game Pokémon Go. The developers of Pokémon Go, Niantic, acquired many AR companies, such as 6D.ai and 8th Wall, and released their public AR SDK for developers worldwide. Their SDK, known as Niantic Lightship ARDK, provides world-scale marker-less AR capabilities to devices regardless of ARCore and ARKit support. They primarily focus on visual positioning and 3D meshing without additional sensors like the LiDAR sensor. Also, their ARDK provides network capabilities to develop shared AR experiences. They have a Visual Positioning System (VPS) that crowdsources environmental data. Any developer who uses VPS can build applications that are world scale and can recognize public places to place AR content. Figure 3.16 features AR apps built using the Niantic Lightship AR Developer Kit:

FIGURE 3.16 Niantic Lightship offers world-scale multiplayer AR.

Throughout this book, the basics of Niantic Lightship will be reviewed to build an area-based AR application that can track a predefined location.

CONCLUSION

Through this chapter, the platforms, tools, and SDKs that allow the building of AR applications have been described. AR developers can now evaluate the requirements and choose the most suitable tool and framework to build apps based on the target platforms. As many platforms support Unity and many SDKs are available for the Unity engine, building AR applications using the Unity engine with example use cases will be the focus from the next chapter onward.

KEY POINTS

- There are different platforms that can run AR applications.
- Wearable devices and smartphones are the leading platforms.
- Developing AR apps that run on these platforms requires tools and development kits.
- Unity Engine is a 3D engine that supports cross-platform development.
- Many AR-supported platforms have SDKs that support the Unity 3D engine.
- This makes Unity 3D a suitable candidate for building AR applications across platforms.

QUESTIONS

From the following list, choose the most suitable tool, platform, and SDK to build an AR application appropriate to the scenarios provided here:

- *Tools*: Unity, Spark AR, Web Development, 8th Wall, Xcode, Android Studio.
- *Platforms*: HoloLens, Magic Leap, smartphones, Web.
- *SDK*: AR Foundation, Windows SDK (and MRTK), Vuforia, Niantic Lightship, Web XR, 8th Wall, No separate SDK.

Scenarios

1. Build an enterprise on-site building inspection tool in AR.

2. Social media campaign with face tracking feature.

3. A multiplayer AR archery game in a shared physical space for schoolchildren.

4. An AR art museum requests people to download an app to scan paintings and see them come to life.

5. A QR code that opens the camera to show tourist waypoints in AR.

Answers appear in the appendix.

UP AND RUNNING WITH UNITY 3D

INTRODUCTION

Now that the tools and frameworks available to build augmented reality (AR) applications have been discussed, the next chapters of this book will focus on building AR apps using the most popular and widely used tools from the ones explored. Unity 3D is one of the best 3D game engines in the world, with expanded capabilities not just for game development but for any sort of interactive development. Allowing an easier interface to build custom components and having direct compatibility with C# (.Net framework), Unity has been picked up by many AR algorithm developers as a base platform. As discussed in the previous chapter, almost all the available AR software development kits (SDKs) support Unity. Moreover, Unity being cross-platform makes it the best candidate to build AR applications that can run on many different operating systems and devices. This chapter will go through the process of installing Unity, explain its basic elements, and describe building two projects to get started with 3D development.

STRUCTURE

This chapter will discuss the following topics:

- Installing Unity 3D
  - Installing Android SDK, Java SDK
- Installing Xcode (MacOS)
- Installing Visual Studio/Visual Studio Code
- Creating a project and setting up the target platform

- Unity engine user interface
- Using the tools to create and manipulate primitive objects
- Understanding lights
- Creating materials
- Manipulating the virtual camera
- Using the Unity package manager
- Importing content into Unity
- Importing assets from the Unity Asset Store
- The structure of the GameObject
- Components of Unity
  - Transform
  - Mesh renderer
  - Colliders
  - Rigid body
- Creating prefabs

OBJECTIVES

After completion of this chapter, readers will be able to install the necessary tools required to build 3D applications, including Unity 3D and other supporting software. There will be explanations of how to use the Unity 3D engine to create 3D environments by using primitives, importing 3D models, using the Unity Asset Store, and an overview of the basic principles of 3D. There will also be a description of how to create a simple obstacle course by downloading assets from the Asset Store, creating custom components with C# language, and using the components to create a simple 3D clock.

INSTALLING UNITY 3D

Currently, Unity provides a manager application to install and manage different versions of Unity as well as manage the projects made in Unity on a local machine. This tool, known as *Unity Hub*, makes it easier for developers to manage Unity licenses, regardless of the version. It also helps manage different Unity versions and modules. The following steps explain how to install the Unity Hub:

1. Go to *https://unity3d.com/get-unity/download*.

2. Click on *Download Unity Hub*, as shown in Figure 4.1:

FIGURE 4.1 Unity download Web page.

3. While Unity Hub is being downloaded, sign up with Unity by creating a Unity ID, which requires an email, name, username, and a password.

4. Install the downloaded Unity Hub software and launch it.

5. Click the profile picture icon and select *Sign in*, as shown in Figure 4.2. This will open a Web page to sign into the Unity profile. Once signed in, it will redirect back to the Unity Hub and one will now be signed in.

FIGURE 4.2 Sign into Unity Hub with Unity ID.

6. Click the same profile icon again, go to *Manage Licenses*, and click the *Add* button to add a license. From here, activate a Unity Pro license key, or get a free personal license by selecting the free option. On agreeing to the license statement, the account will be bound with a free personal license.

7. Unity Window has two main sections: projects and installs. Manage different versions of the Unity program by going to the *Installs* section. Go to the *Installs* tab and select the *Install Editor* option. This will give a list of Unity versions to choose from. Unity, by default, provides three main editor versions. These versions are known as *long-term support (LTS)* versions, and Unity usually provides minor updates for a chosen version for up to 3 years. This book will focus on Unity 2021 LTS version (and the 2022 LTS version in some chapters). If the 2021 LTS or 2022 LTS version are not present, there may be changes in the flows of development as discussed throughout this book. Select the *Archive* option and navigate outside the Unity Hub to download the 2021 or 2022 version. From the *Official releases* section, select the *2021.3.xf1 (LTS)* version and click the *Install* button. Here, the x may be different based on when it was installed, since Unity keeps incrementing it when updating editor versions.

8. As Unity is a cross-platform development tool, one can choose different modules to install with the Unity Editor. For scripting in C#, Unity provides the community version of Microsoft Visual Studio by default. On the next screen, select *Visual Studio IDE* as the development or dev tool and Android Build Support if developing for Android or iOS Build Support if developing for iPhones and iPads. Additionally, install *Windows Build Support* and *Mac Build Support*, depending on the computer operating system.

INSTALLING ANDROID SDK, JAVA SDK

Building Android devices requires Android and Java SDKs to be installed. The recommended option with Unity is to install them within the Unity Hub. Make sure to select *Open JDK* and *Android SDK and NDK Tools* from the platform options. Continue with the following steps:

1. Click the *Install* button, and it will download and install the Unity version. Refer to Figure 4.3:

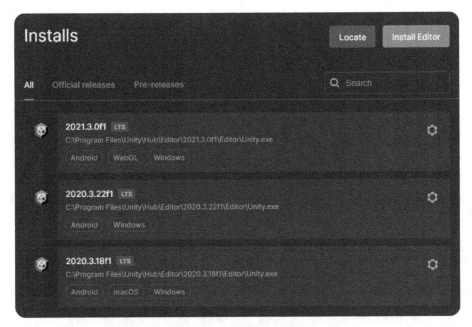

FIGURE 4.3 Installs section of the Unity Hub to manage Unity versions.

If unable to install the specified modules for a Unity version, click the *Settings* button and choose *Add modules* to add them to the editor.

INSTALLING XCODE IN MACOS

When developing iOS devices such as iPhones and iPads, Unity cannot directly manage the final export build. Instead, Unity will generate another project source file, which can only be opened by *Xcode*. Xcode is the only development *integrated development environment* (*IDE*) tailored to develop Apple device-based applications.

To install Xcode, do the following:

1. Open the Mac OS App (only on a Mac OS device) Store and select the *Develop* tab, as shown in Figure 4.4.

2. After noting Xcode as an app, click on *Get* to download the software. This is a large application that requires over 12 GB of disk space. Therefore, make sure there is enough space. Refer to Figure 4.4:

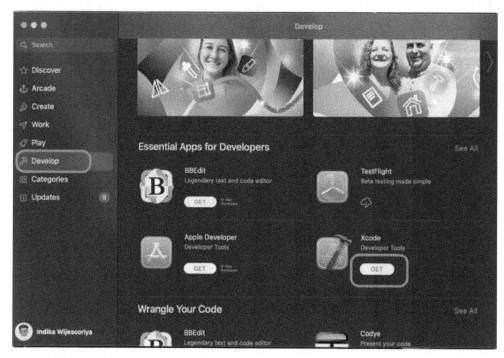

FIGURE 4.4 Xcode installation from the Apple App Store.

INSTALLING VISUAL STUDIO/VISUAL STUDIO CODE

The recommended way to install Visual Studio is through the Unity Hub. Those wanting to use a separate Visual Studio version can go to the link shown in parentheses (*https://visualstudio.microsoft.com/downloads/*) to download the latest community version of Visual Studio. This will open Visual Studio installer to access the IDE.

Once the IDE is installed, open the installer again and click *Modify*. Select the *Game Development with Unity* option from the pop-up window and click *Install while downloading*. This will make sure that Unity support tools are installed to work with Visual Studio. Refer to Figure 4.5:

FIGURE 4.5 Installing Unity modules for Visual Studio using the VS Installer.

It is also possible to use Visual Studio Code instead of Visual Studio; however, VS Code is only a text editor with extended support and requires additional plug-ins and prerequisites to work with Unity.

To install VS Code, follow the listed steps:

1. Install the .NET SDK: *https://dotnet.microsoft.com/download*.

2. For Windows machines, restart the computer. For MacOS computers, install the latest Mono release: *https://www.mono-project.com/download/*.

3. Install VS Code: *https://code.visualstudio.com/*.

4. Open *VS Code*, go to *Plugins* section, and install the C# plug-in. Refer to Figure 4.6:

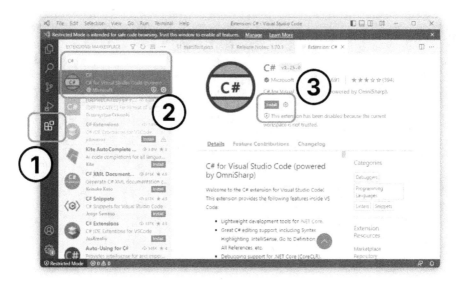

FIGURE 4.6 Steps to customize Visual Studio Code for Unity development.

5. In VS Code, press *Ctrl* + (comma) to get the settings editor. Search for `Omnisharp: Use Modern Net` and uncheck the setting.

There are some additional settings that need to be changed within the Unity Editor, but that requires opening a project. This will be discussed when the first C# script is created.

CREATING A PROJECT AND SETTING UP THE TARGET PLATFORM

New projects can be created using the Unity Hub. To create a new project, go to the *Projects* tab and click *New Project*. This will open a new window to create a project which consists of different templates.

Throughout this book, the 3D *Universal Render Pipeline (URP)* template will be used. This will create a new blank project that uses Unity's URP. URP will be used since the new render pipeline allows exploration of more effects provided by Unity. Moreover, performance-wise, it is better than the standard 3D render pipeline. Those who are using Unity for the first time will be prompted to download the template before using it. Refer to Figure 4.7:

FIGURE 4.7 Steps to create a new URP project in Unity.

At the top of the window displayed in Figure 4.7, make sure the editor version is selected as *2021.3.x*.

Select the *Project name* text field and change it to *Hello Unity*. Now choose a proper location to save the Unity Project and click *Create Project*.

This will create a new Unity Project in the given location. A Unity Project is a combination of files and folders and does not have a single file to launch the project. Unity Editor mainly looks for the `Assets, Project Settings,` and `Packages` folder within the project folder and opens the editor with the information within those folders.

UNITY ENGINE USER INTERFACE

The Unity interface consists of many windows. A 3D view in the Unity Editor shows the currently selected scene. A scene is an entity that holds 3D models, lights, script behaviors, and so on. By default, Unity has generated an empty scene with some content in it. This scene is saved as the `Sample Scene` in the `Assets/Scenes` folder.

Figure 4.8 shows the default layout:

FIGURE 4.8 Unity interface.

An explanation of each window is as follows:

1. *Scene View:* This window shows the currently opened 3D scene information. The default sample scene consists of a main camera (virtual camera), a directional light, and another global volume object.

2. *Hierarchy Window:* This window lists all the objects in the opened scene. The objects listed are called `Game Objects`. A game object consists of `Components`. These components define the behavior of the game objects they are in. Selecting a game object will allow its components to be viewed.

3. *Inspector Window:* Once a game object is selected, all the components attached to the game object are listed in this window. Select the objects in the current scene through the hierarchy window and see how each object consists of different components in the inspector window.

4. *Project Window:* This will show all the files and folders that are within the `Assets` folder of the project. There is also a `Package` folder in it. This

folder content is managed by Unity and other libraries, and thus it is not recommended to modify the content in these folders.

5. *Game Window:* The virtual camera in the scene captures the scene content and projects it onto the game view. This is the camera point of view which can be seen from the game window. When an application is exported, what is seen through the final build will be what is ultimately seen through the game window.

USING THE TOOLS TO CREATE AND MANIPULATE PRIMITIVE OBJECTS

Right-click on an empty area of the hierarchy window or click the plus button at the top left corner of the window, as shown in Figure 4.9. This will open the *Create* menu. Select *3D* object and choose *Cube*:

FIGURE 4.9 Create new objects in the scene using the hierarchy window.

Navigating in the Unity interface can be hard for a beginner but is nevertheless easy to master. The simplest way to move inside the scene is by holding the right click inside the editor and using the W, A, S, and D keys to move forward, backward, left, and right, respectively. While moving, the mouse can be moved (holding the right click) to look up, down, left, and right.

Another method is by selecting the 3D cube and pressing the *F* key to focus on the object. Now holding the *Alt* key or *Option* on Mac, the user will be able to click and rotate around the cube. The right click while holding the keyboard button will zoom in and out of the object selected.

The object transform can be manipulated by choosing the Move, Rotate, Scale, and Transform tools provided on the left side of the default scene window. Switch these tools by pressing W, E, R, and Y, respectively, with the mouse within the Unity scene window. Each tool provides ways to handle gizmos to manipulate the object transform properties. Select each tool to see what is available with each tool within the scene window.

Refer to Figure 4.10 for a better understanding of the basic transformation tools in Unity:

FIGURE 4.10 Basic transformation tools in Unity.

At the top of the *Scene* view, there is a tool settings bar, as shown in Figure 4.11. Each button has configurations that can be changed to aid the 3D building scene:

FIGURE 4.11 Unity scene view toolbar.

1. *Toggle Tool handle position button:* This allows the user to switch between the center point of the selected object and its pivot point. Usually, a 3D model has a defined point in its local space that defines the origin point of the model itself. The position of the 3D model is defined based on the pivot point. When the pivot is not exactly in the center, Unity can estimate a center point if the tool position is selected to center.

2. *Toggle Tool handle rotation button:* This allows one to manipulate the object transform with respect to world space or the object's local space (see the previous chapter's discussion about different spaces). The scale tool only works with local space, as it cannot be scaled along a nonprimitive axis.

3. *Toggle grid visibility:* One can also get X, Y, and Z grids to be visible.

4. *Toggle grid snapping:* One can also set the snapping parameters. Enabling this will allow one to snap objects to a grid.

5. *Snap increment:* Increase the snapping values to change the size of the snapping grid with this tool.

6. *Draw mode:* Choose a draw mode option from the list for 3D design and debugging of the scene details.

7. *2D mode:* Toggle between 2D and 3D mode.

8. *Toggle light:* Toggle the light check in the scene, which is good for designing dark 3D environments.

9. *Toggle sound:* All the audio in runtime can be toggled.

10. *Toggle* different 3D scene options such as skybox, fog, postprocessing, and so on.

11. *Toggle hidden objects.*

12. *Scene camera options:* This allows one to modify the virtual camera properties in the scene.

13. *Gizmos:* Allows one to toggle and modify the icons in the scene representing different objects such as lights, cameras, and so on. Gizmos are visible only in the scene view.

Try adding more objects to the scene and toggle the tools and manipulate them to practice moving around the scene. Users can drag and move objects within objects to make groups; however, child objects scale and transform themselves with respect to their immediate parent object. Try dragging and dropping an object onto another object in the hierarchy window to make groups of objects. Figure 4.12 features the hierarchy of game objects in a parent–child relationship:

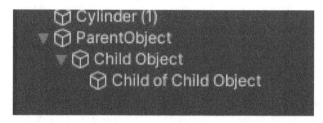

FIGURE 4.12 Hierarchy of game objects in a parentñchild relationship.

A user can build a simple character using primitive objects and transform tools. Figure 4.13 is an example. Notice how the objects are created and placed inside other objects in the hierarchy. A group of groups can be created for easier manipulation of game objects in the scene.

Refer to Figure 4.13:

FIGURE 4.13 Simple 3D character using primitive objects.

UNDERSTANDING LIGHTS

In Unity, the whole scene shades rely on virtual lights. Without an ambience and a light object, one will not be able to see the 3D models in the scene. By default, a Unity scene is lit by an ambient light from the skybox. A skybox is the surrounding colors in the infinite space of the 3D scene.

1. Go to *Window | Rendering | Lighting* to open the lighting window.

2. Go to the *Environment* tab.

3. Under *Environment Lighting*, select *Color* as the *Source*.

4. Now click on the *Ambient Color* bar and choose a different color. Notice how changing the color manipulates the 3D object colors by adding shading. This is the basic light that sets up the scene ambience.

Refer to Figure 4.14:

FIGURE 4.14 Ambient lighting settings in the Lighting window.

Apart from the ambient lights, the directional light acts as a parallel light to the whole scene. Every time a new scene is created, a directional light will be there by default. This is managed by a *Light* component provided by Unity, which is attached to an empty game object. Components will be discussed in a later section of this chapter.

The following experiment may clarify matters:

1. Add a plane object to the bottom of a character such that it appears to be sitting on the floor.

2. Select the *Directional Light* in the scene. Look at the inspector window.

3. Change the intensity to 10 and see how the scene brightens up. Change it back to 2.

4. Change the *Shadow type* to hard shadows, soft shadows, or no shadows, and see how the shadows on the plane change accordingly.

5. At the top of the inspector window, change the rotation values under *Transform* and notice how the direction of the light affects the shadows and the shading of the character. Refer to Figure 4.15:

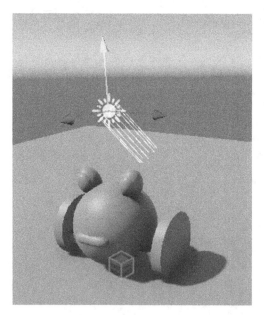

FIGURE 4.15 Impact of the directional light in the scene.

6. Move the directional light closer to the character.

7. Now change the light type from *General* to *Point*. Move the light around and notice how the total scene light has changed to a simple point light. One can also modify the light color by providing color in the *Inspector* window.

8. Similarly, change the light type to spot and notice how the light acts as a flashlight. Try changing the *Inner/Outer Spot* angle and modify the spot-light area. One can also use the rotational tool to rotate the direction of the light.

9. The name of the game object *Directional Light* is independent of the light type configured in the inspector window.

Figure 4.16 features the difference between the point light (left) and spotlight (right):

FIGURE 4.16 Difference between the point light (left) and the spotlight (right).

CREATING MATERIALS

One who is familiar with 3D modeling tools may know the term *materials*. Consider the material as a *paint bucket*. Each 3D mesh can have one or more materials to define the colors of the 3D model. Materials can contain textures to wrap images around 3D models. The textures are known as maps, and based on the material configuration, different maps cause materials to get different looks.

Materials are defined by computer programs called *shaders*. Shaders run in a computer's *graphical processing unit (GPU)* and run parallel for each screen pixel. For this chapter, use a shader known as *Lit* under the Universal Render Pipeline given by Unity.

As a beginning, start coloring the character.

1. Go to the project window and right-click on the `Assets` folder. Choose *Create* and select `Folder.` Now name it as `Materials.` Or name it with any other choice; it is always better to be organized since the project folder can be messy with various files and folders.

2. Now go into the `Materials` folder and right-click on an empty area.

3. Go to *Create | Material*.

4. This will give a new file that has an *orb* icon. Rename it to anything. For this example, name it `Yellow.`

5. Now, select the material created and look in the inspector window. There may be a list of options under the material. Go to the base map under Surface Inputs.

6. Click on the white color bar and choose a yellow color. Notice how it changes the color of the material preview in the project window as well.

7. Now drag and drop the material onto the body of the character. Notice how it changes the color of the object to yellow. Now, changing the color of the original material will change the colors of the objects they are attached to as well. Select the material and change the options in the inspector window. Try changing the surface type and options in Surface Inputs, such as the Metallic map value, Smoothness, Emission, and so on. These values can be manipulated to generate physically based materials such as metal, rubber, plastic, and so on.

8. It is now possible to create multiple materials and assign different colors. Try adding different colors to the character meshes and complete them. The character in color is shown in Figure 4.17.

NOTE *Those reading in paperback may not see color. Please download the digital content provided with this book to view materials in color.*

FIGURE 4.17 Coloring the character with materials.

9. Now, create a new *Sphere* in the scene and a new material in the *Materials* folder. Rename it to `tiled yellow`. Change the color of the material to `yellow`.

10. Now, click the small dot on the left side of the color bar and select *Default-Checker-Gray*.

11. Change the *Tiling* to 10 for both X and Y. Notice how the image selected has wrapped around the sphere as a tile. This is how to use images (textures) and align them onto 3D models using materials. Refer to Figure 4.18:

FIGURE 4.18 Assigning a texture for material.

MANIPULATING THE VIRTUAL CAMERA

Virtual Camera is the only component that captures the objects in the scene with its point of view to render the final output. The output is given through the Game window in Unity Editor. Once exported as an application, it can be viewed through a PC screen, mobile screen, a HoloLens projection, or a virtual reality (VR) headset.

By default, Unity provides a *Main Camera* game object which has a *Camera* component attached to it.

To try how the Camera works with Unity, follow these steps:

1. Dock the Game view by the side of the Unity window, which can be done by dragging from the *Game window* tab.

2. Now select the *Main Camera* and look at the inspector window.

3. Change the position and rotation values of the camera and notice how the view through the game window changes, as shown in Figure 4.19:

FIGURE 4.19 How the user sees the camera and how the camera sees the world.

In AR development, use this virtual camera to move and rotate within the 3D space with respect to the movement of the AR device. All the AR SDKs, as shown throughout this book, have custom components that help the cameras. The cameras will replace the background sky with the device camera input (actual world capture).

There are many options in the camera component to modify:

- Try changing the clipping plane near the value from 0.3 to 4 and moving the camera.
- Also, change the far value to a smaller value, such as 10, and notice how objects cut through the game view output.
- The clipping plane filters only the objects that should be visible in the final view based on distance from the camera.
- Also, go to the *Culling mask* under *Rendering* options and change the value to none. Now, click other values and notice how all the objects are gone from the game view except the sky; selecting *default* shows them all again. This is known as a layer mask, where one can enable and disable

objects being captured from the virtual camera based on the layer that the object is given. There are many use cases for employing a layer mask, and filtering objects through the camera is one of those common uses.

USING THE UNITY PACKAGE MANAGER

Unity is a tool that is capable of many things. By default, the Unity Editor comes with the basics needed to develop a 3D application; however, there are extensions and packages that can extend the capabilities of the editor. For that, Unity has a package manager that works as an extension repository.

1. Click *Window | Package Manager*.

2. There are many ways a package can be installed to a project:

   a. *Unity Registry:* Packages that are already available from Unity.

   b. *Asset Store:* Packages downloaded from the Asset Store.

   c. *External sources:* Sources like GitHub, local packages, and so on.

One can switch between different options by clicking on the package option drop-down at the top, as highlighted in Figure 4.20:

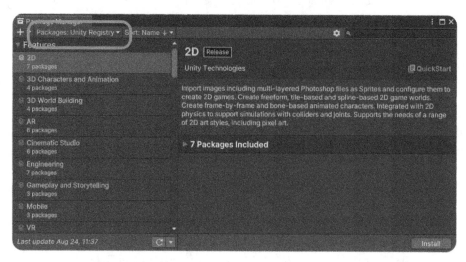

FIGURE 4.20 Selecting the package repository from the package manager.

This window lists the packages that can be installed into a project. Scrolling down, one may see that some packages, such as the Universal Render Pipeline, are already installed.

To install any package, select the package and click the *Install* button at the bottom right corner.

IMPORTING CONTENT INTO UNITY

There are many ways to import assets into Unity. Importing assets into Unity creates a copy of the assets imported within the `Assets` folder of the project. Based on the project target platform, it also generates metafiles related to conversions and other metadata.

1. Download the project files associated with this book, go to *Assets | Chapter 4*, and open the *Smiley* folder.

2. In the Unity Editor, create a new folder and name it `Textures`. Double-click and go into the folder.

3. Now, go to `Assets` | *Import New Asset…*

4. This will open a new window. Navigate to the `Smiley` folder and select all three images. Click *Import*, as shown in Figure 4.21.

This will convert and import three new images into the project `Assets` folder. Now they can be used as textures in the materials:

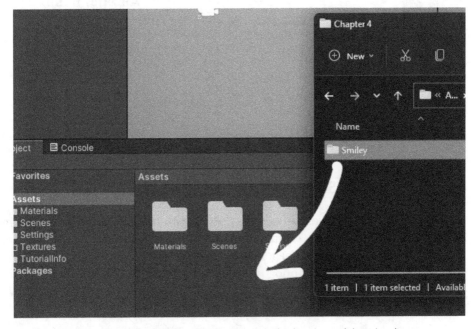

FIGURE 4.21 Importing files into Unity by dragging and dropping them.

Users can also drag and drop the whole folder into Unity's project window. Additionally, one can use the imported textures to create a new material. Name the material as `Smiley`. The material parameters can be as follows:

- *Base map* | Use the Texture image.
- *Metallic Map* | Use the *Metallic Map*. Increase smoothness to 1.
- *Enable Emission* and add the Emission map. Change the emission color to white.

Apply the material to a sphere and notice how each map works with different areas of the sphere. Refer to Figure 4.22:

FIGURE 4.22 Impact of the different maps attached to a material.

IMPORTING ASSETS FROM THE UNITY ASSET STORE

Unity also has a crowdsourced Asset Store with millions of assets containing 3D models, animations, custom components, audio, video effects, and so on. Currently, the package manager can be used to download assets into a project; however, it is necessary to log into the Asset Store to purchase assets with a Unity ID. Follow the listed steps:

1. Head over to the link at *http://assetstore.unity.com* and log in.

2. Search for any free asset available.

3. Click *Add to My Assets*. If there is a license agreement, read it and click *Agree*.

4. Now, go to the package manager window (*Window | Package Manager*). Choose `My Assets` from the drop-down and search for the asset added to the library.

5. Click *Download*. After downloading, click the *Import* button again. This will show a list of all the files that will be added to the project. Click *Import*.

THE STRUCTURE OF THE GAME OBJECT

A Unity scene is made of lighting settings and game objects that fill the scene. A game object, by default, is an empty entity. Game objects can contain many components. These components define the behavior of the game object. The application logic is scripted into the components, and the components will manage the interactions. Unity has provided a list of components to prototype a 3D environment quickly. Refer to Figure 4.23 for a hierarchy of a Unity application:

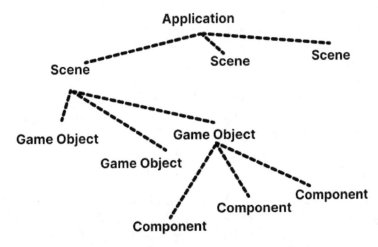

FIGURE 4.23 Hierarchy of a Unity application.

Some of the most used components in Unity are described next.

COMPONENTS OF UNITY

For the Unity scene, create an empty game object (right-click the hierarchy | *Create Empty*) and name it `Component Test`, as shown in Figure 4.24. Now select the game object and look at the inspector window. At the top the name will appear with a tick box. This tick defines the activate/deactivate status of the game object. If a game object is inactive, it will neither be visible in the scene nor run any component logic attached. One can also provide a layer to the game object and a tag that can be used in segmenting game objects in a scene.

FIGURE 4.24 Game object properties in the inspector window.

Transform

Transform is the base component for any game object. Without a transform, there cannot be a game object in existence. The transform component defines the position, rotation, and scale of a game object. Moreover, this component provides useful functions (methods) to move, rotate, translate, and scale objects in local and world spaces. Additionally, a transform component can be used to change the parent of a game object, as the transform component keeps a list of all the child game objects within its transform.

Mesh Renderer

Any game object, by default, can be considered an empty object with just a transform. A mesh renderer can use a 3D mesh and materials to draw a 3D model in the 3D space. A mesh renderer is an inherited component from the *renderer* component. If a 3D model is nondeformable, one may always see a mesh renderer component attached to any 3D model in the scene.

In the 2021, URP, the mesh renderer is divided into materials, lighting, probes, and other additional settings. The materials section will mainly be used to change the material of a 3D model. Also notice that with the mesh renderer, another mesh filter component is attached to it. This component passes the 3D mesh to the renderer, as the renderer and the mesh are independent. Try changing the mesh of the mesh filter component and notice how the game object changes its appearance without changing the color/material. The lighting sections of the component also define whether the 3D model should receive and cast shadows. Carry out the following steps:

1. Add a *Mesh Filter* and a *Mesh Renderer* component to the *Component Test* game object.

2. Click the *dot* next to *Mesh input* and select any mesh from the list. Notice how the object appears in pink. This is because the mesh renderer draws the mesh but does not have a material attached to it.

3. Drag a material to the 3D model or choose a material from the inspector window. Notice how the material now colors the model with the material color.

Colliders

In 3D development, collisions may be needed in various situations. Identifying interactions, detecting physics-based collisions to move objects naturally under simulated forces, and triggering events are some of the use cases of colliders. They work as a virtual boundary for a game object. The task of a collider is to detect if the boundary of the collision area is inside another collision boundary and pass that information to other components attached to the game object. Usually, a collision can be used as a collider or a trigger. Triggers can detect collisions but would not restrict another collider from entering the trigger area. Unity has provided basic collider shapes for 3D. Those are the sphere collider, box collider, capsule collider, and mesh collider. The number of faces of a boundary area increases the mathematical calculations Unity must do to detect a collision. Usually, a sphere collider uses the least amount of computational power, while a mesh collider can have the highest based on the complexity of the collider. Carry out the following steps:

1. Click the component test game object.

2. Add a *Box collider* and notice how it generates a green color boundary gizmo that resembles the boundary areas of the collider. Base collider

components have a button to configure the boundaries visually, known as *Edit collider*. It can be used to change the boundary parameters, which can also be modified using the inspector user interface (UI).

Figure 4.25 shows how different colliders attach to empty game objects:

FIGURE 4.25 Different colliders provided by Unity. The cylinder is a mesh collider.

Rigid body

If a 3D application requires built-in physics by the Unity engine, it will be managed by the rigid body component. Adding a rigid body component to any game object makes it responsive to external forces. The forces can be applied to the object at any given point in any direction; however, without a collider, the engine cannot recognize the external collision-based forces. One can also use a rigid body to apply torques (rotational forces), set the velocity of a game object, detect physics-based collisions, and apply gravity. Carry out the following steps:

1. Select the test game object and add a rigid body. Now click the *Play* button in the editor. Notice how it falls. If there is a plane at the bottom, it will collide with the floor and stop there.

2. Stop the play mode and attach a sphere collider instead of the box collider. Move the object on a plane and click *Play*. Notice how the object rolls despite the mesh resembling another shape. Create a duplicate of the same and try to collide them both together.

Rigid body, by default, responds to a gravity value and will fall toward a negative Y direction. This can be disabled to simulate gravityless space. There is another option to enable and disable the *kinematic* feature of a rigid body. Enabling this will make the object immovable with any external force but will result in collisions. Try changing the values with many duplicates of the game objects in the scene and test them in play mode.

This section has discussed the very few components that Unity offers by default. One can use C# to build custom components for the object and other components to provide custom interactions. A game object can contain as many components as its child objects; however, having many game objects in the scene with many components can be chaotic when there is a need to change the property of a component in a range of game objects. There needs to be a reusable approach to manage game objects.

CREATING PREFABS

Imagine a character game object to duplicate and place around a 3D scene. Their behavior needs to be the same with slight variations. By default, one can create a game object with all the necessary components and custom components, make duplicates of the same object, and place it anywhere.

Now imagine needing to change some values of the parameters of all the character copies. This will be a nightmare if there are many changes to make. Creating prefabs allows creation of a game object with any child object or any component and converting it in a way that allows easy reuse and updating of the components as much as wanted. The changes will affect all the instances (copies) right away.

In Unity, a prefab can also be referred to as a game object. A prefab consists of the same components as a game object. Having a prefab in the scene view is an instance of the prefab.

To create a prefab, follow these steps:

1. Drag and drop a game object from the scene view to the project view.

2. Create a new folder called `Prefabs`.

3. Now drag and drop the `Character` game object into the `Prefabs` folder.

Refer to Figure 4.26:

FIGURE 4.26 Creating a prefab by dragging and dropping a game object from the hierarchy to the project view.

Now one can see how the character is converted into a prefab by changing its icon to a blue cube.

One can delete the character from the scene but drag and drop again into the scene view just like adding a 3D model from the project. The prefab consists of all the child objects and components attached to the original game object.

One can also open the prefab in its own local space to modify it by double-clicking it or choosing the open function in its right-click menu. Any prefab instance can be modified, but the changes need to be applied for the main prefab to be updated. Since the prefabs are defined objects, one cannot delete or remove any objects or components by an instance of the prefab; however, one can append and modify the instance by adding components and game objects at the end.

CONCLUSION

This chapter not only went through the basics of Unity installation but also examined the interface, basic 3D concepts and how components work with each other, properties of different components, and the concepts of creating prefabs. The next chapter will offer an introduction to C# with Unity and learning to create a first custom component.

KEY POINTS

- Unity uses Unity Hub to manage projects and versions.
- Unity is a cross-platform tool, and supportive modules must be installed to enable the platform capabilities.
- One can use Visual Studio or Visual Studio code to write C# scripts for Unity Projects.
- iOS applications can only be built using Xcode, an IDE only available for Mac OS devices.
- A Unity Project can have multiple scenes. A Unity scene consists of game objects. Components define game objects.

QUESTIONS

1. Which of the following is not true regarding Unity 3D engine?

   a. Unity engine is a cross-platform tool and supports multiple platforms, including Android, iOS, Hololens, and Magic Leap.

   b. Unity Hub is an authorizing tool that provides the Unity license and manages Unity projects and versions installed.

   c. Unity uses a *MonoManager* component written in C# language to allow developers to inherit and build custom components.

   d. Unity uses native core language capabilities integrated with .NET runtime.

2. Which of the following is a transformation tool?

   a. Rect tool

   b. Tool handle position

   c. View tool

   d. Gizmo tool

3. What is the most appropriate definition for a prefab?

   a. A prefab is a group of *GameObjects* with transform, renderer, and collider components.

   b. A prefab is a 3D model with materials combined to provide a complex 3D shape.

   c. A prefab is an asset downloaded from the Asset Store, imported using the package manager.

   d. A prefab is a reusable *GameObject* created in a scene and saved in the project assets.

4. Which of the following is not true regarding different components in Unity?

   a. Collider components use a boundary to check whether it is inside another boundary.

   b. Transform component is the base component that allows any object to enable physics.

   c. Renderer components use the material and the GPU to draw the graphics in a 3D scene.

   d. Light component adds illumination in different shapes to all the objects with lit materials in a Unity scene.

Answers appear in the appendix.

5

CREATING A FIRST CUSTOM COMPONENT

INTRODUCTION

C# is a language developed by Microsoft that runs on the .NET framework. This language is primarily used to build Windows applications, but lately, it has also been used for Web, mobile, and game development.

This book is for designers and developers with basic knowledge of C#, including the basic syntax, variables, methods, loops, and conditional statements. For those very new to programming and C#, it is recommended to go over the C# tutorials provided by Microsoft. Go to the following link to learn more about C#:

https://docs.microsoft.com/en-us/dotnet/csharp/

This chapter takes a quick peek at C# within Unity, and how it can be used to create a custom component. It will also show how to communicate with other components and manipulate their values using C#.

STRUCTURE

This chapter will discuss the following topics:

- Introduction to C# in Unity
- Exploring the *MonoBehavior*
- Serialized variables
- Debug class of Unity
- Time in Unity

 ▨ *GetComponent()*
 ▨ Building a simple 3D clock

OBJECTIVES

After completing this chapter, the reader will be able to understand how C# scripts work with Unity, while also understanding some core features of the syntax with Unity, by creating custom components with C# language and using the components to create a simple 3D clock.

INTRODUCTION TO C# IN UNITY

In Unity, a base script is considered as a *component*. Components are defined by Unity based on another C# class file. A basic component script is a class file derived from the *MonoBehavior* class created by Unity.

In order to create a C# component, use the project window to generate a C# class file. Instead of a blank C# class, Unity will generate a class inherited from the *MonoBehavior* class. Due to that, the script now works like a blueprint for a custom component that can be attached to any game object in the scene.

To create an initial component, follow the listed steps:

1. Go to the sample scene with the character and the smiley face sphere.

2. Create a new folder called *Scripts* in the *Assets* folder.

3. Inside the scripts folder, right-click and click *Create | C# Script*.

4. This will generate a default script. Immediately rename it. Change the name to *Spinner*. By clicking somewhere else, Unity will generate a component called *NewBehaviorScript*. This should not be renamed from the Unity editor, as the name of the C# file should be the same as the *MonoBehavior* class name.

5. Chapter 4, "Up and Running with Unity 3D," talked about setting up Visual Studio (VS) and VS code to script in Unity, where the last step to set it up with Unity was paused. Now is the time to continue with that process.

6. Go to *Edit | Preferences*.

7. Select *External tools* from the window that appears.

8. For the *External Script* editor, choose an integrated development environment (IDE). This IDE should support C# development (such as VS and VS code).

9. If there is no editor in the list, browse and choose the location of the editor application.

10. Click on the *Regenerate Project files* button. Now, the Unity editor is configured with the IDE. This is a one-time process and there is no need for it to be done for every project.

11. Close the window, go to the `scripts` folder, and double-click on the script to launch it through the editor.

EXPLORING THE MONOBEHAVIOR

After opening the new C# script, the following template code will appear:

```
1.  using System.Collections;
2.  using System.Collections.Generic;
3.  using UnityEngine;
4.
5.  public class Spinner : MonoBehaviour
6.  {
7.  // Start is called before the first frame update
8.  void Start()
9.  {
10.
11. }
12.
13. // Update is called once per frame
14. void Update()
15. {
16.
17. }
18. }
```

In Unity, the script must be attached to an active game object in the runtime to execute it. There are some imports made by Unity to use Unity-based methods and C# system collection application programming interfaces (APIs). The class name is similar to the file name and is inherited from the

MonoBehavior component. There are two primary methods in any C# template script:

- *start ()*: This method is executed by Unity if this component is attached to an active game object. This method always executes only once at the very moment the game is started. Usually, this method is used to initialize things in the scripts.
- *update ()*: This method is also executed by Unity as long as the application is running. This is a loop method and executes once every frame. The *update* method can be used for any continuous checks, input detection, movement of objects, and so on.

There are other standard methods that Unity executes, such as *Awake()*, *FixedUpdate()*, *OnTriggerEnter()*, and so on; however, they will not be discussed n this chapter.

SERIALIZED VARIABLES

Follow the listed steps for serialized variables:

1. Before utilizing the *start ()* method, create a simple public *float* variable named as *spinnerSpeed* as follows:

   ```
   public float spinnerSpeed;
   ```

2. Now save the script and go back to Unity.

3. Select the smiley sphere created before, and click *Add component.*

4. Type *Spinner* in the search bar and click on the *Spinner* C# component.

5. Now a new custom component *Spinner* may be attached to the sphere, along with a text field to input the spinner speed value. This is a *public* variable. Unity can use its interface to access the public variables and change them, just as other scripts. Sometimes the variable does not need to be public and so must have proper access modifiers. As in this case, the spinner speed can be a *private* variable.

6. Go back to the code, change *public* to *private,* save the script, and go back to Unity.

7. Select the sphere and notice that the variable input is gone. This is because the access modifier is private; Unity cannot access or modify it through the interface anymore.

8. However, developers can use the *[SerializeField]* attribute in order to ask Unity to serialize it. This allows the Unity interface to show and modify the value; however, being a private variable, other scripts do not have permission to access the variable directly.

9. Change the variable to a serialized field by adding the attribute. It should now be like this:

   [SerializeField] private float spinnerSpeed;

10. Save the script and go back to Unity. Notice that the field for *Spinner-Speed* is now back. Refer to Figure 5.1:

FIGURE 5.1 How a script component appears in the inspector window, with placeholders for serialized variables.

DEBUG CLASS OF UNITY

In Unity, one can use the debug class to print messages in the console and draw editor-only gizmos in the scene at runtime. This allows the use of graphics and text to debug code properly.

The most used method of the *Debug* class is the *Log()* method. This is similar to the *Console.PrintLine()* method provided by core C#.

Open the *Spinner* script, and add the following line into the *start* method:

```
Debug.Log("Hello Unity!");
```

Add this to the *update* method:

```
Debug.Log("Hello Update!");
```

Save the script and run the game. Open the console window at the bottom, as shown in Figure 5.2, and see how it prints *Hello Unity* at once and *Hello Update* infinitely (until one stops playing):

FIGURE 5.2. Console window of Unity.

1. Press the *Collapse* button to collapse duplicate logs.

2. It will show the number of iterations that it has logged.

This book will be using the `Debug.Log()` method throughout to debug the code executions. Readers can go to https://docs.unity3d.com/ScriptReference/Debug.html to learn more about the `Debug` class and the methods it offers.

TIME IN UNITY

Unity uses the clock speed of the computer that it is running in order to perform frame-based calculations. Also, Unity uses the internal clock to determine the real time using the *Time* module.

As shown before, the `Update` method executes once per clock cycle assigned to Unity by the processor. This is variable due to the number of processes running in the computer, as the operating system schedules and allocates time to run the Unity app. By default, a good computer can run around 200–300 frames per second, and it totally relies on how the application performs as well.

So how are real times calculated in the `update` method?

This can be achieved by using a variable provided by Unity known as `Time.deltaTime.` This is a `float` value, and it varies between each frame, as it gives the time between two frame updates. Therefore, by continuously appending *Time.deltaTime* to *0* in the *update* method, the resultant value would be the number of seconds that have elapsed since the start of the play mode.

Change the inside of the *Spinner* class to the following, save it, and run:

```
1.  float timeSinceStart = 0;
2.
3.  void Update()
4.  {
5.  timeSinceStart += Time.deltaTime;
6.  Debug.Log(timeSinceStart);
7.  }
```

Notice how the console window prints the time after each iteration and how it matches the real time. The *Time* module in Unity offers various time-related values, such as the current time since level load, frame rate, frame count, and so on.

The *DateTime* module from the C# System core module is also available and can be used within Unity. One of the best features of Unity is the ability to use .NET core modules within the custom components that are built. In the next section, use the *DateTime* method to create a simple 3D clock.

GETCOMPONENT

Out of all the methods that Unity provides, the *GetComponent* can be considered one of the more important methods to be used within components. This method can be used anywhere in a component script to access other components of the game object that the script is attached to.

By default, Unity provides access to the *gameObject* and the *transform* component of the attached game object by using the same keywords. In order to get access to other components, use *GetComponent<T>()*. Here, the *T* stands for the component generic, that is, the class name of the component being referred to. The *Get* component method is costly. Unity iterates through all of the components attached to the game object to look for the needed component. Instead of using *GetComponent* in the *update* method, use it just once in the *Start* method and cache the value to reuse it.

Modify the *spinner* script to the following, change the spinner speed to 100, and play to test it:

```
1.  using UnityEngine;
2.
3.  public class Spinner : MonoBehaviour
4.  {
5.    [SerializeField] private float spinnerSpeed;
6.
7.    private MeshRenderer rend;
8.    float timeSinceStart = 0;
9.
10.   void Start()
11.   {
12.       rend = GetComponent<MeshRenderer>();
13.   }
14.
15.   void Update()
16.   {
17.       transform.Rotate(0, spinnerSpeed * Time.deltaTime, 0);
18.
19.       timeSinceStart += Time.deltaTime;
20.       if(timeSinceStart > 0)
21.       {
22.           timeSinceStart = 0;
23.           rend.material.color = Random.ColorHSV();
24.       }
25.   }
26. }
```

Notice that the smiley sphere starts rotating around its Y axis while changing its color tint to a random color every second. A description for the preceding code is as follows:

- *Line 7:* A *MeshRenderer* reference variable is created.
- *Line 12:* In the *Start ()* method, the attached mesh renderer component of the smiley sphere is cached as the *rend* variable. This provides access to the mesh renderers' methods and variables.
- *Line 17:* The transform component of the sphere is called to rotate around itself by using the Rotate method with *x*, *y*, and *z* parameter values.

- *Line 19 to 24:* The `timeSinceStart` by `Time.deltaTime` is incremented and every time it goes beyond 1, it is pulled back to 0. This way, anything can be executed with a 1-second interval.
- *Line 23:* The material of the mesh renderer is accessed and its color is changed to a random color using `Random.ColorHSV()` method. This is a method provided by Unity under `UnityEngine.Random` module.
- As can be seen, a sandbox of methods and components are provided in order that a user can play with scripts to build any computer graphics visualization. It is always better to follow the C# documentation by Microsoft, as well as Unity's own documentation, to learn more about the components and supporting methods provided by Unity.

BUILDING A SIMPLE 3D CLOCK

Using the content learned in the previous sections, it is now time to try to build a simple 3D clock. Refer to the following steps:

1. Create a new Scene in the *Scenes* folder and rename it to 3DClock.

2. Open the scene and create a cylinder 3D object. Remove the *Capsule collider* component from it by clicking on the *three dots* button on the top right end of the component.

3. Scale the cylinder in such a way that it looks like a clockface.

4. Now inside the clock, add three empty game objects and rename them as *Hours, Minutes,* and *Seconds.* These objects will hold the clock handles inside them separately. The transform components of these empty game objects can be referenced to rotate based on the current system time.

5. Now, add another cylinder inside the main clockface and rename it as *knob.* This will be a good reference game object to know the center of the clockface.

6. Inside each empty game object, create a cube, and scale it in such a way that it looks like a proper clock handle. Because a cube uses its center as the pivot point, it may be necessary to move it away from its parent's origin to *look like* it starts from the knob position.

7. One may use different materials to color each cube inside each empty game object.

8. Finally, a clock model with the time perfectly set to 12:00:00 should appear. All the *hours, minutes, seconds,* and *knob* game objects should be at the 0,0,0 position with 0,0,0 rotation. By selecting any handle game object and rotating it around the Y axis, it will appear that it goes around the clockface. Figure 5.3 shows how the clock and the handles must be set up:

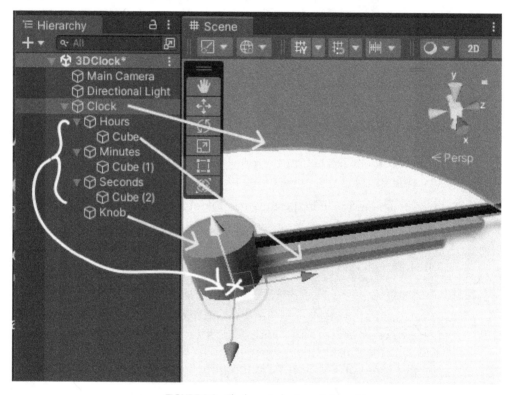

FIGURE 5.3. Clock created using primitive objects.

9. Save the scene.

10. Go to the *Scripts* folder and create a new C# script. Rename it as *Clock* and press *Enter.*

11. Open the script and change it as follows:

```
1.  using UnityEngine;
2.  using System;
3.
4.  public class Clock : MonoBehaviour
```

```
5.  {
6.      [SerializeField] private Transform hoursHandle;
7.      [SerializeField] private Transform minutesHandle;
8.      [SerializeField] private Transform secondsHandle;
9.
10.   DateTime currentTime;
11.   Vector3 hours, mins, secs;
12.
13.
14.   void Update()
15.   {
16.       currentTime = DateTime.Now;
17.
18.       hours = new Vector3(0, (360/12) * currentTime.Hour, 0);
19.       mins = new Vector3(0, (360/60) * currentTime.Minute, 0);
20.       secs = new Vector3(0, (360/60) * currentTime.Second, 0);
21.
22.       hoursHandle.localEulerAngles = hours;
23.       minutesHandle.localEulerAngles = mins;
24.       secondsHandle.localEulerAngles = secs;
25.   {
26.}
```

The following is an explanation of the code:

- *Line 6 to 7:* Transform references were added for the empty game objects that are holding the handles.
- *Line 10:* Cached variable to hold and update the current time.
- *Line 11:* `Vector3` values to hold the rotation of the handles in Euler angles (x, y, z values).
- *Line 16:* Assign the current time to the `currentTime` variable using `DateTime.Now`.
- *Line 18 to 20:* Use the *hour*, *minute*, and *second* values from the current time, divide the full 360° circle by the number of segments and multiply that value to convert the time values to degrees. Here, the rotation was applied only to the *y*-axis; the other two axes are kept at 0. Calculate these vectors and hold them temporarily in the variables created in line 11.
- *Line 22 to 24:* Use the `localEulerAngles` variable of the transform component to assign the rotation directly to its local space. This way, the

rotation of the handles will only be with respect to the *Clock* game object. Therefore, rotating the parent game object will not impact the rotation of the handles.

12. Save the script and go back to Unity.

13. Select the `Clock` object, click *Add Component*, and choose the `Clock` script.

14. Now it has three placeholders to assign *Transform* components. In Unity, this can be done by dragging and dropping the associated game object onto the placeholder. Drag and drop `Hours, Minutes,` and `Seconds` game objects onto the relevant placeholders. Figure 5.4 shows what it should look like after the assignment.

15. Now, click play and see how the clock ticks based on the actual computer time:

FIGURE 5.4 Assigning reference components by dragging and dropping the game object.

CONCLUSION

This chapter took an introduction to C# with Unity and discussed how it works with other components. The next chapter will take a deeper dive into C# with Unity and teach how to create components that can talk to each other to build a complete interactive application. As Unity and C# both contain a large number of modules, this book will limit discussion to the scope of building augmented reality (AR) applications. Therefore, it is highly recommended to read the C# documentation and Unity documentation to understand how scripting can be used effectively in projects.

KEY POINTS

- C# scripts are inherited from a *MonoBehavior* class, which makes it a blueprint for a component.
- A *MonoBehavior* class has default methods, such as *start*, *update*, *awake*, *FixedUpdate*, executed (if available within components) by Unity, as a part of the program's runtime process.
- A script can use the *Get* component to get access to other components and manipulate their values to create logic and implement interactions.

QUESTIONS

1. Which of the following variables cannot be modified using the inspector window?

   a. `[SerializeField] public int health;`

   b. `[SerializeField] private string name;`

   c. `private bool useGravity;`

   d. `public float gravity;`

2. What is the difference between the start and the update methods?

   a. The *start* method runs before enabling the component as soon as it enters runtime. The *update* method runs once every second.

   b. The *start* method runs when the component becomes available in play mode. The *update* method runs once per frame.

    c. The *start* method runs once every second, and the *update* method runs per every frame.

    d. The *start* and *update* methods both get executed once, one after the other.

3. What is the use of the *GetComponent<T>()* method?

    a. It goes through all the objects in the scene to find the *T* component and returns it.

    b. It goes through all the components in child objects to find the *T* component and returns it.

    c. It returns the transform *(T)* component attached to the game object to which the script is attached.

    d. It returns the component of *T* type attached to the game object to which the script is attached.

Answers appear in the appendix.

6

REFRESHING C# CONCEPTS WITH UNITY

INTRODUCTION

A major goal of this book is to develop 3D applications that can run in an augmented reality (AR) world. Before that, understanding C# concepts with Unity and the capabilities of different components will make it possible to build any interaction that can be done within an AR world. The previous chapters provided a thorough introduction to Unity's ecosystem and a simple implementation of a custom component using C#.

This chapter of the book goes through all the essential components discussed before and attempts to manipulate the values to build a simple top-down shooter game. Using this game will lead to an ability to understand a simple structure of a 3D application, accomplished by moving through different scenes and using physics, coded animation, audio, and particle effects. There will also be a lot of coding in this chapter.

STRUCTURE

▪ This chapter will discuss the following topics:
▪ Setting up the scene
▪ Movement of the player
▪ Creating a bullet for the player to shoot
▪ Shooting bullets
▪ Setting up the enemy
▪ Setting up the player

- Spawning and destroying enemies
- Game user interface (UI)
  - Game manager
- Adding audio and polishing
  - Adding the main menu
  - Switching scenes
  - The next steps

OBJECTIVES

Completion of this chapter will lead to an understanding of how to use different components for different system behaviors, how to employ design patterns to access the code, how to apply use cases of different components, and finally how to polish an application, making it ready to be published as a first prototype.

SETTING UP THE SCENE

The requirement is to build a simple top-down shooter game that is similar to the Capcom 1942 game. To create a straightforward version of it but in 3D, the idea is straightforward. The player will be controlling a spaceship that shoots bullets at timely intervals and keeps shooting at the enemy spaceships that are approaching from the opposite side, as shown in Figure 6.1. Occasionally, the enemy ships will also shoot at the player, who can block the bullets by shooting at them. There will be different enemy ships with different levels of difficulty. The goal is to get the highest score possible during a single run. To get started, first refer to Figure 6.1:

FIGURE 6.1 Simple sketch of the final output of the game.

First create a new Universal Render Pipeline (URP) project in Unity and load up the sample scene. It is recommended to download all the asset files provided with the book before trying out this chapter. Import the *Top-Down Shooter* Unity package within the `Chapter 6` folder of the assets. This has all the necessary assets and prefabs that are required for the completion of the project.

The project needs a player, enemies, bullets, and an enemy spawner to generate enemies. For the moment, use primitives to set up the basic scene. Create a sphere for the enemy with a scale of a unit vector (1,1,1), another sphere for the player, a small cube for the bullet, and a big cube in front of the player. The collider bounds of this cube will be used to randomly generate and spawn enemies that fly in the player's direction. Also, the main camera should be moved to the top of the scene, looking down at the player. The arrangement of the setup should be as shown in Figure 6.2:

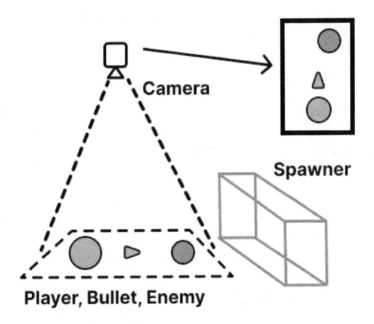

FIGURE 6.2 Sketch of the scene setup.

Make sure that the player's forward direction is toward the enemy and the enemy's is toward the player. In this game, keep the player's position within the screen space and move the enemies and the background to visually mimic the movement of the player along an endless path forward.

MOVEMENT OF THE PLAYER

Add a rigid body to the player. This allows the use of physics to move the player's object. Change the sphere collider radius to 0.5 since 1 meter seems too big. Eventually, the mesh filter and mesh renderer will be removed but keep that for now.

Create a C# script and name it *PlayerMovement.cs*. This class is going to capture the touch input and move the player. Open the script and update the script as follows. The descriptions of the major lines will be given after the code:

```
1.  public class PlayerMovement : MonoBehaviour
2.  {
3.    [Range(0,.3f)]
4.    [SerializeField] private float touchSpeed = 0.5f;
5.    [SerializeField] private Camera cam;
6.
7.    private Rigidbody playerBody;
8.    private Vector3 worldPos;
9.    private Vector3 touchPos;
10.   private float playerZ;
11.
12.   void Start()
13.   {
14.     playerBody = GetComponent<Rigidbody>();
15.     playerZ = cam.transform.position.y - playerBody.trans-
    form. position.y;
16.   }
17.
18.   void FixedUpdate()
19.   {
20.     if (!cam || !playerBody)
21.       return;
22.
23.     if(Input.touchCount>0)
```

```
24.    {
25.       touchPos = Input.GetTouch(0).position;
26.       touchPos.z = playerZ;
27.       worldPos = cam.ScreenToWorldPoint(touchPos);
28.
29.       MovePlayer(worldPos);
30.    }
31. }
32.
33.  void MovePlayer(Vector3 target)
34.  {
35.    playerBody.MovePosition(Vector3.Lerp(playerBody.position,
   target, touchSpeed));
36.  }
37. }
```

The script here is using linear interpolation to slowly move the player toward the touch position using the *Vector2.Lerp* method. A linear interpolation running in the update method moves the player toward a given point by a provided fraction, which is a variable that can span between *0* and *1*.

Line number 4 references that as *touchSpeed* and has given a restriction range to be within 0 and 0.3. In order to move the player, use the *rigidbody* object's *MovePosition* method instead of the *transform* component. This way, the movement will give priority to any physics-based movements, such as collisions. Also, cache the *rigidbody* of the player's game object by using *GetComponent* in the *start* method.

The *Camera* reference is also needed. Since the touch point is in screen space, use the camera to convert that point to one in world space; however, this will give a position too close to the camera. Therefore, it is necessary to get a distance from the camera, and usually, it is better to have the distance set up by default in the scene. Therefore, calculate a *z* value to position the player with a *z* offset with respect to the camera. This is captured in line 15, and the value is stored in a variable.

Now select the player game object and attach a *Rigidbody* and the *PlayerMovement* script. In the *rigidbody* component, enable rotation constraints for all *x*, *y*, and *z* under the constraints section. This will restrict the player from rotating due to external forces.

CREATING A BULLET FOR THE PLAYER TO SHOOT

Now that the player's movement is ready, it is necessary to create another component to shoot bullets while the screen is being touched; however, first of all, it is necessary to create a bullet.

Select the cube created for the bullet and attach a *Rigidbody* component to it. The bullet needs to be instantiated by both the player and the enemy. Therefore, the bullet should be given damage and information on the initiator of the bullet (whether it is the player or the enemy who owns the bullet). Create a new C# script and name it *Bullet.cs*:

```
1. public class Bullet : MonoBehaviour
2. {
3.    [SerializeField] private GameObject bulletHitParticle;
4.    [SerializeField] private int bulletDamage = 20;
5.    [SerializeField] private Material bulletMaterialEnemy;
6.    [SerializeField] private Material bulletMaterialPlayer;
7.    [SerializeField] private MeshRenderer bulletMeshRenderer;
8.
9.    public enum BulletInitiator
10.   {
11.     ENEMY,
12.     PLAYER
13.   }
14.
15.   private BulletInitiator initiator;
16.
17.   public void SetBullet(BulletInitiator bulletInitiator,
   int damage)
18.   {
19.     bulletDamage = damage;
20.     initiator = bulletInitiator;
21.     bulletMeshRenderer.material = initia-
   tor == BulletInitiator. ENEMY ? bulletMaterialEnemy :
   bulletMaterialPlayer;
22.   }
```

```
23.
24.  private void OnTriggerEnter(Collider other)
25.  {
26.        if(other.CompareTag("Enemy") &&  initiator.
     Equals(BulletInitiator.PLAYER))
27.      {
28.      //destroy the enemy
29.      other.GetComponent<Enemy>().ReduceHealth(bulletDamage);
     //add score
30.        GameManager.instance.AppendScore(1);
31.      }
32.    else if(other.gameObject.CompareTag("Player") && initia-
     tor. Equals(BulletInitiator.ENEMY))
33.      {
34.      //reduce health or game over
35.      other.GetComponent<Player>().ReduceHealth(bulletDamage);
36.
37.      }
38.
39.      // Initiate a simple puff particle
40.      Instantiate(bulletHitParticle, transform.position, trans-
     form. rotation);
41.      Destroy(gameObject);
42.  }
43. }
```

The bullet manages the following tasks:

- *Keeps track of the initiator of the bullet*: This is done using an `enum` called `BulletInitator` and a variable of the same `enum` type `initiator`. The `public` method `SetBullet` requests a `BulletInitiator` parameter to assign a value to the initiator.
- *Changes the material based on the initiator*: The `SetBullet` method will check what the initiator is and assign different materials—for example, create a blue and a red material such that the enemy will spawn red bullets while the player would spawn blue.
- *Checks the collision*: Use the `OnTriggerEnter` method in line 24, which is executed by Unity when there is a collision with triggers. Here, check

the `tag` associated with the other game object that the bullet collides with. Based on the `tag`, specify whether it is the player or the enemy and provide damage by calling `ReduceHealth()` methods in both `Player` and `Enemy` components. Note that those components have not been made yet. Those methods will be discussed when they are needed.

▪ *Adds the score*: Every time the bullet hits an enemy, the script will call a function in a `GameManager` component to append the score by one. In line 31, directly call the `GameManager().instance` and call its method instead of a direct drag-and-drop reference. This will be discussed in the *Game manager* section.

▪ *Spawns a particle prefab at the time of collision*: Use the `Instantiate` method to instantiate a bullet particle when the bullet collides with anything. Once done, the bullet will destroy itself.

Now attach the script to the bullet. Errors will probably appear since there is reference to scripts that are not available yet. For the moment, just comment on the lines in the script that contain calls to components that are not created.

In the inspector window, assign a bullet hit particle from the project window (`Asset package | Prefabs | BulletHit`), two materials for the player, and the enemy bullets (`Asset package | Materials | Enemy_Bullet/Player_Bullet`). Set the `Bullet` damage to 20 and assign the mesh renderer component of the bullet as the `Bullet` mesh renderer. The component should look as shown in Figure 6.3:

FIGURE 6.3 Bullet component attached to the bullet object.

Additionally, select the collider of the bullet and tick `Is Trigger`.

SHOOTING BULLETS

As explained before, the bullets can be shot by two objects: the player and the enemy. This section will delineate how to instantiate bullets and shoot at the enemy:

1. Before creating a new component for this, it is necessary to convert the bullet into a *prefab*. Once done, the bullet can be removed from the scene.

2. Now create an empty game object within the player and move in front of the player. This is going to be a reference point for the bullet to be instantiated. Because the object is inside the *Player* as a child, it moves with the player.

3. Rotate the game object in a way that its local forward direction is pointing forward. Figure 6.4 shows how the spawn point is added inside the player game object:

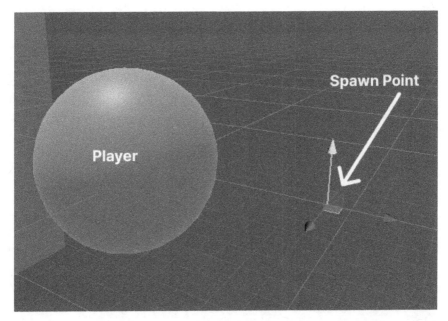

FIGURE 6.4 Player and the spawn point.

4. Create a new C# script and name it *PlayerShoot.cs*. This component will instantiate and shoot bullets with a given frequency while the screen is being touched:

```
1. public class PlayerShoot : MonoBehaviour
2. {
3.   [SerializeField] private GameObject bulletPrefab;
4.   [SerializeField] private Transform spawnPoint;
5.   [SerializeField] private float shootFrequency;
6.   [SerializeField] private float shootForce;
7.
8.   private float timer = 0;
9.   private GameObject tempBullet; 10.
11.  void Update()
12.  {
13.    if(Input.touchCount>0)
14.    {
15.      Shoot();
16.    }
17.  }
18.
19.  void Shoot()
20.  {
21.    if (shootFrequency <= 0)
22.      return;
23.
24.    timer += Time.deltaTime;
25.    if(timer>= 1/shootFrequency)
26.    {
27.      tempBullet = Instantiate(bulletPrefab, spawnPoint. posi-
  tion, spawnPoint.rotation);
28.  tempBullet.GetComponent<Rigidbody>().AddForce(spawnPoint.
  forward * shootForce);
29.      tempBullet.GetComponent<Bullet>().SetBullet(Bullet.
  BulletInitiator.PLAYER, 20);
30.
31.      AudioManager.instance.PlaySFX("fire");
32.
33.      Destroy(tempBullet, 5);
34.
```

```
35.     timer = 0;
36.   }
37.  }
38. }
```

This component will check for the touch input and run a *Shoot()* method in the update loop. The shoot method contains a timer that increments and resets to 0 after each *1/shootFrequency* second. If the shot frequency is 2, the timer will reset every 0.5 seconds, and every time the timer resets, it shoots a bullet. Lines 21 to 25 are used for the time increment and frequency check.

From line 27 to 29, a bullet is instantiated on the spawn point (transform reference variable) and a force added on its *rigidbody* component by getting the forward direction of the spawn point and multiplying it by the shoot force variable value. Finally, the *Bullet* component of the spawned object becomes accessible in order to set its values: the initiator and the damage.

Line 31 calls an *AudioManager* to play a sound effect. This will be discussed at the end of the chapter. For the moment, comment out the line.

5. Before resetting the timer to zero, register the bullet to be destroyed after 5 seconds. If it is not destroyed and if the bullet does not hit an enemy, it will be loaded into memory, which will increase memory usage and hinder the performance of the game. Therefore, use the *Destroy* method with the temp bullet and the number of seconds as parameters.

6. Go back to Unity and assign this component to the *Player*. Drag and drop the *Bullet* prefab from the project window onto the *Bullet Prefab* option and the *BulletSpawn* game object onto the *Spawn Point* option. Figure 6.5 shows a sample configuration to spawn 13 bullets per 10 seconds and a shoot force of 400:

FIGURE 6.5 Player shoot component attached to the player.

SETTING UP THE ENEMY

The enemy uses the most basic setup. Once the enemy is spawned, it will move in the forward direction with a given speed and shoot a bullet in random time frequencies. The enemy will have a health value that will be reduced when it collides with a bullet. If the health goes below 0, the enemy will explode and be destroyed. In order to indicate the enemy's health, use a simple world space canvas with a tiny health bar attached to the top of the enemy:

1. Select the enemy game object created before. Right-click and `Add UI | Canvas`. This will add a fairly big 2D element inside the enemy.

2. Change the scale of the canvas to 0.01. In the canvas component, change the render mode to `World Space`.

3. Add two image game objects in the canvas by using `UI | Image`. Name one as `HealthBarBackground` and the other as `HealthBar`. For both images, set the left, right, top, and bottom to 0 in the `Rect` transform component, 0 for Min, and 1 for Max, while keeping the pivot to 0.

4. Now select the `HealthBar` and make sure that it is at the bottom. Select its `Image` component and change the `Source Image` to `HealthBar` sprite from the assets package (`UI Images | HealthBar`). Refer to Figure 6.6.

5. Set the `Color` to red and `Image` type to `Filled`. Change the `Fill Method` to `Horizontal`. Now if the `Fill amount` of the component is changed, it will be possible to see a small progress bar that looks like a mini health bar.

6. Position the canvas on top of the enemy in a way that it is visible from the top camera.

Refer to Figure 6.6 to see the setting up of the health bar:

FIGURE 6.6 Setting up the health bar with filling UI image.

7. Now like the player's spawn point, add an empty game object inside the enemy as well, and make sure that it is rotated toward the forward direction of the enemy; however, the enemy can still look in the opposite direction just as the player can.

8. Create a new C# script and name it *EnemyMovement.cs*. Open it and add the following:

```
1.  public class EnemyMovement : MonoBehaviour
2.  {
3.    [SerializeField] private float enemySpeed;
4.
5.    private Rigidbody enemyBody;
6.    private Vector3 nextPosition;
7.
8.    public void SetSpeed(float speed)
9.    {
10.     enemySpeed = speed;
11.   }
12.
13.   public float GetSpeed()
14.   {
15.     return enemySpeed;
16.   }
17.
18.   void Start()
19.   {
20.     enemyBody = GetComponent<Rigidbody>();
21.   }
22.
23.   void Update()
24.   {
25.   nextPosition = enemyBody.position + enemyBody.transform.
      forward * enemySpeed * Time.deltaTime;
26.     Move(nextPosition);
27.   }
28.
```

```
29.  void Move(Vector3 target)
30.  {
31.    enemyBody.MovePosition(target);
32.  }
33. }
```

This script will capture a given speed and move the player in the forward direction. The next position of the enemy is calculated in line 25, where it adds a forward position multiplied by the enemy's speed.

9. Also add a couple of *set* and *get* methods to manage the *speed* variable. The rigid body added to the enemy will be cached at the *start* method, using the *GetComponent* method.

10. In order to manage the rest of the enemy functions, create another C# script and name it *Enemy.cs*. Add the following:

```
1.  using UnityEngine.UI;
2.  public class Enemy : MonoBehaviour
3.  {
4.    [SerializeField] private int enemyHealth;
5.    [SerializeField] private GameObject bulletPrefab;
6.    [SerializeField] private Transform spawnPoint;
7.    [SerializeField] private GameObject destroyParticle;
8.    [SerializeField] private Vector2 bulletTime;
9.    [SerializeField] private Image healthUI; 10.
11.   private GameObject tempBullet;
12.   private EnemyMovement enemyMove;
13.   private float startHealth;
14.
15.   private void Start()
16.   {
17.     enemyMove = GetComponent<EnemyMovement>();
18.     StartCoroutine(ShootBullets());
19.   }
20.
21.   public void SetHealth(int value)
22.   {
```

```
23.    enemyHealth = value;
24.    startHealth = enemyHealth;
25.    UpdateHealthUI(1);
26.  }
27.
28.  public void ReduceHealth(int reductionAmount)
29.  {
30.    enemyHealth -= reductionAmount;
31.    UpdateHealthUI((float)enemyHealth / (float)startHealth);
32.    if(enemyHealth <= 0)
33.    {
34.      Instantiate(destroyParticle, transform.position, trans-
    form.rotation);
35.      AudioManager.instance.PlaySFX("explode");
36.      Destroy(gameObject);
37.    }
38.  }
39.
40.  private IEnumerator ShootBullets()
41.  {
42.    while (gameObject.activeSelf)
43.    {
44.      yield return new WaitForSeconds(Random.
    Range(bulletTime.x, bulletTime.y));
45.      tempBullet = Instantiate(bulletPrefab, spawnPoint. posi-
    tion, spawnPoint.rotation);
46.      tempBullet.GetComponent<Bullet>(). SetBullet(Bullet.
    BulletInitiator.ENEMY, 20);
44.      tempBullet.GetComponent<Rigidbody>().AddForce(
45.        spawnPoint.forward * enemyMove.GetSpeed() *
    2,ForceMode.VelocityChange
49.        );
50.      Destroy(tempBullet, 5);
51.    }
52.  }
```

```
53.
54.   void UpdateHealthUI(float value)
55.   {
56.     healthUI.fillAmount = value;
57.   }
58.
59. }
```

This script will be using `UnityEngine.UI` to manipulate the fill amount of the health bar. For initializing the health value of the enemy, the `SetHealth` method is added with a parameter. This will reset the start health of the enemy, as well as reset the health bar.

The `ReduceHealth` method in line 28 will take any amount as a parameter and reduce that amount from the current health of the enemy. If the current health is below 0, the enemy will be destroyed while instantiating an exploding particle and playing an audio effect. Comment line 35 for the moment. This method also will call the `UpdateHealthUI` method to change the health bar values.

The `UpdateHealthUI` method changes the fill amount by getting the fraction of the current health from the start health of the enemy. This will give a value between 0 and 1 and will be used as the fill amount of the health bar.

`ShootBullet()` is an *IEnumerator* method that returns a yield. The yield can be represented as a wait. It can be dynamic or configured. Inside the *IEnumerator*, the loop will work indefinitely until the enemy is active. The loop returns a yield wait time that is a random number between the x and y values of the `bulletTime Vector2` method. A `Vector2` was used here to store two values in one variable.

Once the wait time is over, similar to the player, it will shoot a bullet by instantiating and adding force to the bullet while setting the damage and the initiator. The force of the bullet is calculated by doubling the speed of the enemy. `ForceMode.VelocityChange` will apply a force in a way that the starting velocity matches the value in the first parameter of the `AddForce` method. This `IEnumerator` is called to run by initiating a coroutine, as in line 18.

11. Now select the enemy and add both `EnemyMovement` and `Enemy` components. Assign all the necessary references to the `enemy` component, as shown in Figure 6.7:

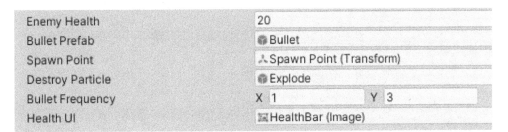

Enemy Health	20	
Bullet Prefab	⊕ Bullet	
Spawn Point	⚘ Spawn Point (Transform)	
Destroy Particle	⊕ Explode	
Bullet Frequency	X 1	Y 3
Health UI	⊠ HealthBar (Image)	

FIGURE 6.7 Enemy component.

The `Bullet Prefab` is the same as players; `Spawn Point` is the empty game object within the enemy, and `Destroy Particle` as `Explode`, which can be found from the `asset package | Prefabs | Explode`, and the `Healthbar` is the `Image` game object added inside the health bar canvas.

SETTING UP THE PLAYER

Now it is time to finalize the player object by adding a new *Player.cs* script. Similar to the enemy component, this method will take care of the health of the player and end the game once the player gets destroyed. The player will immediately be destroyed if it collides with an enemy. Open the C# script and add the following:

```
1.  public class Player : MonoBehaviour
2.  {
3.     [SerializeField] private int playerHealth = 100;
4.     [SerializeField] private GameObject destroyParticle;
5.
6.     private void Start()
7.     {
8.       GameManager.instance.DisplayHealth(playerHealth);
9.     }
10.
11.    public void ReduceHealth(int reductionAmount)
12.    {
13.      playerHealth -= reductionAmount;
14.
15.      if (playerHealth <= 0)
```

```
16.    {
17.       Instantiate(destroyParticle, transform.position,
          transform.rotation);
18.       Destroy(gameObject); 19.
20.       // Game Over
21.       GameManager.instance.GameOver();
22.    }
23.    else
24.    {
25.       GameManager.instance.DisplayHealth(playerHealth);
26.    }
27.  }
28.
29.  private void OnCollisionEnter(Collision collision)
30.  {
31.    if(collision.gameObject.CompareTag("Enemy"))
32.    {
33.       // Reduce max health
34.       ReduceHealth(100);
35.    }
36.  }
37. }
```

In this component, use the *GameManager* to set the display health in the UI and end the game. This will come later; for the moment, just comment on the lines. Like the enemy component, the *ReduceHealth* method deducts health from the player and destroys it once it reaches the 0 health limit. The *OnCollisionEnter* method will check if the player collides with the enemy and reduces the max health amount to immediately end the game.

Assign the player component to the player and assign the destroy particle (choose *Asset pack* | *Prefabs* | *Explode*). Now is the time to uncomment lines 29 and 36 from the bullet C# script.

Since all the base components are set up, convert the enemy into a prefab and remove it from the scene.

SPAWNING AND DESTROYING ENEMIES

Now that the base enemy setup has been accomplished, it is time for spawning and destroying the enemies. Create a new C# script and name it *EnemySpawner.cs* and open it:

```
1. public class EnemySpawner : MonoBehaviour
2.  {
3.    [SerializeField] private GameObject enemyPrefab;
4.    public bool isPlaying = true;
5.
6.    private BoxCollider spawnArea;
7.    GameObject enemy; 8.
9.    void Start()
10. {
11.    spawnArea = GetComponent<BoxCollider>();
12.    }
13.
14.    public void StartSpawning()
15.    {
       isPlaying = true;
16.    StartCoroutine(Spawner());
17.    }
18.
19.    private IEnumerator Spawner()
20.    {
21.    yield return new WaitForSeconds(3);
22.    while(isPlaying)
23.    {
24.      SpawnEnemy();
25.      yield return new WaitForSeconds(Random.Range(1, 3));
26.    }
27.    }
28.
29.    void SpawnEnemy()
```

```
30.  {
31.    enemy = Instantiate(enemyPrefab, GetRandomPosition(),
transform.rotation);
32.    enemy.GetComponent<EnemyMovement>().SetSpeed(Random.
Range(1f, 10f));
33.  }
34.
35.  private Vector3 GetRandomPosition()
36.  {
37.    return new Vector3(
38.        Random.Range(spawnArea.bounds.min.x, spawnArea.
bounds.max.x),
39.        Random.Range(spawnArea.bounds.min.y, spawnArea.
bounds.max.y),
40.        Random.Range(spawnArea.bounds.min.z, spawnArea.
bounds.max.z)
41.      );
42.  }
43. }
```

Using the spawner cube created earlier, its box collider is bound to generate a random position to spawn the enemy. In line 36, create a *GetRandomPosition* method to generate a random *vector3* that values inside the collider bounds. Cache the box collider as the *spawnArea* from the *start* method.

Just like the enemy bullet shoot, use an *IEnumerator* here to initiate a coroutine. The *IEnumerator* will run while the *isPlaying* variable is *true*. *isPlaying* is a public variable that can be modified by a game manager component. The coroutine will spawn an enemy with a random speed, as stated in lines 32 and 33. After every enemy spawn, the coroutine will wait for a random period before instantiating the next enemy.

Now attach the component to the spawner cube that has been placed. Make sure that the box collider of the spawner is a *Trigger* (*Is Trigger* | *Ticked*).

Now that the game can spawn enemies, there is a high chance that the enemies can bypass the player and be in the scene, even outside the camera bounds. Therefore, it becomes necessary to destroy the enemies that go beyond the player. Just like the spawner, create another cube that is placed behind the player.

Create a new C# script and name it as *DestroyBounds.cs*:

```
1.  public class DestroyBounds : MonoBehaviour
2.  {
3.    private void OnCollisionEnter(Collision collision)
4.    {
5.      Destroy(collision.gameObject);
6.    }
7.  }
```

This component will destroy any game object that it collides with. Add this component to the cube that was created.

GAME UI

Now that all the game elements are ready, it is time to put everything together. Before setting up the game manager, set up additional game objects in the scene.

1. Create a new `Canvas` object. In the `Canvas Scaler` component, change the UI scale mode to scale with `Screen Size`. Inside the canvas, create two `Text-TextMeshPro` UI game objects. Import any additional packages if Unity requests to do so.

2. Now using the 2D mode and the `Rect` transform tool, place the text objects on top of the screen. These two text objects are going to show the current health and the score of the player.

3. Inside the canvas, create a UI panel and add a `Button` and a text object into the panel. Change the text to `GameOver` and also change the color of the panel to be semitransparent black if wanted. Change the colors of the text objects as required. Figure 6.8 shows a sample configuration of the UI; in this case, a custom font was used for the sample project.

FIGURE 6.8 UI of the game scene including the game over overlay.

Now deactivate the panel in the inspector window.

Game Manager

Create a new C# script and name it as *GameManager.cs*. Notice that it takes a new icon. Open it and add the following script:

```
1.  using TMPro;
2.
3.  public class GameManager : MonoBehaviour
4.  {
5.    public static GameManager instance;
6.
7.    [SerializeField] private TMP_Text scoreText;
8.    [SerializeField] private TMP_Text healthText;
9.    [SerializeField] private GameObject GameOverUI;
10.   [SerializeField] private EnemySpawner enemySpawner;
11.
```

```
12.   private bool isRunning = false;
13.   private int score = 0;
14.
15.   private void Awake()
16.   {
17.     if(instance != null && instance != this)
18.     {
19.       Destroy(this);
20.     }
21.
22.     instance = this;
23.   }
24.
25.   private void Start()
26.   {
27.     StartGame();
28.   }
29.
30.   public void StartGame()
31.   {
32.     isRunning = true;
33.     score = 0;
34.     enemySpawner.StartSpawning();
35.   }
36.
37.   public void AppendScore(int value)
38.   {
39.     score += value;
40.     scoreText.text = score.ToString();
41.   }
42.
43.   public void DisplayHealth(int value)
44.   {
45.     healthText.text = value.ToString();
```

```
46.    }
47.
48.    public void GameOver()
49.    {
50.      isRunning = false;
51.      GameOverUI.SetActive(true);
52.      AudioManager.instance.PlaySFX("gameOver");
53.    }
55.    public bool IsRunning()
56.    {
57.      return isRunning;
58.    }
59. }
```

Game manager should be a component that can be referenced by any other component without assigning it manually. Also, there can only be one game manager in the scene. In order to overcome this, use a *Singleton* design pattern along with public access to its methods. Line number 5 added a blank static object of the same *GameManager* variable called *instance*. Since this is a *static* variable, there can only be one variable as *instance* of type game manager, and any object can directly reference the instance by calling *GameManager.instance*. In the *Awake* method, check if the instance has been assigned, and if so, any other duplicated game objects will be destroyed. If not, the only available *GameManager* instance in the scene will be referred to by the *instance* variable (line 22).

TMPro is used here since Text Mesh Pro updates health and score. The game manager can perform the following tasks:

- *Start the game*: In line 30, the *StartGame()* method resets the score, sets the *isRunning* variable to true, and requests the *enemySpawner* to start spawning enemies.
- *Append and display the score*: In line 37, the *AppendScore()* method requests an integer parameter and adds that value to the score. Also, it displays the score by changing the text of the *scoreText* TMPro-referenced component.
- *Display the health of the player*: The player can call this method to update the current health of the player.

- *Ends the game*: Once the player is destroyed, the player can request the game manager to end the game. In line 48, the `GameOver()` method sets `isRunning` to false, plays a game over sound, and activates the `GameOver` UI panel that was deactivated in the scene.

Once the script is complete, attach that to a new empty game object in the scene. Rename the game object as `GameManager`. Drag and drop the necessary UI components from the scene view to the game manager.

Now that the game manager is ready, the game will still not work without adding proper tags. Select the `Layers` drop-down at the top right corner of the Unity editor window, and select `Edit Layers`, as shown in Figure 6.9. Now from the tree view, expand `Tag` and add the `Enemy` tag by clicking the plus button:

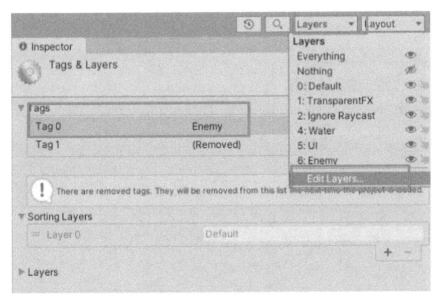

FIGURE 6.9 Adding new layers.

Select the `player` object and assign the `Player` tag from the top of the inspector window. It is a drop-down right under the name of the game object. Similarly, select the `Enemy` prefab from the project window and assign the `Enemy` tag previously created.

Finally, revisit the previous scripts and uncomment all the places where the `GameManager` reference lines were commented.

ADDING AUDIO AND POLISHING

It may have been noticed that a singleton instance of the *AudioManager* and its *PlaySFX()* method has been called from different other components. It is time to create that component and the relevant methods. Create a new C# script and name it as *AudioManager.cs*. Open it and add the following:

```
1.  public class AudioManager : MonoBehaviour
2.  {
3.    [SerializeField] private AudioSource foregroundAudioSource;
4.    [SerializeField] private AudioClip shootSFX, explodeSFX,
      buttonClick, gameover;
5.
6.    public static AudioManager instance;
7.
8.    private void Awake()
9.    {
10.     DontDestroyOnLoad(gameObject);
11.
12.     if (instance == null)
13.     {
      instance = this;
14.     }
15.     else
16.     {
17.       Destroy(gameObject);
18.     }
19.   }
20.
21.   public void PlaySFX(string name)
22.   {
23.     switch (name)
24.     {
25.       case "button":
26.         foregroundAudioSource.PlayOneShot(buttonClick);
27.         break;
```

```
28.        case "fire":
29.            foregroundAudioSource.PlayOneShot(shootSFX);
30.            break;
31.        case "explode":
32.            foregroundAudioSource.PlayOneShot(explodeSFX);
33.            break;
34.        case "gameOver":
35.            foregroundAudioSource.PlayOneShot(gameover);
36.            break;
37.        default:
38.            break;
39.    }
40.  }
41. }
```

Similar to the game manager, the *Audio* manager also can be referenced by other components without a manual drag and drop of any other methods; however, this component awake method is a little bit different, as it is a *DontDestroyOnLoad()* method. This will keep the game object without destroying it, even if the scene is changed. This will become handy in the next stage.

Moreover, instead of checking whether the instance is assigned, check here whether it is not assigned and immediately assign it. Any other *AudioManagers* in the scene will be destroyed immediately this way, as well as preventing this from duplicating when coming back to the first scene. Loading the same scene will duplicate the *AudioManager* object's game object due to *DontDestroyOnLoad()*.

In order to play the audio, an *AudioSource* component is needed that references to a set of *AudioClips*. Since this is a small game, use four different sound effects, as can be seen in line 4.

The *PlaySFX()* method takes a string as the parameter, and based on the value, it plays the selected audio clip just once by using the *PlayOneShot()* method.

This will not be attached to the *Game* scene. Instead, create a new scene for the main menu and have it there.

Adding the Main Menu

In the scenes folder of the project window, right-click and select scene to create a new scene. Rename it as *MainMenu*. Also, rename the game scene as *Game*. Now follow the listed steps:

1. Double-click and open the *MainMenu* scene.

2. This scene will only use a canvas with the name of the game and a button to load the game. Create a new *Overlay* canvas and change its UI scale mode to *Scale with Screen Size*.

3. Inside the canvas, add a UI Image. Use the *rect* tool to scale the image to cover the whole canvas. The *Galaxy Background* image from the asset pack can be used as the background.

4. Now add a new *Image* object inside the canvas. Use the *SPACE FORCE* image in the UI *Images* folder of the *asset* package. Use the anchoring points to anchor the title image to the center.

5. Similarly, add a button and change the text inside the button to *PLAY* and also use the *Button* image in the asset back as the button background button. Once done, change the image type of the button's *Image* component to Slice. Once everything is set up, the final result should be as shown in Figure 6.10:

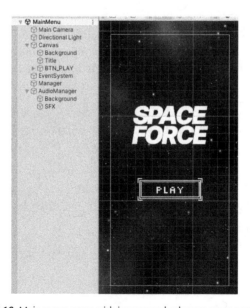

FIGURE 6.10 Main menu setup with images and other manager game objects.

Now it is time to set up the audio manager. To set up the audio manager, follow the listed steps:

1. As in the preceding figure, create an `Empty game` object for the `Audio Manager`, and add two more empty game objects to play the background music and the SFX.

2. Select the background game object and do the following in the inspector window:

   a. Add an `AudioSource` component.

   b. Assign the `BackgroundMusic` audio clip from the asset pack as this `AudioClip`.

   c. Enable *Play on Awake and Loop*.

   d. Select the SFX game object and add an `AudioSource`—disable *Play on Awake*. This audio source will be used to play all the SFX.

3. Now select the main `AudioManager` game object and add the `AudioManager` script component.

4. Assign the SFX game object's audio source as the `Foreground Audio Source`. Now other audio clips can be assigned as per the component references. The asset pack contains sound effects for shooting, explosions, button clicks, and game over.

Switching Scenes

Finally, a way is needed to switch from one scene to another. This is to be performed by the *PLAY* button in the main menu and the *MENU* button in the game scene. To be generic, create a C# script and name it `SceneChanger.cs`:

```
1. using UnityEngine.SceneManagement;
2.
3. public class SceneChanger : MonoBehaviour
4. {
5.    public void ChangeScene(string sceneName)
6.    {
7.      SceneManager.LoadScene(sceneName);
8.      AudioManager.instance.PlaySFX("button");
9.    }
10.}
```

Once the script is created, follow the listed steps:

1. Use the `SceneManager` by Unity to switch the scene by the name of the scene. Additionally, call the `Audiomanager` to play the button sound effect.

2. Go back to Unity, attach this component to a `Manager` empty game object, and select the Play button.

3. In the button component under the `OnClick()` event, click the + (plus) button and drag and drop the `Manager game` object on top of `None(Object)` prompt. To the right of the event, the drop-down list will show all the components attached to the `Manager object`, including the `SceneChanger` component. Select it and choose the `ChangeScene()` method.

4. Now since the parameter requests a string, the UI will show a text box to add the name of the scene. Since the Game scene is wanted, type `Game` in the text box. The event should be as shown in Figure 6.11:

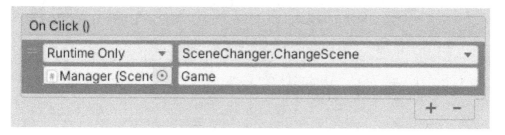

FIGURE 6.11 Using the OnClick Unity event.

5. Now go to the `Game scene`, select the *Menu* button in the game over panel, and assign the same with a manager game object in the `Game scene`.

6. The `SceneManager` uses the scenes listed in the build settings in order to switch from one to another. Therefore, both scenes need to be added to the build settings.

7. Click `File | Build Settings`.

8. From the project window, drag and drop the Game and the `MainMenu` scene into the Scenes in the `Build` panel. Make sure to keep the `MainMenu` scene on top of the list.

The Next Steps

Now everything is almost ready. A player can click play from the main menu and play the game; however, the models do not look nice, and the liveliness of the game is lacking. The final finished project that comes with the book has additional features added to the game, such as the following:

- Autoscrolling background in the game view.
- 3D models for enemies and the player.
- Adding difficulty by increasing the health of enemies over time.
- Spawning different enemies with different strengths.
  Refer to Figure 6.12:

FIGURE 6.12 Final completed project gameplay.

CONCLUSION

This chapter went through the process of adding game objects, developing C# scripts that work with each other, employing design patterns, using prefabs with collisions, and establishing simple scoring mechanisms as well as touch input. The next chapter will provide instructions on building the game on Android and Apple devices and how to play properly with the touch input. From the next chapter onward, this book will not prioritize Unity editor interactions and instead focus more on AR integrations with Unity.

KEY POINTS

- The instantiate method is used to spawn game objects in the scene.
- `OnCollisionEnter` detects collisions if a `rigidbody` and a collider are present in both objects.
- `OnTriggerEnter` detects triggers that do not have a force impact.
- Any game object can be converted to a prefab and can be instantiated from the project window during runtime.
- Input-based methods can be used in update methods to capture mouse and touch inputs.
- `IEnumerators` can be used to run coroutines within Unity, which work similarly to parallel processes alongside the main application.
- Game UI can be an overlay or world space. The overlay UIs render in screen space, while the world space UI uses the 3D scene to render the UI elements.
- The audio source can play one audio clip at a time.
- Buttons in Unity use `UnityEvents`, such as `OnClick`, to capture events and execute methods directly from the inspector window.
- Unity UI images can use filled, tiled, stretched, and sliced methods to present the final texture.

QUESTIONS

1. What is the purpose of using the [`SerializeField`] attribute in Unity scripts?

   a. It allows a variable to be visible in the inspector window and be editable.

   b. It makes a variable private and inaccessible from other scripts.

   c. It automatically initializes a variable with a predefined value.

   d. It forces a variable to be updated every frame.

2. In Unity's image component, what does the fill amount property represent?

   a. The current opacity level of the image

   b. The percentage of the image's visibility on the screen

   c. The amount of memory used by the image asset

   d. The fill level or progress displayed within the image

3. Which Unity function is used to detect collisions between two `GameObjects` with colliders?

   a. `OnTriggerEnter`

   b. `OnTriggerExit`

   c. `OnCollisionEnter`

   d. `OnCollisionExit`

4. In Unity, how can one play an audio clip only once using the `AudioSource` component attached to a `GameObject`?

   a. Call the `PlayOneShot()` method on the `AudioSource` component.

   b. Attach an `AudioListener` component to the `GameObject`.

   c. Call the `PlayOnce()` method on the `AudioSource` component.

   d. Instantiate the audio clip and attach it to the `GameObject`.

5. What is the purpose of Unity's Scene Management system?

   a. To manage the rendering of objects in the scene

   b. To control the lighting and shading of the scene

   c. To handle interactions between different scenes in the game

   d. To manage the physics simulations within a scene

Answers appear in the appendix.

7

TRYING OUT A FIRST 3D MOBILE APP DEVELOPMENT

INTRODUCTION

The previous chapter discussed how to develop a simple mobile game using the Unity engine. It further covered the basic components and the steps of creating custom C# components; however, the game was not tested on a mobile device to check the touch input. In augmented reality (AR) application development, one of the major steps is to iteratively test the application on actual devices for usability as well as optimization. The way the app features in the development environment will never be the same as on an actual mobile device.

This chapter goes over the steps of building mobile applications on Android and iOS devices. First, there will be a review of the necessary tools discussed during Chapter 4, "Up and Running with Unity 3D," prior to development. Furthermore, the debugging steps required to check the status of the app while running on mobile devices will be discussed as well. Since the game was not an AR application, there are some additional steps required for such builds, which will be discussed in other chapters.

STRUCTURE

This chapter will discuss the following topics:

- Unity build settings

- Android build settings
- iOS build settings
- Building Unity apps
  - Building for Android
  - Building for iOS
- Unity script debugging with Visual Studio
- Debugging the app for both platforms

OBJECTIVES

After completion of this chapter, readers will be able to optimize and build for mobile devices that run on Android and iOS operating systems. They will also be able to connect their devices to the computer and debug the code and test for complications. Additionally, readers will be able to connect script debugging tools to Unity directly to test the code more effectively.

UNITY BUILD SETTINGS

This section discusses Android build settings as well as iOS build settings. These settings are used to customize the build and include the build tools, icon and splash screen information, scaling information, rendering, operating systems, and device-based features.

Android Build Settings

Chapter 4 discussed installing the necessary tools to build Android apps using Unity. The Android development architecture allows the *software development kit (SDK)* and the *native development kit (NDK)* to be used by other applications, such as Unity, to build the app from within. The previous chapter introduced how to open the build settings folder to add the necessary scenes for the scene manager.

Go to `File|Build Settings`.

From here, switch to the platform for which the app is being built; however, switching is not necessary to set up the build settings. For this section, select `Android` and check the settings, but first, before moving to the settings in this window, it is necessary to click the `Player Settings` button at the bottom left corner.

This window can also be opened by going to *Edit | Project Settings* and choosing the *Player* tab from the left sidebar.

The player settings consist of shared settings across all the platforms, such as the name of the app, the version, the developer's name, and the icon. Add items such as the icon and any other preferred information. If the shared assets are accessible, use the *ICON* texture in the *Textures* folder.

Underneath the shared settings, look for the icon tabs of the platform modules previously installed with Unity. Click the *Android* tab and check the settings for Android, as shown in Figure 7.1:

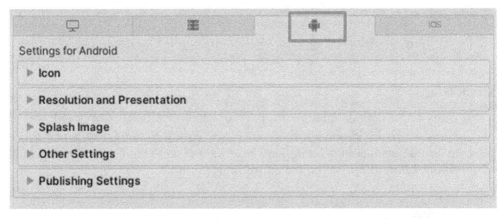

FIGURE 7.1 Android tab of the build settings window.

Icon

This is important if different icons are needed for different devices with various screen sizes. Like the shared settings icon, it is possible to upload different icons that match several resolutions, as requested by the interface.

Resolution and Presentation

This defines how the screen should appear when built on an Android device. There are various options to enable and disable full-screen window mode, hide the navigation bar, and allow forced aspect ratios. It may be necesary to keep the default settings except for the *Orientation* and *Allowed Orientation*. Usually, it is better to lock the orientation of AR apps to portrait, as it allows users to view a large AR viewport through the screen. This also depends on the application. This scenario only requires enabling portrait rotation. It can be locked to just one orientation or one can allow autorotation and tick only the *Portrait* and *Portrait Upside Down* options. Refer to Figure 7.2:

Orientation	
Default Orientation*	Auto Rotation ▾
Allowed Orientations for Auto Rotation	
Portrait	✓
Portrait Upside Down	✓
Landscape Right	
Landscape Left	

FIGURE 7.2 Resolution and presentation section of build settings.

Splash Image

Unity has a default splash with its logo, which can be removed with a paid Unity license; additionally, there are a few customizations that can be made to add a personal logo alongside Unity, as well as to change the background colors. Leave them on the default settings for now.

Other Settings

This is the most important section when it comes to building AR applications. Many settings can be left as default, but this section will point out the necessary settings required to build AR apps for Android.OS. Choose the following for the options under *Other settings*:

- *Rendering | Color Space:* Set this option to Linear color space.
- *Rendering | Graphics APIs:* Currently, many Android-based AR SDKs do not support Vulkan or OpenGLES2 graphics application programming interfaces (APIs) since they are upgraded to the latest. Select them and click the "-" button underneath to remove it. Only keep OpenGLES3 available. If these options are not visible, untick *Auto Graphics API* over it to make them appear.
- *Identification | Package Name:* This is the unique package name for the project. Upon uploading it to any app store, this will be used to uniquely identify the app. There cannot be two apps under the same package name. Therefore, enter a unique value here. Usually, it is recommended to use

    com. companyname.appnickname to make it unique. A sample identifier one can use is *com.indikawijesooriya.spaceforce*.

- *Identification | Versions:* If it is necessary to update the app for the next versions, this can be used to add the version as a meta value. This will help make the latest build version of the app recognizable.
- *Identification | Minimum API level:* Android keeps on updating its operating systems, and each operating system has its own API level. Depending on hardware and software capabilities, different OS versions do not support AR applications. Some APIs discontinue their support for newer features. Currently, the minimum API required to build an AR app is limited to API Level 25 (Android 7.1 Nougat). If the app is not AR, choose the default version to build the app; however, devices with a low OS version will not be able to run the app.
- *Configuration | Scripting backend:* Many recent Android devices now support 64-bit architecture. In order to support 64-bit hardware, compiling must be done by a backend that supports it. The default Mono can be used only to create Armv7 architecture-based apps for Android. Therefore, change it to *IL2CPP*.
- *Configuration | Target Architectures:* Switching to IL2CPP will allow the option to choose the target architecture. Only select *ARM64* since AR apps will not work with any other architecture.
- If the app does not require any AR capabilities, use Mono and Arm v7 as the scripting backend and the target architecture.

Publishing Settings

    Android uses a *keystore* to sign the app when building. The signing binds a certificate made by the developer, which can be used to recognize who built the final executable file. This is used by the app stores to verify the developer. Currently, the Google Play store has the capability to manage the keystores within its developer console. Once an app is signed with a certificate, every new update should be signed using the same certificate.

    This can be left as it is for just testing the app on a phone. This uses a debug key and a certificate which is already there in one's computer. If one uses a different computer to build the app, the debug key certificate would be different, and the app cannot be considered as an update even if it is the same project.

    It will be necessary to make a new key to upload this app to the app store. For Android, Unity has created the necessary interfaces to create a personal keystore for an app.

For those hoping to publish the build in an app store, click the *Keystore Manager* button to launch the keystore window, as shown in Figure 7.3. Here, one can load an existing keystore file or create a new one. It is recommended to use one key per application within a keystore and save it securely within secure repositories. One can also password-protect the keystore. Once the keystore is saved, it is possible to add keys to the store. These keys can then be used to sign the app. Refer to Figure 7.3:

FIGURE 7.3 Steps to create and set up an Android sign key.

In Figure 7.3:

1. *Keystore Manager* is used to create a new keystore and a key.

2. Choose an existing keystore with its passkey.

3. Add the password to authenticate the key loaded from the keystore.

Add new key values and load them to sign the app. Always keep in mind that once an app is saved using a key, the same key must be used for further updates. Once the keystore is loaded, the loaded key can be used under the *Project Key* section. Select the key and add the password to authenticate the signature.

Additionally, more settings may help you to customize the manifest of the Android app. Since Unity manages the manifest of the application, leave the settings as default for now.

If the app is large, `Split application binary` can be used to build the app in multiple parts. This allows app stores to distribute an app in chunks rather than streaming a large app file. For those planning to build a large AR app that could be uploaded to the Google Play Store, it is recommended to enable `Split application Binary` at the bottom of the `Player Settings` section.

iOS Build Settings

Compared with Android, iOS build settings are different. Apple has not provided an SDK to use their APIs to build the iOS app on their behalf. Instead, Apple requests the final build as an Xcode project to build and deploy to devices. All the settings for icon, resolution, and splash image are similar to Android. Therefore, it is only necessary to look at the other settings section in the iOS tab of the player settings.

Identification | Bundle Identifier

This property is similar to the package name property in Android. One can use the same identifier here since it is the same app on different platforms. For iOS, each version can have multiple build numbers for testing purposes. Usually, a developer build is given a Unity incrementing number for a specific version.

Identification | Provisioning Profile and Signing Team ID

Apple manages the keys and certificates in the device keychain. This is similar to an Android keystore, but it cannot be made within Unity. For development purposes, an Apple ID is needed to test the app on devices, but for those needing to publish the app in the app store, a developer account with a team ID should be obtained from Apple Developer Connect. Since that is beyond the scope of this book, that option will not be considered for now.

Configuration | Target Device, SDK and Minimum iOS Version

Currently, any AR app that uses ARKit must be over iOS 11.0. AR apps cannot be run on an iOS simulator. Therefore, it is good to keep *Device SDK*. For an app intended to be installed only on one of several device types, such as the iPhone and the iPad, select the target device option here as well. For the moment, keep them as default.

Configuration | Camera Usage Description

Any app that uses the camera must add a camera request message to seek the user's permission to allow camera usage. Similar requests go to location usage as well as microphone usage. Since the AR app requires the camera to work, it is necessary to add a camera usage description to show the message to the user. This is not needed for the Space Force project, but a similar message for the description can be as follows: *We are using your camera to enable Augmented Reality support.*

Configuration | Requires ARKit Support

This is not needed for any app that does not require ARKit. For the Space Force project, it can be left alone, but when going through the AR Foundation section, ARKit support must be enabled to allow the camera to work in the app.

These are the necessary settings that can be set up from the Unity side; however, for iOS, some changes can be made after building the Xcode project. This is explored in the next section of this chapter.

BUILDING UNITY APPS

Now that the different necessary settings required to build Android and iOS applications have been described, it is time to go through the process of building and loading the app on devices. Both devices use different methods for the build process.

Building for Android

When building for Android, an Android package file, also known as an *APK file*, is created and can be loaded and installed on an Android device. It is also possible to use the `Build and run` method, which uses the *Android device bridge (ADB)* to connect to a device over a cable or Wi-Fi, to install and launch the app without touching the APK file oneself. For the purpose of understanding both options, both ways will be described.

Building for Android without ADB

Open the build settings window. Make sure that the current target platform is Android. If not, select *Android* and click *Switch Platform* at the bottom of the window. After a while, the project will be ready to be built.

Ensure that the scenes in build are properly listed and ticked in the window and click the *Build* button at the bottom with default settings. Now this will ask for a folder location to save the APK file. Choose a location and a name (the name here is not important; it can be anything like *build.apk* and so on) and click *Save*, as shown in Figure 7.4:

FIGURE 7.4 Saving an Android build APK.

If one is building this app for the first time, Unity may take some time to compile the assets and scripts. Once the process is completed, a *build.apk* file will be saved at the location given before.

Now, connect an Android device, copy the APK file into it, and open it in a file browser. By default, Android has locked the capability to install apps from third parties. Therefore, there will be a redirection to enable *Unknown Sources* to install this application on a device.

Figure 7.5 shows how to enable unknown sources and the prompt shown when one taps on the *build.apk* from within the file manager:

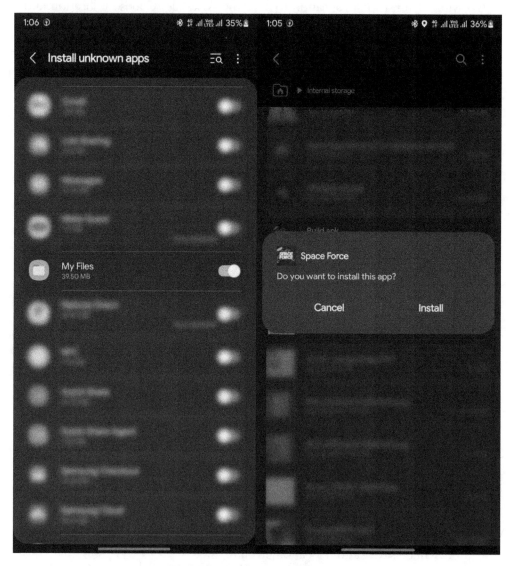

FIGURE 7.5 Enabling USB debugging on Android.

Now, this process will be overwhelming when one wants to iteratively test the app on a device. Therefore, a quick way is to directly build and install the app on the device. In order to enable this, it is necessary to enable the developer settings of the device. To do this, check the following steps. These steps, however, can be slightly different based on the Android device manufacturer and the model:

1. In the Android device, go to `Settings` and find the `About Phone` section.

2. Find something that indicates `Build Number`. This can be inside the `About Phone` section or inside another menu, such as software information.

3. Now tap on the build number five or six times until a small message appears at the bottom that says `Developer mode enabled`.

4. Now, go back to settings, and observe the `Developer` options at the bottom. Open it and enable `USB Debugging`. Make sure to turn it off when not developing since it can lead to security issues if one's device is lost.

5. Now, connect the device using a USB cable. It will show a message on the mobile screen to allow USB debugging with the computer. Allow it and click the refresh button in the build settings window, right next to the `Run Device` drop-down.

6. Now select `Build and Run`. Choose the location to save the APK file and click `Save`. This will take the same build process, but it will launch the app directly on the device, and it can be tested seamlessly. Refer to Figure 7.6:

FIGURE 7.6 Choosing the connected Android device to build and run.

For building to test iteratively, directly select `Build and Run` from the `File` menu without opening the build settings window.

Building for iOS

Unlike Android, building for iOS requires a Mac OS device and Xcode installed along with it. Depending on the plug-ins installed in Unity, this may require installing additional packages into Xcode as well. Fortunately, the AR SDKs used throughout this book will not require additional Xcode-based pod packages.

1. Similar to Android, open up `Build settings` and switch the platform to iOS for building. One can also select `Build and Run` here, but it is safe to do a manual build once to set up the build certificates using Xcode.

2. Select the `Build` button to initiate the build process. One can choose a new folder to export the build. Unlike Android, this will not give a single executable file to install. Instead, it will generate the Xcode project to build the app another time to run on a device/emulator.

3. Once the build process is completed, go to the build folder and open `Unity-iPhone.xcodeproj` Xcode project file, as shown in Figure 7.7. This will open the Xcode project generated by Unity:

FIGURE 7.7 The Xcode project built by Unity.

4. Once the Xcode project is open, head over to the `Unity-iPhone` in the left side tab, as shown in Figure 7.8. Select `Signing & Capabilities` tab in the middle view and select `All` from the window underneath.

5. Now tick on the `Automatically manage signing` option and enable automatic signing. Make sure the bundle identifier is correct. Once the tick box has been enabled, select a team. If logged in to Xcode with an Apple account, it will be possible to see one's name and *(Personal Team)* right next to it. Refer to Figure 7.8 to verify the flow:

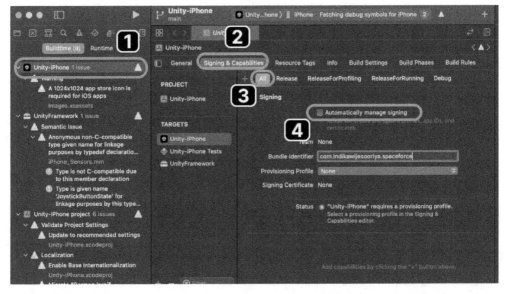

FIGURE 7.8 Signing an iOS app with a certificate before building.

6. Once this has been selected for the first time, Xcode will generate a certificate. Now, connect the iOS device to a MacBook using the cable.

7. Select the specified device from the top breadcrumbs bar, as shown in Figure 7.9:

FIGURE 7.9 Breadcrumbs bar.

8. Then, click on the *Play* button, as shown in Figure 7.10:

FIGURE 7.10 Play button.

This will initiate a secondary build process, which generates an IPA file, that will be automatically installed on the Apple device. Launch it, and once launched, the Debug log within Xcode itself will be available for viewing. This will be discussed in the next section.

UNITY SCRIPT DEBUGGING WITH VISUAL STUDIO

Having learned how to build and run an app on mobile devices developed using Unity, take a step back and look at how to properly debug codes with Unity and Visual Studio. Script debugging allows checking for issues in the code and the status of the variables properly. This can be done in development time using both Windows and Mac environments. Follow the listed steps:

1. For this exercise, use the *Game Manager* script and check the *Append-Score(int)* method created in the previous chapter.

2. Double-click and open the *Game Manager* script.

3. In order to check and debug a certain line of code, it is necessary to create a *breakpoint*. Clicking on the leftmost column on the *score+=value* line of *AppendScore* method causes a circle to appear under the mouse pointer. Click it, and it will make a breakpoint. Now, when the game is running, and it reaches this point, the game will pause, and it will be possible to analyze the code and variable values in that line.

4. Once the breakpoint is made, select *Attach to Unity* from the top panel. This will initiate debugging and connect to Unity (in macOS, click the play button in Visual Studio). Now go back to Unity and click the *Play* button.

5. Figures 7.11 and 7.12 show how to add breakpoints and attach them to Unity:

FIGURE 7.11 Script debugging on Visual Studio6Windows.

Refer next to Figure 7.12:

FIGURE 7.12 Script debugging in Visual Studio6MacOS.

Now when a score is taken, the game will pause and launch Visual Studio with the current status of the game at that point. It will be possible to see all the components attached to the game object and the values of each variable.

This will become very useful when the project has scaled, and one needs to understand how the scripts behave. Figure 7.13 shows how the debug view is represented in Visual Studio when the game hits a breakpoint:

FIGURE 7.13 Debugging a breakpoint at runtime.

DEBUGGING THE APP FOR BOTH PLATFORMS

One of the challenges in developing mobile applications is the limited ability to debug what happens when the app runs outside the development environment. This section will discuss some of the tools that are available for both iOS and Android platforms to view the console log while the app is running on the device.

Using the ADB Console for Android

Unity comes bundled with the Android SDK, which includes the Android device bridge tool to connect and push data into the device. The same can be used to open the console log, also known as the logcat, which logs details of every process on the device. We can also use certain parameters to filter the data log, to show only particular logs from the app, as shown in the following steps:

1. Connect the Android device running the Unity app created for the specified computer.

2. In Unity, go to *Edit* | *Preferences* (in MacOS, it is *Unity* | *Preferences*). Select External Tools and scroll down to the *Android SDK path*. Click *Copy path*.

3. Now open the Windows terminal or MacOS terminal. Open the path copied by this command. Make sure to add *\platform-tools* to the end of the copied path

   ```
   cd <<The path you copied>>\platform-tools
   ```

4. Now type the following:

   ```
   ./ adb logcat -s Unity ActivityManager PackageManager dal-
   vikvm DEBUG
   ```

This will show a complete real-time log of the device and only log lines containing the above-mentioned keywords. Whenever the game prints something on the console, it can be viewed through the log.

Using the Xcode Console for iOS

Compared to Android, Xcode provides a cleaner log-checking system by immediately opening the console within Xcode as soon as it starts running on the device. When one connects the device and clicks the play button to build the app onto the device, it becomes possible to see the filtered console log on Xcode until one clicks the stop button.

CONCLUSION

This chapter discussed the fundamentals of building and testing a mobile application on a mobile phone running either Android or iOS. It also went through debugging basics and explored the console log of the Unity editor. This will help in easily looking for issues that one may encounter when the AR apps run on mobile phones.

KEY POINTS

- There are different build settings requirements for different operating systems.
- Unity used the Android SDK directly to build and install the app on a mobile phone.
- Unity exports an Xcode project that can be later customized, signed, and deployed on an iOS device.
- Visual Studio debugger can be connected with Unity to test and debug the code at runtime.
- The console log can be viewed using the ADB logcat and Xcode runtime console

QUESTIONS

1. What is the tool used by Unity to build for Android?

2. What should be enabled in an Android device to seamlessly deploy the app directly from Unity?

3. What is a necessary step in Xcode before building the app on an iOS device?

4. What should be placed in Visual Studio to check a certain script line in script debugging?

Answers appear in the appendix.

CHAPTER 8

BUILDING MARKER-BASED AR APPS WITH VUFORIA

INTRODUCTION

The previous chapters introduced AR, 3D development concepts, Unity 3D, C# development with Unity, and debugging and building applications for mobile platforms. This will be the first chapter to introduce core AR development concepts used throughout the rest of the book.

This chapter will discuss building augmented reality (AR) projects that use the *Vuforia software development kit*. Vuforia was briefly introduced in Chapter 3, "Exploring Tools and Development Platforms," but this chapter dives into marker-based AR app development with Vuforia, explaining different kinds of markers, considering identification-based events, and finally, building a simple AR treasure hunt game involving physical marker-based tracking for clues.

STRUCTURE

This chapter will discuss the following topics:

- Introduction to Vuforia
- Using image targets
- Using cylinder targets
- Using multi targets
- Development of an AR treasure hunt game

OBJECTIVES

After completing this chapter, one will be able to design and develop marker-based AR apps for mobile devices. Not only will this allow users to scan, but it will also help them learn to develop logic around marker-based AR recognition, such as tracking and losing events. Additionally, users will learn different tricks to design illusions around AR.

INTRODUCTION TO VUFORIA

As mentioned in Chapter 3, Vuforia is a leading marker-based AR software development kit (SDK) provider, as well as one of the oldest in the world. Their SDK supports both iOS and Android, as well as any other device with a Web camera, and it does not rely on hardware limitations. Therefore, it is possible to test and run any AR application within the development environment just by using a webcam.

Create a Vuforia Developer Account and Login

Vuforia is a third-party library. Therefore, it allows developers to develop and publish applications without paying for the SDK, while charging for commercial and industry-related applications. Vuforia offers different license categories, which vary with their business goals; however, any AR application that uses Vuforia should register and obtain a license key to authenticate it for use. This requires registering on their platform. Follow the listed steps:

1. Go to *https://developer.vuforia.com/*.

2. Click `Register` and create a new account using one's email address. The same link can be used to log in to the license dashboard.

3. Once logged in, a user will be redirected to the `License Manager`. This is the page needed to buy premium licenses or get a basic developer license.

4. Click the `Get Basic` button to create a new license key.

5. Now add a name for the license key, tick the developer agreement box, and click `Confirm`.

6. Now it will be possible to choose the selected license and copy the license key. Depending on the Vuforia version, the services they offer for the basic license could differ; however, it will always allow stand-alone AR tracking for an unlimited number of markers.

Downloading and Installing the Sdk

To download and install the SDK, follow the listed steps:

1. Click on the `Downloads` tab and download the Unity Vuforia package. As of writing this book, the latest version of the SDK is 10.11.

2. Create a new Unity URP 3D project.

3. Import the Unity SDK package by either double-clicking or dragging the Unity package into the project or choosing the `Assets | Import Package` menu.

4. This will install Vuforia SDK in the selected packages folder. Those using the Git version controlling for projects may have to add the SDK archive to the `.gitignore` file or enable *Git large file storage (Git LFS)*; otherwise, there will be problems in pushing updates to the repository. This archive is over 250MBb and may not be compatible directly with Git.

5. Once the package is installed, go to `Window | Vuforia configuration.`

Figure 8.1 shows the configuration page for Vuforia. Under the `Global` category, there appears an input for `App License Key`. Copy the license key created from the developer account and paste it here. Now the application is ready to work with AR:

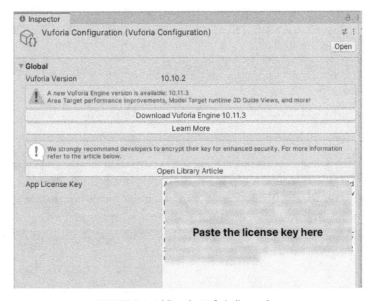

FIGURE 8.1 Adding the Vuforia license key.

For those paying for a license key, note that adding the key to this window is not secure. Moreover, for those hosting the project in a shared repository, be aware that sharing keys will exploit them, and therefore, they must be kept outside of the project. Use C# to load the key from an external file and load it before the runtime in order to avoid any of the keys being exposed to unauthorized access.

One can create a script as follows to load the license key from an external source securely and add it in an *Awake* method:

```
1.  void Awake()
2.  {
3.    VuforiaConfiguration.Instance.Vuforia.LicenseKey =
      "MyLicenseKey";
4.  }
```

Setting up a Basic AR Scene

There are two main game objects required to set up the most basic AR scene:

- AR camera
- A trackable to track something in the space

To set up a basic AR scene, follow the listed steps:

1. Create a new scene and remove the *Main Camera*. This will be replaced with an AR camera, which is the same main camera but with additional components.

2. Right-click an empty area in the hierarchy and select *Vuforia Engine | AR Camera*.

3. This will create a new AR camera in the scene.

4. Now right-click again and choose *Vuforia Engine | Image Target*.

5. This will show a basic blank AR setup with an *Image Target*. Click *Run* to play, and this should open up the webcam in the game view as the background. If a black screen appears, make sure that there is proper access to the webcam by selecting the *Camera Device* in the *Play Mode* section of the *Vuforia Configuration* window, as shown in Figure 8.2:

FIGURE 8.2 Changing the camera to run Vuforia in the editor.

USING IMAGE TARGETS

There are a couple of ways that an image target can be loaded into the project:

- Database method
- Image method

If it is necessary to quickly prototype with any image target, choose the *From image* option when adding a Vuforia image target *GameObject* into the scene; however, the number of features and the tracking ability of the image will be unknown. The database method is relevant to generating pretrained targets that have proven tracking ability.

To get an AR marker running with a 3D model, follow the listed steps:

1. Import an image into the project. This figure also should be printed and be present physically to test it. Usually, a book cover with an image works well. This section will be using Figure 8.3 as the target:

FIGURE 8.3 Image target (plane marker).

2. Select the `Image Target` in the hierarchy, drag and drop the image from the project window onto the `Image property` in the `Image Target Behavior` component. One can also specify a unique name for the target name. Now, the image target representing the same image that was added will be visible.

3. Now, right-click the `Image Target` and add any 3D object. For this exercise, add a sphere with a scale of 0.1. Move the sphere above the image target so that it looks as if it is on top of the figure.

4. Once everything is set up, the configuration is as shown in Figure 8.4:

FIGURE 8.4 Vuforia Image Target implementation.

5. With Vuforia, this is all that is needed to get an AR marker running with a 3D model. Click the `Play` button and show the same marker physically to the camera, and a sphere will appear on top of the figure, as depicted in Figure 8.5:

FIGURE 8.5 Result of Vuforia Image Target.

To use the database method to add an image target, follow the listed steps:

1. Go to the Vuforia console and select the `Target Manager` tab.

2. In this tab, marker databases can be created. Create a new database by pressing the `Add Database` button.

3. Once pressed, add a name to the database without spaces and choose `Device`. A device database will generate a list of images that can be integrated into the application. The next chapter will further discuss Cloud and VuMark.

4. Now select the created database. Here, one can upload different types of targets alongside image targets. Click on the `Add Target` button.

5. Make sure that the `Image` option is selected. Browse and choose the image target, add the width of the target (in meters), add a name, and click the `Add` button. For this section, there will be two different image targets, as shown in Figure 8.6:

FIGURE 8.6 Image target with good features (left) and not enough features (right).

6. Once both of them are uploaded and processed, check the database table, and focus on the rating column. Note that the first one has five stars while the second one with circles has just one star.

7. Go into each target by clicking on the name and select the `Show Features` option at the bottom of the image target. A number of unique features that the algorithm has identified will appear. Chapter 1, "Getting Started with Augmented Reality," discussed the underlying technology of tracking features instead of a figure. Vuforia uses a similar algorithm, and

the database visually shows how each target is seen by the AR SDK. Feature distribution and the star ratings of both are presented in Figure 8.7:

FIGURE 8.7 Image target feature distribution.

Keep in mind that any target with a lower rating will have a hard time being recognized and tracked by Vuforia. Vuforia recommends at least four stars for an AR application to track the images seamlessly.

Choosing the Best Markers/Targets

As seen in the previous section, the rating of the image target depends on the number of trackable features of the image. There are some best practices to follow in order to get the best results. Some of them are as follows:

- Pointy corners of the shapes are better features than rounded features of the image. This is visible in Figure 8.7.
- The features are enhanced more if the contrast of the image is higher, as can be seen in Figure 8.8:

FIGURE 8.8 Contrast check for image targets.

■ The features should be distributed throughout the whole image, as shown in Figure 8.9:

FIGURE 8.9 Image target feature distribution comparison.

■ Patterns with similar features are hardly recognizable since the algorithm cannot define the corners of the marker figure. Refer to Figure 8.10:

FIGURE 8.10 Pattern distribution.

▪ Nonrectangular images perform less well compared to rectangular images, a s can be seen in Figure 8.11:

FIGURE 8.11 Example of a nonrectangular target.

Additionally, Vuforia has a descriptive list of all the best practices in the following link: *https://library.vuforia.com/objects/best-practices-designing-and-developing-image-based-targets*.

If the application uses only image targets, one can easily use the asset library of the project instead of the online database library. Although one will not get an insight into how the target would perform, it will be easier to quickly drag and drop the image from the project window to the component. To do that, simply set the `Type` under `Image Target Behavior` to `From Image` and add the image under `Image` field, as shown in Figure 8.12:

FIGURE 8.12 Using an image target directly within Unity.

Additional Features of Image Targets

Imagine that an AR effect requires the 3D models to be hidden under the image. Just placing the 3D object on top of the image target and moving it under the target will not hide it. This is because the AR effect will only consider the physical target as a reference, and it will not occlude the tracker. Therefore, the object will be visible under the target image. This can be resolved by the following methods:

- *Adding an occlusion object:* By clicking on the `Add Occlusion Object` of the `Image Target Behavior` component, Unity will add an invisible plane on top of the target image and align it. This invisible plane will hide anything that is under that plane. This is done using an occlusion material added to the invisible plane:

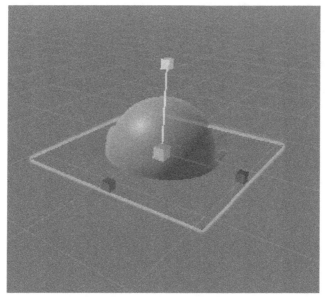

FIGURE 8.13 Occlusion object to cover the other side of the image target.

■ *Adding a similar target image*: By clicking on the `Add Target Representation`, Unity will add an image similar to the target image on top of the target. This way, a similar image will be tracking the image target, hiding anything underneath.

■ *Scan multiple image targets at once*: Users may realize that they can add more than one image target, but only one gets scanned at a time. This can be changed by going to `Window | Vuforia Configuration` and changing `Max Simultaneous Tracked Images` from 1 to the number wanted.

NOTE *The higher the number of multiple image targets that are defined to track, the higher the processing power required to check for image targets. Therefore, use it only when necessary and use the minimum number of targets that the project needs to scan.*

USING CYLINDER TARGETS

Vuforia SDK can recognize cylinder targets in addition to image targets. Imagine the AR application requires the user to scan a beverage can trigger a

3D animation on top of it. This is comparatively harder to achieve with a flat 2D image used as a target. The cylinder target method in Vuforia matches the curvature of the cylinder-shaped object to match any virtual objects perfectly. Figure 8.14 is a still image of an AR game known as *Beer Invaders* made by `immertia.io` that uses a similar tracking system to detect the beverage can:

FIGURE 8.14 Sample cylinder target implementation.
Source: Beer Invaders (https://*immertia.io/beer-invaders/*).

As for the next step, use the sample beverage can in Figure 8.15 to implement a cylinder scan. Compared to an image target project, this can be troublesome since the images uploaded to Vuforia should exactly match the label of the curved cylinder beverage. The cylinder object being used in this project has a circumference of 1,000 units at the edges. Its height is 451.85 units with respect to the circumference. The diameter of the circle was taken as 318.31 units. These values should be measured and used according to the size of the cylinder shape.

Additionally, the labels must appear correctly around and at the sides of the cylinder. Vuforia cylinder tracker can not only scan perfect cylindrical objects but also cone-shaped objects as well. Therefore, the label dimensions should be added with the correct unit measurements. Refer to Figure 8.15:

FIGURE 8.15 Sample cylinder target.
Source: "Soda Can"(https://skfb.ly/6WTvu) by Sunich, licensed under
Creative Commons Attribution (*http://creativecommons.org/licenses/by/4.0/*).

Follow the listed steps:

1. Go to the `Target Manager` of the Vuforia portal and click `Add Target`.

2. Select the `Cylinder` option for the *Type* and add the correct dimensions in units and name the target with a proper name. In Vuforia, the units are in meters, so once imported into Unity, the size can be large. The dimensions can be added by scaling them uniformly. Refer to Figure 8.16. The object will be scaled within Unity once imported:

Add Target

Type:

Image	Multi	Cylinder	Object

Dimension:

Bottom
Diameter: 318.31

Top Diameter: 318.31

Side Length: 451.85

Enter the dimensions of your target in scene units. The size of your target shall be on
the same scale as your augmented virtual content. If you enter '0' for the top or
bottom diameter, your target will be cone shaped.

Name:

Soda Can

Name must be unique to a database. When a target is detected in your application,
this will be reported in the API.

Cancel   Add

FIGURE 8.16 Adding a new cylinder target.

3. Once added, the list of targets will be populated with a new cylinder target without previews. Click on the name of the marker and open the 3D view of the cylinder target. This is where the side label image and the top and bottom images are uploaded. Click on each button on the right side of the 3D viewport and add the images. In this case, blank grey images have been added to the top and bottom since the object does not have any textures for them. The final 3D viewport appears as shown in Figure 8.17:

Soda_Can

FIGURE 8.17 Cylinder target preview.

4. Now, go back to the target manager and download all the targets for Unity.

5. Import the `unitypackage` to Unity and update the Vuforia marker database.

6. Now, along with the AR Camera, add a `Cylinder Target` by going to `Game Object` Menu | `Vuforia Engine` | `Cylinder Target`.

7. If the database has been imported correctly, the cylinder target will be populated and added to the scene. If there are multiple targets, they can be chosen from the `Cylinder Target Behavior` component. If high values have been added when creating the target, the size of the target object within Unity will be enormous compared to other objects. It is not recommended to scale a Vuforia target. The best way to scale it down is by expanding the `Advance` section of the cylinder target behavior and changing one value by dividing any number. Other values will change

proportionally. Figure 8.18 (1) shows how the units were divided by 100 and changed to scale down the cylinder target.

8. Also, as shown in Figure 8.18 (2), a simple low poly tree group was added around the cylinder to appear when tracked; however, the cylinder will not be there when it is scanned. Therefore, the trees on the other side will be visible on top of the actual cylinder target. As explained in the previous section, one can add an occlusion object or a target presentation to occlude the back of the cylinder object and make it believable when tracked:

FIGURE 8.18 Adding AR content to appear around a cylinder target.
Source: "Low Poly Tree Concept" (https://skfb.ly/6VosA) by sycoinc, licensed under Creative Commons Attribution (*http://creativecommons.org/licenses/by/4.0/*).

9. Now when *Play* is clicked and the can is scanned with the camera, the trees will appear around the cylinder. Minor adjustments to the scale of the cylinder can be made by changing the scale of the tracking objects and the occlusion object. Figure 8.19 shows the sample output of the cylinder can being scanned:

FIGURE 8.19 Demonstration of cylinder target tracking.

USING MULTI TARGETS

Multi targets in Vuforia are similar to cylinder targets but allow multiple image targets to work around a single cubic object. A multi target object has width, length, and height. A multi target can be used to spawn AR content on top of or around a box-shaped object such as a packaging box.

Similar to how cylinder targets are added, the developer must enter the dimensions of the cubic object to create a multi target. Figure 8.20 shows how to add them to create a new multi target reference:

Add Target

Type:

Image   Multi   Cylinder   Object

Dimension:

Width: 3.53

Height: 6.39

Length: 3.53

Enter the width, height and length of your target in the same unit as your augmentation. The size of the target shall be relative to the size of the augmented virtual content.

Name:

tea_box

Name must be unique to a database. When a target is detected in your application, this will be reported in the API.

Cancel   Add

FIGURE 8.20 Adding a multi target to the database.

Similar to how cylinder target images are uploaded, images for back, front, top, bottom, left, and right should be uploaded when the created target is clicked to upload reference images. Figure 8.21 shows the rectangular images uploaded to the target and the corresponding ratios. The dimensions are given in inches:

FIGURE 8.21 Textures of the multi target in correct dimensions.
Source: Artwork design by pikisuperstar from Freepik.

NOTE *The aspect ratio of the images uploaded for each side should exactly match the dimension values added when creating the marker.*

Once uploaded, a 3D model of the multi target with the uploaded textures will appear. Figure 8.22 shows the viewport once all the images are uploaded:

FIGURE 8.22 Multi target preview.

Similarly to how cylinder targets are imported, download the complete database, and import it back into the project. A different scene is being used to demonstrate multi target tracking. Once the database is imported, along with the AR Camera, add a `Multi Target` by going to `Game Object` menu | `Vuforia Engine` | `Multi Target`.

Users will be able to select the database and the available multi target to get the visual 3D box reference with the texture attached. Use this object as the base and populate any 3D content to spawn, once scanned in AR.

Figure 8.23 shows how a 3D model of a parrot is added into the multi target, along with the occlusion object that was added by using `Add occlusion object` within the `Multi Target Behavior` component:

FIGURE 8.23 Adding AR content to appear when the target is scanned.
Source: "African Grey Parrot" (https://skfb.ly/6GuRt) by Gert-Jan van den Boom licensed under Creative Commons Attribution-ShareAlike (*http://creativecommons.org/licenses/by-sa/4.0/*).

Now click on `Play` and scan the physical box of the same artwork, and the 3D model on top of the box may be seen, as shown in Figure 8.24:

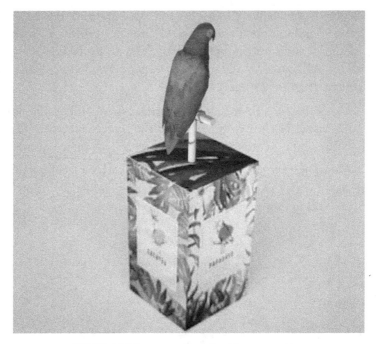

FIGURE 8.24 Demonstration of multi target tracking.

Vuforia has a highly intuitive and developer-friendly structure for building an AR app without much coding knowledge. All the different targets perform in the same manner and use a straightforward approach to show and hide AR content that has been placed in reference to the targets.

Vuforia supports more types of targets that increase the spectrum of what it can scan in a real physical environment. Some of the extended tracking features are as follows:

- Model target
- Cloud recognition (this will be covered in the next chapter)
- Barcode scanning
- Area targets
- Ground plane
- Device tracking
  Complete documentation for Vuforia SDK is provided on the library page (*https://library.vuforia.com/*).

In the next section, use the `Default Observer Event Handler` to set up trigger events and build a simple AR treasure hunt game.

DEVELOPMENT OF AN AR TREASURE HUNT GAME

This section will use the knowledge that has been gained by making image targets to create a simple AR treasure hunt game. This will be a self-paced exploration game and the rules of the game will be as follows:

- The challenge will be to find all the posters placed around the city and reach the final poster. There will be X number of posters and the final poster will provide the treasure.
- The game will provide a hint to find the first poster.
- Scanning a poster will activate a new hint and an AR experience to find the next poster.
- Scanning posters that are not relevant for the hint will not trigger anything.

Although only three posters will be used, one can make any number of them. In this case, the third poster will be the final one. Figure 8.25 shows the flow of the hunt and the posters along with the hints and the augmented content that will be used:

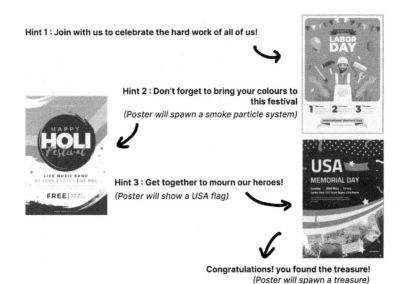

Hint 1 : Join with us to celebrate the hard work of all of us!

Hint 2 : Don't forget to bring your colours to this festival
(*Poster will spawn a smoke particle system*)

Hint 3 : Get together to mourn our heroes!
(*Poster will show a USA flag*)

Congratulations! you found the treasure!
(*Poster will spawn a treasure*)

FIGURE 8.25 Treasure hunt game plan.
Source: Posters designed by Freepik.

Based on the knowledge gained in the previous sections, add three images for the posters to Unity and make them Image targets. Figure 8.26 shows how the assets are added under each image target. A particle system was used within the first poster target and two 3D models inside other posters. Now, all these image targets will activate the content added within them when scanned in play mode; however, it is not yet understood which marker has been tracked and how functionality has been set up around it to make this a game:

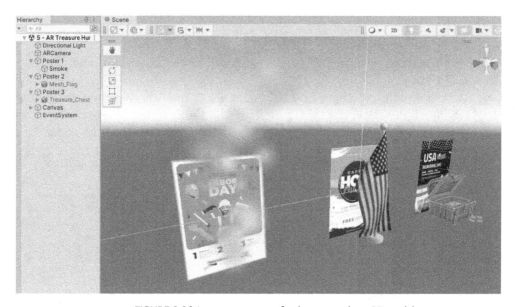

FIGURE 8.26 Image target setup for the treasure hunt 3D models.
Sources: "Treasure Chest—3d Game asset (mobile game)" (*https://skfb.ly/6WOHL*) by brainchildpl and "US flag on pole" (*https://skfb.ly/ouOIu*) by ecto, licensed under Creative Commons Attribution (*http://creativecommons.org/licenses/by/4.0/*).

The hints will use a simple canvas text and once someone wins the treasure hunt, another text box will be activated. Based on the knowledge gained in Chapter 6, add a screen space overlay canvas to the hierarchy and add two `TextMeshPro` objects. Figure 8.27 shows how to configure the canvas:

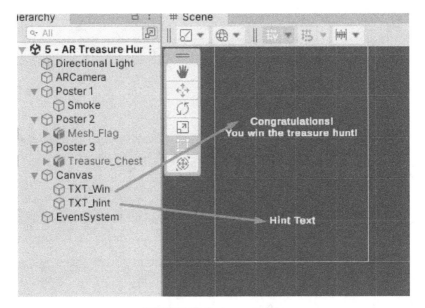

FIGURE 8.27 Setting up the game canvas.

Once someone wins the treasure, all the posters will show the AR content when scanned, but no hint will be displayed. To manage this, create a simple game manager:

```
1. using System.Collections;
2. using System.Collections.Generic;
3. using UnityEngine;
4. using TMPro;
5.
6. public class GameManager : MonoBehaviour
7. {
8.
9.    [SerializeField] private TMP_Text TXT_win;
10.   [SerializeField] private TMP_Text TXT_hint;
11.
12.   // The list of all the image targets
13.   [SerializeField] private HintTarget[] targets;
14.
15.   // State management variables
16.   private int state = 0;
```

```
17.  private bool isWin = false;
18.
19.  // Singleton pattern to retrieve the game manager by the
     targets
20.  private static GameManager instance;
21.
22.  private void Awake()
23.  {
24.    if (instance != null && instance != this)
25.    {
26.        Destroy(this);
27.    }
28.    instance = this;
29.  }
30.
31.  // Returns the global instance
32.  public static GameManager GetInstance()
33.  {
34.    return instance;
35.  }
36.
37.  void Start()
38.  {
39.    //Initialize the state of the game
40.    state = 0;
41.    TXT_win.gameObject.SetActive(false);
42.
43.    //Show the first hint
44.    TXT_hint.text = targets[state].getHint(); isWin = false;
45.  }
46.
47.  // This method will be called when an image target is
     tracked
48.  public bool CheckWin(HintTarget target)
49.  {
50.    if(target == targets[state])
51.    {
```

```
52.     if(state == targets.Length-1)
53.     {
54.       //win
55.       TXT_hint.gameObject.SetActive(false);
56.       TXT_win.gameObject.SetActive(true);
57.       isWin = true;
58.     }
59.     }else
60.     {
61.       //correct target, move next
62.       TXT_hint.text = "Correct! wait for the next hint";
63.
64.       state++;
65.       //show the hint after 3 seconds
66.       Invoke("ShowHint", 3);
67.     }
68.     return true;
69.   }
70.   else
71.   {
72.     // tracking the wrong target
73.     TXT_hint.text = "Wrong target!";
74.     return false;
75.   }
76. }
77.
78. // Method to show the hint of the current state
79. public void ShowHint()
80. {
81.   TXT_hint.text = targets[state].getHint();
82. }
83.
84. public bool IsWin()
85. {
86.   return isWin;
87. }
88. }
```

Game manager is a component written on a singleton pattern for the image targets to trigger the commands. The game manager mainly tracks the current status of the game. This is done using the *CheckWin()* method. This checks if the target that has been tracked is the same as the reference index of the *targets* array. If the status is not the number of the targets available, it is not a win since there are more targets to scan. Otherwise, it will be the correct target for the hint, which increments the status to move to the next target.

If the status and the target are both not in alignment, it is the wrong target. Therefore, it will show an error message. The *CheckWin()* method is being called by the targets when tracked. If the treasure has not been found, it can only show the content of the correct hint. The return value of the *CheckWin()* method determines the visibility of the AR content within the tracked image.

Now, errors may be produced for the *HintTarget*-related references. Therefore, create the *HintTarget* C# script, as follows:

```
1.  using System.Collections;
2.  using System.Collections.Generic;
3.  using UnityEngine;
4.  using Vuforia;
5.
6.  public class HintTarget : MonoBehaviour
7.  {
8.
9.    [SerializeField] private string hintName;
10.
11.   [SerializeField] private GameObject ARObject; 12.
13.
14.   public string getHint()
```

```
15.   {
16.     return hintName;
17.   }
18.
19.   public void OnTargetFound()
20. {
```

```
21.    if (GameManager.GetInstance().IsWin())
22.      return;
23.
24.    ARObject.SetActive(GameManager.GetInstance().
   CheckWin(this));
25.  }
26.
27.  public void OnTargetLost()
28.  {
29.    Debug.Log("lost");
30.    GameManager.GetInstance().ShowHint();
31.    ARObject.SetActive(true);
32.  }
33. }
```

The target mainly holds the hint that is to be identified by the player. Game manager will get the hint and display on the screen. There are two methods added to this script, which are *OnTargetFound()* and *OnTargetLost()*. These two methods are public and will be used by Vuforia to execute when the target has been found and lost. In line 24, the target will check if it is either the correct target or the winning target, and if not, it will hide the AR content by deactivating the game object. Before that, as in line 21, the target will check whether the game has already been beaten. If the game is beaten, it will not check for hints and will not hide the game objects within the target.

Go back to Unity and add the *HintTarget* component to all three image targets. For each image target, do the following:

1. Add the hint in the *Hint Name* parameter. This should be the hint that describes the same poster.

2. Add the child object as the *AR object*. If there is more than one object, add all of them into a parent empty object and assign that.

3. Now, check the *Default Observer Event Handler* component within the target. For both *On Target Found()* and *On Target Lost ()* methods, assign the public methods created within the *HintTarget* component. Make sure to assign the methods within the same game object.

4. However, when tracking, *OnTargetLost* may not be triggered. This is due to the extended tracking feature of Vuforia keeping the AR content available even if the marker is not in the viewport. To fix it, it is necessary to

change the `Consider target as visible if its status is:` option within the `Default` object event handler component to `Tracked`.

5. Now, repeat the same procedure for all the posters/image targets. Figure 8.28 is an example of the component setup for poster 1:

FIGURE 8.28 Hint target parameter setup.

6. Now create an empty game object and add the `GameManager` component.

7. Set up all the text box references and the targets. Make sure to add all the targets to the `Targets` parameter based on the correct flow. Figure 8.29 shows how the parameters are set up.

8. In this section, the main intention was to get an introduction to the target found and lost events. The methods were manually added to the events provided by Vuforia. This is a simple task for just three targets, but it can

be overwhelming if there are more targets. Therefore, one can remove the methods from the events (remove the added *OnTargetFound* and *Lost* methods) and assign them within the *start* method. This can be done by adding the following to the *start* method of the *HintTarget* script. Make sure to add *using Vuforia;* at the top of the script:

```
1. private void Start()
2. {
3.   DefaultObserverEventHandler eventHander =
   GetComponent<DefaultObserverEventHandler>();
4.   eventHander.OnTargetFound.AddListener(OnTargetFound);
5.   eventHander.OnTargetLost.AddListener(OnTargetLost);
```

9. Click play to try it on an editor or build and run on a mobile device to test the flow of the game. What was built was a basic implementation of marker-based AR. Another chapter will look into polishing techniques and other enhancements, in order to enhance the quality of the AR experience.

CONCLUSION

This chapter implemented multiple practical marker-based AR exercises using the Vuforia SDK. Unity and AR can be treated as two separate entities in the same room. Use all the Unity-based functionalities considering the tracked AR target as a local environment space. The next chapter will check how to build dynamic AR applications with Vuforia that do not require importing image targets into a Unity project.

KEY POINTS

- The Vuforia SDK uses a license key to check the validity of the use of their tool.
- Vuforia image targets get processed by the database manager from Vuforia Cloud.
- Image targets must have certain details and should adhere to best practices in order to be scanned by the SDK properly. This is known as the *trackability rating*.
- By uploading images to the Vuforia database, one will be able to see how the target would perform in play mode.

- Image targets can also be added locally within the project without using the database method. This is done in *Image Target Behavior* by changing the target mode to *From Image*, instead of *From Database*.
- Testing cylinder targets and multi targets requires a physical object with proper printed surfaces.
- Vuforia targets emit events when the targets are tracked and untracked. These events can be used to add interactivity to applications that trigger marker scans.

QUESTION

1. Increase the number of targets in the project and add more interactions and puzzle elements to the treasure hunt game. Use different targets, such as multi targets and cylinder targets.

Developing Marker-based Dynamic AR Apps

INTRODUCTION

Now that previous chapters have established a basic overview of how Vuforia works within Unity, readers are capable of developing any Unity-based application logic that can run within a local space around a trained marker (image target, cylinder targets, and so on); however, building enhanced augmented reality (AR) applications effectively requires additional knowledge on how data can be manipulated and transferred across platforms.

This chapter looks at building two AR projects while developing concepts on data processing and retrieval. One project will be an AR machine inspection tool that uses only one AR image target but with a method to identify each marker using an encoded method called *VuMarks*. One can use the encoded data to retrieve more data using an *application programming interface (API)* and convert that raw data to usable methods within Unity. The second project involves building an AR billboard app that does not rely on image targets imported into Unity, instead using Vuforia Cloud targets to dynamically update the image target and retrieve the content accordingly.

STRUCTURE

This chapter will discuss the following topics:

- Machine inspection tool
  - Unity serialization and deserialization

- Creating a simple mock API
- Using UnityWebRequest to request data based on input
- Vuforia VuMark introduction
- Designing a VuMark using Adobe Illustrator
- Connecting the marker recognition with networking to request dynamic data and displaying them in AR
- Dynamic AR billboard
  - Setting up the AR poster project
  - Implementing Vuforia Cloud targets
  - Creating Asset Bundles in Unity
  - Uploading the Asset Bundles in the cloud
  - Updating meta files to update the AR experience
  - Downloading content and displaying in AR

OBJECTIVES

After completing this chapter, readers will be able to design and develop AR applicationsthat use distributed systems to load data dynamically and visualize them in a 3DAR space. Readers will also be able to develop marker-based dynamic AR apps that do not require users to update the app every time a new experience has been created. Readers will be able to use cloud storage for their data and load them to an AR application during runtime.

MACHINE INSPECTION TOOL

Imagine being supposed to build an AR-based machine inspection tool to retrieve the current data of each machine, just by pointing an AR camera or a wearable at it. Moreover, the requirement is to do it using marker-based tracking when there are over 50 machines that must be scanned to attach a marker (image). Putting the data retrieval process for each machine aside along with a decision to use the traditional way of using image targets to build the application, one must first design 50 different image targets for each machine.

Additionally, two image targets cannot create similar features since the AR algorithm may misidentify the target if both look similar. Even if there are 50 different image targets, one must add all of them to the database and set up every image target within Unity manually. In addition to that, the application will not be scalable to serve new machines that will require the AR inspection.

In order to overcome this challenge, Vuforia has introduced a new marker-based detection system known as VuMark. This allows anyone to encode data into an image marker and load that decoded data into the application using their software development kit (SDK). Keeping the same image marker aesthetics, a portion of the image target can be modified to encode any data.

The project to be built will use VuMark as the detection system and employ data retrieval methods to dynamically load data from a remote system. Figure 9.1 gives an overview of the flow of the machine inspection tool:

FIGURE 9.1 Flow of the machine inspection AR app.

As per Figure 9.1, there are three machines with the same image target pasted onthe surface of each. Occasionally, the machines send sensory data to cloud storage. A cloud storage can be a database or a raw storage based in a remote location, and the machines will be using a connected network (Internet) to send data along with its unique ID through an API.

The VuMark system can encode the machine IDs inside the target images without hindering the aesthetics of the marker. Now the AR application will be able to decodethe IDs when scanned using the Vuforia SDK. The decoded

ID will be used to filter and request the same machine data from the cloud storage, and the data will be shown over the machine with other 3D elements, over the VuMark image target.

This way, the AR developer can use a single image target and dynamically show different data on different machines. The display of AR content can also be customized based on the data that will be retrieved from the cloud.

As can be realized, apart from AR development, this application requires knowledge of methods for the following reasons:

* *Request data from an external source dynamically:* Each machine has its own ID. Therefore, data requests should be different for each machine.
* *Retrieve data from the external source dynamically:* Data from each machine can be dynamic and raw.
* *Convert data into a format that can be visualized:* Convert raw data to a usable data format, such as variables (string, int, float, and so on).
* Visualize data in AR, within the image target.

Unity Serialization and Deserialization

Before requesting data from an external source, one must identify the structure of a data format, and how the structure can be helpful in terms of splitting it into individual segments of information. There are different ways to present data in a structured format. There are many data structures that have been used all over the world, but *extensible markup language (XML)* and *JavaScript object notation (JSON)* are two of the most-used data structures to represent data in a text format; however, a text string is not data. The text data structure should be converted into a format that can be saved within an object format. This conversion is known as *data serialization*. Converting an object into a textual format is called *data deserialization*. Text data can be converted into bits that can be transmitted through any data transmission method, such as the Internet. Therefore, data serialization and deserialization are processes that many software applications use to exchange data. Unity directly supports JSON serialization with its API. JSON is a lightweight data structure that is built on two structures:

* *A collection of key-value pairs:* A key can be the name of a variable and the value is the value of the variable. The value can be anything, such as a number, an integer, a string, a Boolean, or even another JSON.
* A list of values, consisting of an array, list, or a sequence of objects.

The following is a simple JSON that represents the basic data of a machine:

```
1.  {
1.    "machine_id": 1,
2.    "name": "Xtract ABC 123",
3.    "make": "CAT",
4.    "version": 1.3
6.  }
```

Notice how the JSON is wrapped by curly brackets ({ and }). Within the JSON object, there are four variables: the machine ID, name, make, and the machine version. See how each variable type is presented, based on the type of variable. An extended version of the data structure can be seen as follows:

```
1.  {
2.    "machine_id": 1,
3.    "name": "Xtract ABC 123",
4.    "make": "CAT",
5.    "version": 1.3,
6.    "is_running": true,
7.    "location": {
8.      "building": "A",
9.      "isle": "X5",
10.     "section": 10
11. },
12.   "current_data": [{
13.     "id": 1001,
14.     "name": "temperature",
15.     "unit": "C",
16.     "value": 66.45
17. },
18.   {
19.     "id": 1002,
20.     "name": "humidity",
21.     "unit": "%",
22.     "value": 78
23. },
```

```
24. {
25.    "id": 1003,
26.    "name": "Units processed",
27.    "unit": "unit/min",
28.    "value": 3.4
29. }
30. ]
31. }
```

The preceding JSON includes strings, integers, floats, Booleans, and another JSON, as well as a list of JSONs. Visit *https://www.json.org/* to learn more about JSONs. In Unity, use C# to create scripts that are by default inherited from the *MonoBehavior* class. The components added using a *MonoBehavior* class are the instances of that class. One can use C# classes to create instances of any object that is defined by the script. Instances can hold actual variables. Serialization converts the text data into defined C# instances, which can be used in data visualization. The following C# script called *MachineData.cs* is a serializable class that can be used to serialize the data of the first JSON:

```
1. [System.Serializable]
2. public class MachineData
3.
4. {
5.    public int machine_id;
6.    public string name;
7.    public string make;
8.    public float version;
9. }
```

If one compares the JSON object, the key names are similar to the variables of the serializable class. Unity needs to know that is a serializable class by adding *[System. Serializable]*.

For the extended user data, three data types can be seen, including the parent object, which is *MachineData*, *Location*, and *CurrentData*. Here, *CurrentData* objects are placed in an array. To cater to this, it is necessary to create two more classes to define the objects that can be generated. In C#, multiple classes can be added within one script as long as they are not for Unity components. The standard is to create separate files to increase maintainability; however, for this example, add two more classes and modify the *MachineData.cs* script as follows:

```
1.  [System.Serializable]
2.  public class MachineData
3.  {
4.    public int machine_id;
5.    public string name;
6.    public string make;
7.    public float version;
8.    public bool is_running;
9.    public Location location;
10.   public SensorData[] current_data;
11. }
12. [System.Serializable]
14. public class Location
15. {
16.   public string building;
17.   public string isle;
18.   public int section;
19. }
20.
21. [System.Serializable]
22. public class SensorData
23. {
24.   public int id;
25.   public string name;
26.   public string unit;
27.   public float value;
28. }
29.
```

As can be seen, all the classes are noted as serializable and the machine data class has two new data types, which are defined as *SensorData* and *Location*. After converting the complete JSON into one serialized object, there will be one instance that contains one *Location* instance and three *SensorData* instances.

In order to test the conversion within Unity, it is necessary to load the JSON as a string. One can store a file and load it in runtime using *StreamingAssets* in Unity. Create a new folder in the *Assets* folder and name it *StreamingAssets*.

Now open the folder and add a new text file and rename it to *data.json*. This extension is optional for reading the file but it is better for maintainability. Now, open the text file and add the previous extended JSON string as the text and save the file.

Create a new C# script called *DataSerializationTest.cs* and add the following:

```
1.  using System.IO;
2.  using UnityEngine;
3.
4.  public class DataSerializationTest : MonoBehaviour
5.  {
6.    void Start()
7.    {
8.      string json = File.ReadAllText(Application.
      streamingAssetsPath
+ "/data.json");
9.
10. MachineData machineData = JsonUtility.
      FromJson<MachineData>(json);
11.
12.      Debug.Log(machineData.name);
13.      Debug.Log(machineData.location.building);
14.      Debug.Log(machineData.current_data.Length);
15.      Debug.Log(machineData.current_data[0].name);
16.  }
17. }
```

Add this to an empty game object and run the scene. The script will print:

```
Xtract ABC 123
A
3
temperature
```

System.IO was used to read the text file from the streaming assets path as a string. The text string is converted to an object by using the *JsonUtility*, which is a feature provided within the *UnityEngine*.

One can iterate through the whole instance and pick each individual value and use it to represent data within Unity. The machine inspection project will be mostly using data serialization. If it becomes required to convert an object into the JSON format, it will be necessary to deserialize the object. A sample test script for data deserialization is as follows:

```
1.  using UnityEngine;
2.
3.  public class DataDeserializationTest : MonoBehaviour
4.  {
5.    void Start()
6.    {
7.      MachineData machineData = new MachineData();
8.      Location location1 = new Location();
9.      SensorData temperatureData = new SensorData();
10.
11.     temperatureData.id = 1;
12.     temperatureData.name = "temperature";
13.     temperatureData.unit = "F";
14.     temperatureData.value = 456.3f;
15.
16.     location1.building = "b1";
17.     location1.section = 1;
18.     location1.isle = "A";
19.
20.     machineData.machine_id = 1;
21.     machineData.is_running = false;
22.     machineData.name = "Machine 1";
23.     machineData.make = "AXG";
24.
25.     machineData.location = location1;
26.     machineData.current_data = new SensorData[1];
27.     machineData.current_data[0] = temperatureData;
28.
29.     string json = JsonUtility.ToJson(machineData);
30.     Debug.Log(json);
31. }
32. }
```

Notice how an individual object is created and added to the parent machine data object array. When this is run, the console will display the following JSON. The variables with no values in the objects have taken default values, as shown:

```
{"machine_id":1,"name":"Machine
    1","make":"AXG","version":0.0,"is_
running":false,"location":{"building":"b1","isle":"A","sec-
tion":1},"current_data":[{"id":1,"name":"temperature",
    "unit":"F","val-
ue":456.29998779296877}]}
```

Creating a Simple Mock API

The previous example used a JSON file stored within the application to serialize data; however, the data must be retrieved from a remote service. A method to request and retrieve data from another source is known as an API. *Representational state transfer* (*REST API*) is a popular and widely used network-based API. Read more about REST API from the following link:

https://www.redhat.com/en/topics/api/what-is-a-rest-api

In order to test the data retrieval process with Unity, one would build a simple virtual remote server (computer) within one's own computer. This is usually known as the `localhost`. This can be achieved by using a simple software application known as *Mockoon*. Visit the following link and download and install the mockoon application:

https://mockoon.com/

One may see a sample project setup in the app when it is opened for the first time. In this scenario, one would add one datapoint to retrieve information about a machine.

In Mockoon, go to `File` and select New Environment. Save it in any location with any preferred name. In this case, it was `Machines`. As shown in Figure 9.2, add the path `machines/1` as in (1) and copy the complete JSON that was used before into the inline section (2). Once done, click on the `Play` button to start the server.

Now, open any Web browser window and type `localhost:<port>/` `machines/1` into the address bar. Here `<port>` means the number seen under `Machines` in Mockoon right next to `0.0.0.0`:

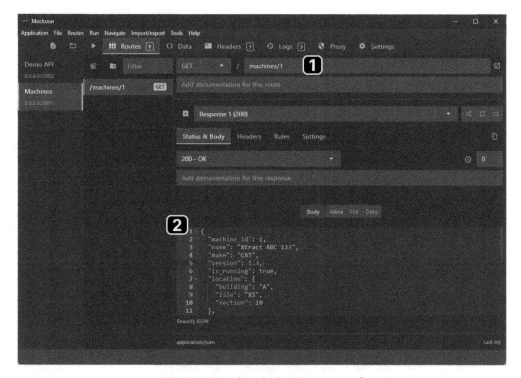

FIGURE 9.2 Mockoon basic GET request configuration.

Now, create more paths that resemble the following pattern with different data:

```
localhost:<port>/machines/<machine_id>
```

This provides an opportunity to request mock data for different machines based on the machine id. The next subsection examines how to get this data into Unity.

Using Unity WebRequest to Request Data Basedon Input

Unity WebRequest is a library provided by Unity that lies within Unity networking features to send and receive data through the HTTP protocol. It uses *DownloadHandler* and *UploadHandler* to send REST API requests such as *Get*, *Post*, *Put*, and *Delete*. In the previous subsection, a mock *API endpoint* (*API path*) was created that returns a *GET* response. In this subsection, use

Unity WebRequest to send a *GET* request and retrieve data into Unity as a string. Then use the knowledge gained previously to convert it into an object.

Create a new C# script and call it *DataConnector.cs* and add the following:

```
1.  using System.Collections;
2.  using UnityEngine;
3.  using UnityEngine.Networking;
4.
5.  public class DataConnector : MonoBehaviour
6.  {
7.    void Start()
8.    {
9.      StartCoroutine(RequestData());
10.   }
11.
12.   Ienumerator RequestData()
13.   {
14.     UnityWebRequest getMachineDataRequest = UnityWebRequest.
Get("http://localhost:3001/machines/1");
15.     yield return getMachineDataRequest.SendWebRequest();
16.   DownloadHandler hander = getMachineDataRequest.
   downloadHandler;
17.     Debug.Log(hander.text);
18.   }
19. }
```

In the preceding example, the link should be the one created with Mockoon. Make sure it is running before testing this script.

As can be seen, the request is added into an *Ienumerator* instead of a method, and it has been called a coroutine. This is because an API request is not real time and will take time to process. Therefore, it is necessary to wait until it returns a response. If this works without any issues, one will be able to see the JSON getting printed in the console.

The preceding material should clarify an understanding of the makeup of text-based data structures, how to retrieve them from a remote service using *GET* REST API methods, and how to convert them to objects usable within

Unity. The idea of this application is to request data dynamically, based on an AR scan. Different machine data can be requested changing the `machine_id` of the path. This machine ID can be encoded into an AR marker, which can be retrieved using Vuforia VuMarks.

Now it needs to be clarified what VuMark is, to create a VuMark, and how to retrieve data encoded within a VuMark.

Vuforia VuMark Introduction

VuMark is similar to a QR Code or a bar code but with added customized designs. A VuMark can serve as a barcode as well as a logo of a trademark or a company.

Compared to a normal image target, a VuMark is a vector image in the Scalable Vector Graphics (SVG) format that has light and dark components in the middle to encode a value. A sample VuMark image can be seen in Figure 9.3:

FIGURE 9.3 A VuMark.

A VuMark consists of multiple sections listed as follows:

- *Border*: A dark border that surrounds a VuMark.
- *Contour*: The line where clear space inside the border meets the surrounding border. Vuforia mainly uses the contour for the initial marker recognition.
- *Clear space*: This is the clear space under the VuMark.

- *Code elements*: These are the dark and light elements that are placed on top of each other to represent two states. The number of elements within a VuMark depends on the length of the encoded data. When designing, it is better to optimize the encoded data to have fewer elements in the design.
- *Background*: This is the area inside the code elements, or outside the VuMark, that does not involve any tracking purpose. This can be a logo or any design element.

Designing a VuMark Using Adobe Illustrator

Augmented reality is the designer's as well as the developer's job. Therefore, getting used to a design tool comes in handy when building AR applications. In order to design a VuMark, Vuforia has created a designer tool that works only with Adobe Illustrator. A free trial version of Adobe Illustrator is available for download by visiting *https://www.adobe.com* and signing up for a Creative Cloud account.

It will also be necessary to download the VuMark Designer tool by visiting the following link:

https://developer.vuforia.com/downloads/tool

Now, extract the ZIP file downloaded as the VuMark Designer tool and copy the three JSX files within the VuMark folder into the following folders:

- *MacOS*: `/Applications/Adobe Illustrator CC folder/Presets/en_US/Scripts` (Right-click the Illustrator icon and select `Show Package Contents` to go into the `application-content` folder).
- *Windows*: `<Illustrator Installation path>\Presets\en_US\Scripts`

Now, open Adobe Illustrator and go to *File | Scripts | VuMark-Setup*.

This will give the window shown in Figure 9.4, where it is possible to set up a template. In the window, name the design and choose the type of the encoded values in VuMark. The number of elements required for each type is different. At the bottom of the window, notice the number of encoding elements required within the design. In the example under discussion, `Numeric` has been chosen to hold the ID of the machines, and as the maximum value, 10 has been added. This VuMark now requires the user to create 28 encoding dark and light elements for the VuMark.

Refer to Figure 9.4:

VuMark Template Setup

This script will create an Illustrator template for your VuMark based on the Name, Type and ID Length that you choose.

Name: `myVumark`

Max length of 255 characters. Valid characters are a-z, A-Z, 0-9, and underscores.

Type: ○ String • Numeric ○ Bytes

Numeric is for serial numbers in range of [0..maximum ID]. Enter maximum ID.

Maximum ID: `10`

Elements required: 28   [Cancel] [Continue]

FIGURE 9.4 VuMark setup dialog.

Design step 1

Select the `VuMark-ClearSpace` layer and draw a rectangle that should include one's VuMark logo. Make sure the background color of this is white and does not have a stroke. Figure 9.5 shows a sample clear space layer.

NOTE *The stroke (border) of the VuMark target is added for showcasing only. If wanted, change the colors of the background and borders by the top panel.*

Refer to Figure 9.5:

FIGURE 9.5 VuMark Clearspace.

Design Step 2

Select the `VuMark-Border` layer and add the shape of the chosen logo. This should be a darker element and the contrast between the clear space and the border should be more than at least 40%. Test this by choosing `File | Scripts | VuMark-Verify`. The VuMark properties section next to the design will update the status as to whether the design is passed or failed. Figure 9.6 shows how one design border has been passed:

FIGURE 9.6 VuMark border.

Design Step 3

Select the `VuMark-Contour` layer and add a border (only the stroke) that goes around the border shape added before. In the selected case, the same object was copied, the background color was changed to transparent, and the stroke color was set to black only. Now, verify the design. This will update some of the other layers of the design, adding more magenta-colored elements. A designer should not overlap the magenta elements since these elements are important for Vuforia to track the marker. Figure 9.7 shows how the contour of the selected design has been verified. Check the digital assets for the color images:

FIGURE 9.7 VuMark contour.

Design Step 4

This is the most important step of the design: adding the coded elements. In the left side `Properties` section, the `Elements Required` number must be the number of elements needed in the design. A single code element has a dark element and a bright element. These two subelements should be placed exactly on top of each other. Select both `VuMark-DarkElements` and `VuMark-BrightElements` layers and move them above the contour. If only these two layers could be isolated, that would be great. Now select the dark elements layer and add a single small element in a dark color.

The color was made black since it is easier to distinguish. Now copy the element and paste the same in place (`Edit | Paste` in place). Move the copy into the bright elements layer and change the color to a light one. White was chosen in the specified design. Figure 9.8 shows how one code element with dark and bright subelements was added:

FIGURE 9.8 Bright and dark single element.

Design Step 5

Now copy dark and bright elements within the contours to fill up the required elements. Always make sure that the bright and dark elements are on top of each other in two different layers, as in the previous step. Now click and verify. Make changes as required by the tool. Once this step is done, it is possible to export the design; however, one can still add more design elements in the *VuMark-Background* and move the layer above the border as well. Verify again to check any issues. Figure 9.9 shows the final design once verified:

FIGURE 9.9 Final VuMark verified design.

Now, go to *File | Scripts | VuMark-Export*. This will create an SVG file in a chosen location. This is the file necessary to upload to the Vuforia target manager.

Learn more about VuMark design considerations from the following link:

https://library.vuforia.com/vumarks/vumark-design-guide

Now follow the listed steps:

1. Go to the Vuforia developer portal and make a new VuMark database.

2. Add a new target and upload the SVG file generated from Illustrator.

3. Download the complete database for *UnityEngine* and import it into the project.

4. Similar to previous Vuforia target setups, add a VuMark object into the scene hierarchy by going to *GameObject | Vuforia | VuMark*. Figure 9.10 shows how the VuMark target is placed in the scene. This can be considered as an image target with an added encoded data element:

FIGURE 9.10 VuMark added into Unity with the Vuforia SDK.

Connecting the Marker Recognition with Networking to Request Dynamic Data and Displaying Them in AR

Based on the flow discussed in Figure 9.1, users will know how to access mock data and encode that data into a VuMark; also, the principles of retrieving data from the remote location and deserializing it to a comfortable format should be known. This section will show how to decode the VuMark data and display relevant data based on the decoded data.

Downloading VuMark Targets

In order to test the VuMark, download targets that have different encoded data. Recall that the VuMark held numbers from 1 to 10. Therefore, when downloading an encoded VuMark to test, it will be necessary to add the encoded data. Follow these steps:

1. Go to Vuforia target manager and open the VuMark database added before.

2. Click on the `Generate VuMark` link next to the uploaded VuMark.

Here, it is necessary to add the encoded value to download the image, as shown in Figure 9.11. It is also possible to choose the graphic format wanted for the image target. This target can be printed and pasted on a machine for testing:

Generate VuMark

Name: acmevumark
ID Type: Numeric
ID Length: 4 (Max ID = 10)

ID

| 1 |

This is what will be encoded in the VuMark and must match the Type and Length defined above.

Graphic Format

| PNG ∨ |

Cancel   Download

FIGURE 9.11 Add the number as the ID to encode.

In the case under discussion, download the three image targets that encoded 1, 2, and 3 numbers, respectively, as shown in Figure 9.12:

ID : 1   **ID : 2**   **ID : 3**

FIGURE 9.12 VuMark targets with IDs 1, 2, 3.

Decoding VuMark Data

In this section, decode the data and log in to the console. Create a new C# script and name it *VuMarkDataRetriever.cs* and add the following:

```
1.  using UnityEngine;
2.  using Vuforia;
3.
4.  public class VuMarkDataRetriever : MonoBehaviour
5.  {
6.    private VuMarkBehaviour vuMarkBehaviour;
7.    private DefaultObserverEventHandler vuObserver;
8.    private string data = "";
9.    private VuMarkInstanceId instance;
10.
11.   void Start()
12.   {
13.     vuMarkBehaviour= GetComponent<VuMarkBehaviour>();
14.     vuObserver = GetComponent<DefaultObserverEventHandler>();
15.
16.      if(vuObserver!= null)
17.        vuObserver.OnTargetFound.AddListener(OnTargetFound);
18.  }
19.
20.   public void OnTargetFound()
21.   {
```

```
22.      if(vuMarkBehaviour)
23.      {
24.        instance = vuMarkBehaviour.InstanceId;
25.        switch (instance.DataType)
26.        {
27.          case InstanceIdType.STRING:
28.            data = instance.StringValue;
29.            break;
30.          case InstanceIdType.NUMERIC:
31.            data = instance.NumericValue.ToString();
32.            break;
33.          case InstanceIdType.BYTE:
34.                  data = System.Text.Encoding.Default.
GetString(instance.Buffer) ;
35.            break;
36.          default:
37.            data = "";
38.            break;
39.        }
40.      }
41.
42.      Debug.Log(data);
43.    }
44.
45.  public string GetData()
46.  {
47.    return data;
48.  }
49. }
```

This is an intermediate yet simple script to call *VuMark Behavior* and retrieve the *InstanceID* of the target scanned.

In lines 13 and 14 appear references to *VuMarkBehavior* and *DefaultObserver EventHandler* components, which are both included default components of a VuMark object.

In lines 16 and 17, check if there is a valid observer component. If the component is available, add the public method *OnTargetFound* as a listener to the *OnTargetFound* event in the observer. Now, every time Vuforia identifies a new image, this method will be executed. Now, look at the *OnTargetFound* method.

VuMarkBehavior only provides the ID of the instance. This does not mean it is the data encoded within the image. Therefore, it is necessary to retrieve the data from the instance. In line 24, a temporary instance was created and referenced to the instance retrieved by the *VuMarkBehavior*. Using a switch case, check the *Type* of the encoded data. In VuMark, encoded data can be a number, a string, or a byte array, as discussed earlier. This script can identify different types and convert the data into a string stored in the *data* private variable. If no identifiable type is retrieved, the data value will be defaulted to an empty string.

There is also another *Get* method to return what is saved in the data variable.

Now, add the script to the VuMark target *gameobject* alongside other components, as shown in Figure 9.13 (1). Click on the *Play* button and show different target images of the same logo to the camera. Figure 9.13 (2) shows that different ID data are captured and logged in the console:

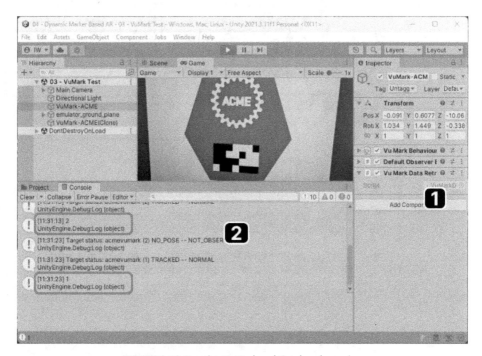

FIGURE 9.13 Running VuMark and Get decode preview.

Using Decoded Values to Retrieve Data from the
RemoteServer through API

Now that the ID can be decoded within the image target, it is time to retrieve data relevant to the ID and show them in AR. First of all, look at the structure of the JSON made earlier. It has basic information about the machine, the location information, and an array of sensor data that consists of the name, unit, and the value. Creating a data structure like this helps transmit data effectively; also, it is scalable. If a new machine is added with different kinds of sensory data, there is the flexibility to add one to the sensor data array.

Figure 9.14 is a simple sketch to define how to display sensory data in AR around the marker. Here, there are static data types that are machine information and dynamic types that are sensor data:

FIGURE 9.14 AR information display sketch.

All the data sent across the previous JSON have been added to the AR information display sketch. In Unity, this can be represented by a world space canvas placed inside the VuMark game object.

Create an empty world space canvas inside the VuMark game object and add the panels and `TextMeshPro` user interface (UI) objects as shown in Figure 9.15 (1). The required assets for the canvas can be found within this chapter's GitHub repository:

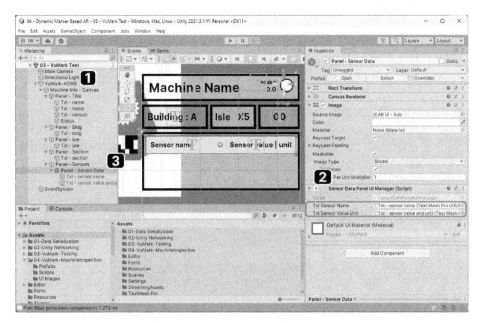

FIGURE 9.15 Setting up the AR canvas within VuMark.

The world space canvas added inside the VuMark contains images as panels and `TextMeshPro` UI objects as placeholders to fill with machine data. The amount of sensor data differs from machine to machine. Therefore, those panels must be instantiated at runtime. In order to do this, create a simple script called `SensorDataPanelUIManager.cs`. This script will refer to the two text objects within a sensor data panel and open a public method to set the values of the text boxes. Then attach the text objects to the properties as shown in Figure 9.15 (2) and convert the sensor data panel to a prefab, as shown in Figure 9.15 (3). The code for `SensorDataPanel` is as follows:

```
1.  using TMPro;
2.  using UnityEngine;
3.
4.  public class SensorDataPanelUIManager : MonoBehaviour
5.  {
6.    [SerializeField] private TMP_Text txtSensorName;
7.    [SerializeField] private TMP_Text txtSensorValueUnit;
8.
9.    public void SetData(string sensorName, string valueUnit)
10.   {
11.     txtSensorName.text = sensorName;
```

```
12.    txtSensorValueUnit.text = valueUnit;
13.  }
14. }
```

Select the UI panel that sensor data will be populating and also add a *VerticalLayout Group* component. This component will automatically arrange the populated sensor data prefabs vertically. Set the padding and spacing as needed. Also, set the *Child Alignment* as *Upper Center* and untick *Height* from *Child Force Expand*. Now remove the prefab from the main canvas panel. This will be instantiated during data retrieval.

Similarly, create a script for the complete canvas data visualization. Create another script called *MachineDataUIManager.cs* and add the following:

```
1. using TMPro;
2. using UnityEngine;
3. using UnityEngine.UI;
4.
5. public class MachineDataUIManager : MonoBehaviour 6. {
7.    [Header("Text Boxes")]
8.    [SerializeField] private TMP_Text txt_MachineName;
9.    [SerializeField] private TMP_Text txt_MachineMake;
10.   [SerializeField] private TMP_Text txt_MachineVersion;
11.   [SerializeField] private TMP_Text txt_Building;
12.   [SerializeField] private TMP_Text txt_Isle;
13.   [SerializeField] private TMP_Text txt_Section;
14.
15.   [Header(""Machine Status"")]
16.   [SerializeField] private Image imgMachineStatus;
17.   [SerializeField] private Color turnedOnColor;
18.   [SerializeField] private Color turnedOffColor; 19.
20.   [Header("Machine Sensor data")]
21.   [SerializeField] private Transform sensorDataPanel;
22.   [SerializeField] private GameObject sensorDataPanelPrefab;
23.
24.   public void SetMachineData(MachineData machineData)
25.   {
26.     txt_MachineName.SetText(machineData.name);
27.     txt_MachineMake.SetText(machineData.make);
28.     txt_MachineVersion.SetText(machineData.version.
   ToString());
```

```
29.    txt_Building.SetText("Building : "+machineData.location.
   building);
30.    txt_Isle.SetText("Isle : "+machineData.location.isle);
31.    txt_Section.SetText("Section : "+machineData.location.
   section.ToString());
32.
33.    //Set machine status
34.    imgMachineStatus.color = machineData.is_running ?turne-
   dOnColor : turnedOffColor; 35.
36.    //Set machine sensor data
37.    foreach (SensorData item in machineData.current_data)
38.    {
39.       //Create a new sensor data element
40.       SensorDataPanelUIManager dataElement =
41.         Instantiate(sensorDataPanelPrefab, sensorDataPanel)
42.           .GetComponent<SensorDataPanelUIManager>();
43.
44.       dataElement.SetData(
45.         item.name,
46.           string.Concat(item.value.ToString(), " ", item.
   unit));
47.    }
48. }
49.
50. public void OnClearData()
51. {
52.   txt_MachineName.SetText("");
53.   txt_MachineMake.SetText("");
54.   txt_MachineVersion.SetText("");
55.   txt_Building.SetText("");
56.   txt_Isle.SetText("");
57.   txt_Section.SetText("");
58.
59.   imgMachineStatus.color = Color.white;
60.
61.   foreach (Transform item in sensorDataPanel)
62.   {
63.       Destroy(item.gameObject);
```

```
64.     }
65.   }
66. }
```

This script provides references to all the text fields inside the canvas element, the rounded image to display the machine status, a transform reference to populate the sensor data of the machine dynamically, and the previously made prefab to instantiate within the sensor data display panel at the bottom.

In line 24, the `SetMachineData` method will get a `MachineData` as a parameter input. The variable values within the parameter value will be distributed among the text fields and populate other content within the canvas.

In line 34, the color of the image used to visualize the machine status will be either `turnedOnColor` or `turnedOffColor`, based on the value.

In line 37, a `foreach` loop will iterate through the `current_data` array of `SensorData` object type, and instantiate new prefab instances. It will also refer the `SensorDataPanelUIManager` component of the prefab and execute the `SetData` method created in the previous script.

There is also a method called `OnClearData()` that will be called when the marker is moved away from the camera. This will clear all the data, and destroy the sensor data instances created, if there are any. Now add the script to the main function and attach all the reference objects. Figure 9.16 shows how each `GameObject` is referenced in the component:

FIGURE 9.16 Machine data UI manager.

Now, it is time to request data from the local server based on machine ID 1. Open the `VuMarkDataRetrieved` script again and add the following to the top:

```
using UnityEngine.Events;
```

1. Add this secondary class before the `Monobehavior` class. Here, a custom `UnityEvent` that takes a string as a parameter is being made, as shown below:

```
[System.Serializable]

public class StringEvent : UnityEvent<string>

{}
```

2. Create a public `StringEvent` variable within the `Monobehavior`:

```
public UnityEvent OnDataReceived;
```

3. Instead of logging data, replace the `Debug.Log` line with the following:

```
OnDataReceived?.Invoke(data);
```

This creates a Unity event that can be invoked whenever VuMark data isreceived and the machine ID is passed to the listeners.

4. Now, create a new C# Script called `MachineDataRequester` and add that to the VuMark alongside the `VuMarkDataRetriever` component.

The script should be as follows:

```
1.  using System.Collections;
2.  using UnityEngine;
3.  using UnityEngine.Networking;
4.
5.  public class MachineDataRequester : MonoBehaviour
6.  {
7.    [SerializeField] private MachineDataUIManager
      machineDataUI;
8.    private void Start()
9.    {
10.     GetComponent<VuMarkDataRetriever>().OnDataReceived.
        AddListener(RequestMachineData);
11.     GetComponent<DefaultObserverEventHandler>().OnTargetLost.
        AddListener(machineDataUI.OnClearData);
12.   }
13.
```

```
14.   private void RequestMachineData(string machineID)
15.   {
16.     StartCoroutine(RequestData(machineID));
17.   }
18.
19.   Ienumerator RequestData(string machineID)
20.   {
21.   UnityWebRequest getMachineDataRequest =
22.       UnityWebRequest.Get("http://localhost:3001/machines/"+
    machineID);
23.
24.       yield return getMachineDataRequest.SendWebRequest();
25.       DownloadHandler handler = getMachineDataRequest.
    downloadHandler;
26.
27.       MachineData machineData = JsonUtility.
    FromJson<MachineData>(handler.text);
28.
29.       machineDataUI.SetMachineData(machineData);
30.
31.   }
32. }
```

As was done before, this script has a data requester that requests data from the remote server. The preceding script registered the *RequestMachineData* method to the *OnDataReceived* method that was created before, and it also registered the *OnClearData* method to the *OnTargetLost* method of *DefaultObserverEventHandler* by Vuforia:

```
"localhost:<port>/machines/<machine_id>"
```

As with the preceding link, the machine ID is the dynamic section that changes based on the VuMark ID. Line 22 used the machine ID that is invoked from the previous class to change the link for every data request. If the data is available, line 27 will set up the response into a C# object and pass the data to the *SetMachineData* method from the referenced *machineDataUI* component. This component must be assigned to the Unity interface before testing. Make sure that the Mockoon app is running along with the mock API with the correct path and click play. Figure 9.17 shows how the attached VuMark sticker provides mock data in AR with proper colors and text data within the UI panel.

NOTE *The scripts added to the project require refactoring to handle different kinds of unexpected data inputs. Read Unity's documentation on UnityWebRequest and JsonUtility classes to learn more about their properties and functions.*

Refer to Figure 9.17:

FIGURE 9.17 Dynamic AR app with VuMark displaying data on a machine.

NOTE *Downloading VuMarks one by one from the developer console can be an overwhelming process. Vuforia has a VuMark generation Web API that can generate VuMark instances using a POST REST API call. This API can be used in a recurring manner to generate and download many instances within a short period of of time.*

Go to the following link to learn more about the API:

https://library.vuforia.com/web-api/vumark-generation-web-api

DYNAMIC AR BILLBOARD

Imagine being supposed to build an AR application that requires marker-based recognition without app updates. As an example, consider a billboard that changes over time and an AR app that dynamically supports the content in the billboard, which shows related AR content. In a standard way, new markers must be added into the project and the app must be updated with additional content.

This section of this chapter is going to be about building an AR app that does not require app updates, but one that can recognize new markers via Vuforia Cloud targets and download content from an external source using Unity Asset Bundles. Figure 9.18 shows the flow of how Vuforia Cloud targets can be integrated with Unity Asset Bundles:

FIGURE 9.18 Flow of the dynamic billboard AR app.

Setting Up the AR Poster Project

For this project, use two AR markers that are not added to the app but uploaded separately to Vuforia Cloud. Before that, it will be necessary to set up the project and the scene with Vuforia Cloud targets.

Go to Vuforia developer console and create a new target database. This time, choose `Cloud` as the database type and choose the license key created in the beginning. For cloud detection, the license key is important since it determines the cloud detection usage allocated for the license plan.

Inside the database, click on the `Database Access Keys` tab and check for `Client Access Keys`. These keys are required to be added into the project as these keys are used by the app to be made to check for image targets in the cloud.

In Unity, open a new scene and add the following two game objects from the hierarchy: `GameObject | Vuforia Engine | Cloud Recognition | Cloud Recognition & Cloud Image Target`.

Select the `Cloud Recognition` game object and copy the `Access Key` and the `Secret Key` from the developer portal checked before into the required properties in the `Cloud Reco Behavior` component.

Now, upload some markers to the database in the developer dashboard. Here, one is supposed to upload not only the `Image Target` but also another text file known as the `metadata` file. As shown in Figure 9.18, the metadata text will be sent to the app when the image target is recognized. This allows easy identification of the image target tracked and any additional data such as the following:

- An updatable link to a video that can be played on the target image
- Dynamic data that can be changed from time to time
- Links to assets (3D models, sounds, images, and so on) that can be downloaded and placed on the image target

This metadata text file can contain a JSON with anything one prefers to retrieve once the target is recognized. For the sample project, use the billboard designs with the respective JSON as metadata as in Figure 9.19:

FIGURE 9.19 Cloud image targets and metadata example.

Go to the target database and upload both the images along with the metadata text files. Both the images and text files are given with this book. Once uploaded, it will be possible to go in and doublecheck if target rating is good and the metadata are uploaded correctly.

Implementing Vuforia Cloud Targets

For cloud recognition, it is necessary to use the cloud reco behavior and register for its events to manage different statuses of the target detection, since this is a network-based scenario that leads to many errors occurring during the process. When the cloud reco behavior is enabled, it starts scanning immediately, which costs one `reco` from the license. Scanning the same image target multiple times without disabling the component will lead to wasting the `reco` session given by Vuforia. Therefore, it must be used carefully.

Create a new C# script, name it `CloudTargetDataReciever.cs`, and add the following:

```
1.  using UnityEngine;
2.  using UnityEngine.Events;
3.  using Vuforia;
4.
5.  [System.Serializable]
6.  public class CloudTargetSearchResultEvent :
    UnityEvent<string>{}
7.
8.  public class CloudTargetDataRetriever : MonoBehaviour
9.  {
10.    [SerializeField] private ImageTargetBehaviour imageTarget;
11.    public CloudTargetSearchResultEvent OnMetaDataReceived;
12.    CloudRecoBehaviour cloudRecoBehaviour;
13.    bool isScanning = false;
14.    string targetMetaData = "";
15.
16.    void Awake(){
17.      cloudRecoBehaviour = GetComponent<CloudRecoBehaviour>();
18.      cloudRecoBehaviour.
    RegisterOnInitializedEventHandler(OnInitialized);
19.      cloudRecoBehaviour.
RegisterOnInitErrorEventHandler(OnInitError);
20.      cloudRecoBehaviour.
    RegisterOnUpdateErrorEventHandler(OnUpdateError);
21.      cloudRecoBehaviour.
    RegisterOnStateChangedEventHandler(OnStateChanged);
```

```
22.    cloudRecoBehaviour.
   RegisterOnNewSearchResultEventHandler(OnNewSearchResult);
23.  }
24.
25.  private void Start(){
26.    cloudRecoBehaviour.enabled = false;
27.  }
28.
29.  void OnDestroy(){
30.    cloudRecoBehaviour.
   UnregisterOnInitializedEventHandler(OnInitialized);
31.    cloudRecoBehaviour.
   UnregisterOnInitErrorEventHandler(OnInitError);
32.    cloudRecoBehaviour.
   UnregisterOnUpdateErrorEventHandler(OnUpdateError);
33.    cloudRecoBehaviour.
   UnregisterOnStateChangedEventHandler(OnStateChanged);
34.    cloudRecoBehaviour.
   UnregisterOnNewSearchResultEventHandler(OnNewSearchResult);
35.  }
36.
37.  public void OnNewSearchResult(CloudRecoBehaviour.
   CloudRecoSearchResult newSearchResult)
38.  {
39.      targetMetaData = newSearchResult.MetaData;
40.      Debug.Log(targetMetaData);
41.
42.      OnMetaDataReceived?.Invoke(targetMetaData);
43.
44.      if(imageTarget){
45.        cloudRecoBehaviour.EnableObservers(newSearchResult,
   imageTarget.gameObject);
46.      }
47.
48.      cloudRecoBehaviour.enabled = false;
49.  }
50.
51.  public void OnStateChanged(bool scanning){
52.      isScanning= scanning;
```

```
53.      if(scanning){
54.        //Clear previously scanned targets
55.        targetMetaData = "";
56.
57.      }
58.    }
59.
60.    public void OnInitialized(CloudRecoBehaviour behaviour)
61.    { Debug.Log("Cloud recognition initialized : " +
       behaviour. name); }
62.
63.    public void OnInitError(CloudRecoBehaviour.InitError
       initError)
64.    { Debug.Log("Cloud recognition initializion error : " +
       initError.ToString()); }
65.
66.    public void OnUpdateError(CloudRecoBehaviour.QueryError
       queryError)
67.    { Debug.Log("Cloud recognition update error : " + query-
       Error.ToString()); }
68.
69.     public void StartScanning(){
70.      cloudRecoBehaviour.enabled = true;
71.      isScanning= true;
72.      targetMetaData = "";
73.    }
74.
75.    public bool ScanStatus(){
76.      return isScanning;
77.    }
78. }
```

In this code, there is a reference to the cloud reco behavior component (line 12) that gets initialized in the Awake method. Once initialized, the Awake method registers the following events with methods within the class:

- *On initialized event:* This gets called once the cloud recognition is initialized and working properly.
- *On init error event:* This gets called if the initialization has an error, such as network issues, license issues, and so on.

▪ *On update error event:* This gets called if there is an error in the recognition update.
▪ *On state changed event:* This gets called every time there is a state change in the scanning.
▪ *On new search result event:* This is the main event needed, which gets called once it recognizes an image target from the cloud. This can be used to retrieve the metadata associated with the tracked target.

In the code five methods were created that are registered to all the five events with necessary parameters. For the first three events mentioned above, only a log will be made in the console. `OnStateChanged` method will clear data if preparing for a new scan.

The `OnNewSearchResult` method has a `CloudRecoSearchResult` parameter that contains the image target information with the metadata.

In this method, there is a string set with the metadata (line 39) passed to a custom Unity event. In line 5 the inherited Unity event takes a string parameter and in line 11, a public variable instance of the same custom event object (`CloudTargetSearchResultEvent`) is made so that the other components can listen to this event. In line 42, this event gets invoked, passing the metadata to any actions that are listening to the event.

In line 45, the observers are enabled by referring to the cloud image target. This will enable the visuals of any game object attached inside the `Cloud Image Target` object to be added in the Unity scene. This image target is dynamic and enables the observers will register the latest scanned image to this target. Simply said, a cube is added inside the image target, the cube will be visible only when this is called, and it will also be the same cube for all the markers uploaded to the cloud database.

In line 48, the cloud reco behavior is disabled since the scanned image is already cached until scanning a new image target becomes required. This also spares any spending of additional recos from the license.

In the start method, the reco behavior is disabled. Therefore, one can manually initiate scanning by calling the `StartScanning` method in line 69.

In order to maintain any memory leaks, unregister all the events previously registered when unloading this scene. This is done in line 29 within the `OnDestroy` method.

Go back to Unity and add this component onto the `Cloud Recognition` game object, next to the cloud reco behavior component. Drag and drop the `Image Target` from the scene onto the `ImageTarget` variable. Add a `UI` button to start scanning and attach the `Start Scanning` method to the button. Hide the button when tapped on using the `SetActive` method and show it again when metadata are received.

It is also possible to add a cube inside the image target and scale it down to match the placeholder image `Cloud Reco`. This was added within another empty game object as seen in Figure 9.20. It can also be seen how the keys and the cloud image target are added onto the properties:

FIGURE 9.20 Setting up the scene for cloud target recognition.

Now click on the `Play` button, show the camera to a poster, and press the `Scan` button and observe how the metadata JSON is displayed in the log and the appearance of the cube on the marker.

Creating Asset Bundles in Unity

Now that the cloud target works perfectly, there is a new problem to solve. It only shows a cube for all the targets. The plan is to build an app that does not need app updates to show content. Now that the process is halfway through, a way is needed to download and show 3D content on the AR marker based on the poster scanned. This can be done easily by using Asset Bundles.

Asset Bundles are a feature in Unity that allows one to package and manage assets and scripts for Unity projects. An Asset Bundle is essentially a collection of assets that are stored in a single file and can be loaded and unloaded dynamically at runtime. This allows one to easily manage and distribute assets, as well as optimize a game's loading times by only loading the assets that are required at any given moment.

With Asset Bundles, assets such as models, textures, audio clips, and animations can be packaged into a single file and then loaded into the app at runtime. This makes it easy to manage and update the content of an app without an app update. One can upload these Asset Bundles in cloud storage and load them to the app externally.

The plan is to build two Asset Bundles to download for both the billboards. In the project under discussion, both of the cloud targets are 5 meters in width. In a new scene a quad was added and rotated on the origin plane scaled to match the image target size and placed as a size reference.

Now, add an empty game object and name it *billboard-1*. Position it on the origin and add any 3D model inside of it with reference to the quad and convert the parent to a prefab. Repeat the same for *billboard-2* as well. This project uses an iPhone and a 3D pizza for both billboards.

Installing the Asset Bundle Browser

To install the Asset Bundle browser, follow the listed steps:

1. Go to the *Package manager* and click the *plus* button to the top left and choose *Add package by name*. Then type *com.unity.assetbundle-browser* and press *Add*. This will install the Asset Bundle generator.

2. Now open the Asset Bundle explorer from the Window menu.

3. In the *Configure* tab, right-click on the new window and click *Add new bundle*. This will create a new bundle to which assets can be added. In

this project, the intent is to build a bundle per image target. Therefore, two bundles are needed, named `billboard-1` and `billboard-2`.

4. From the `Prefabs` folder, drag each prefab and drop on top of the Asset Bundle name created in the Asset Bundle browser window. In Figure 9.21, notice how two prefabs are added into the browser window, along with the previews of the prefabs created. Notice that all the dependent files are included in the package along with the prefab:

FIGURE 9.21 Creating Asset Bundles with prefabs.
Source: 3D Models used for this project: "iPhone 12 Pro" (*https://skfb.ly/6WoUB*) by DatSketch, and "Pizza" (*https://skfb.ly/6DGT6*) by Jeremy E. Grayson, licensed under Creative Commons Attribution.

Now go to the `Build` tab, provide a build target and an output path, and click `Build`. Please note that Asset Bundles are platform-specific. If building for iOS and Android, two bundles will be needed for both the platforms. Also, choosing different build targets will convert the complete project to that platform. It is always better to use a different Unity project to build Asset Bundles. The current example will be demonstrating on the Windows machine, and therefore the stand-alone Windows platform will be the build target. Once the Asset Bundles are built, go to the output path and check if both bundles are available.

Now, upload these Asset Bundles and load them onto the targets when scanned.

Uploading the Asset Bundles in the Cloud

There are many options in terms of uploading data to a cloud server:

- Google Cloud Storage (Buckets)
- Amazon S3
- Azure Storage
- Dropbox

Out of these options, Dropbox, is free and easier for setting up a public folder to host all the Asset Bundles. To use Dropbox, follow these steps:

1. Go to *https://www.dropbox.com/* and create a new account.

2. Once the free account is set up, create a new folder in the files and share it publicly by choosing `Anyone with this link can view`.

3. Go into the new folder and upload both the Asset Bundles. Adding other generated files is not necessary.

4. Nowcopy the public links of the bundles and update the meta files for Unity to download them in runtime. Right-click each bundle in Drop box and `Copy Link`.

5. In Dropbox share links, there is a URL parameter at the end—`dl=0`. Change it to `dl=1` to get direct access to the file. One of the sample links is as follows:

https://www.dropbox.com/s/xxxxxxxxxxx/billboard-1?dl=1

Updating the Meta Files to Update the AR Experience

In order to download an Asset Bundle and display it in AR, it is necessary to know the URL of the bundle and the name of the asset. The current example uses two bundles and two added prefabs named `billboard-1` and `billboard-2`. The meta files are going to be updated with the respective names and the Asset Bundle link and other information. The following are the two updated metafiles:

```
1.  {
2.    "message" : "Flash Sale!",
3.    "link" : "https://www.dropbox.com/s/xxxxxx/
      billboard-1?dl=1",
4.    "name" : "billboard-1"
5.  }
```

```
1.  {
2.    "message" : "Italian Pizza",
3.    "link" : "https://www.dropbox.com/s/xxxxxx/
      billboard-2?dl=1",
4.    "name" : "billboard-2"
5.  }
```

NOTE *The links in the JSONs are modified and will not work by copy and paste.*

Go to the Vuforia Cloud database created earlier. Open each image target, delete the meta file, and upload the new one. Test in Unity for both the targets before moving further.

Downloading Content and Displaying in AR

Delete the cube added inside the image target. Create a new script called *BillboardData.cs* and add the following:

```
1.  [System.Serializable]
2.  public class BillboardData
3.  {
4.    public string message;
5.    public string name;
6.    public string link;
7.  }
```

The preceding script will be used to deserialize the JSON to an object. Create a new script called *BillboardContentLoader.cs* and add the following:

```
1.  using System.Collections;
2.  using UnityEngine;
3.  using UnityEngine.Networking;
```

```
4.
5.  public class BillboardContentLoader : MonoBehaviour
6.  {
7.    [SerializeField] private Transform contentHolder;
8.
9.    public void ExecuteMetaData(string metadata)
10.   {
11.     BillboardData data = JsonUtility.
    FromJson<BillboardData>(metadata);
12.     Debug.Log(data.message);
13.
14.     StartCoroutine(DownloadAssetBundle(data.link, data.
    name));
15.   }
16.
17.   Ienumerator DownloadAssetBundle(string url, string
    assetBundleName)
18.   {
19.     UnityWebRequest assetBundleRequest =
    UnityWebRequestAssetBundle.GetAssetBundle(url);
20.
21.     yield return assetBundleRequest.SendWebRequest();
22.
23.     if (assetBundleRequest.result == UnityWebRequest.Result.
    ConnectionError
24.        || assetBundleRequest.result == UnityWebRequest.Result.
    ProtocolError
25.        || assetBundleRequest.result == UnityWebRequest.Result.
    DataProcessingError)
26.     {
27.       Debug.LogError("Error downloading asset bundle: " +
    assetBundleRequest.error);
28.     }
29.
30.     //Log the download progress
31.     while (!assetBundleRequest.isDone)
32.     {
33.       Debug.Log("Download progress: " + (assetBundleRequest.
    downloadProgress * 100f).ToString("0.0") + "%");yield return
    null;
```

```
34.    }
35.
36.    //Load the asset bundle
37.    AssetBundle bundle = DownloadHandlerAssetBundle.
   GetContent(assetBundleRequest);
38.    GameObject asset = bundle.
   LoadAsset<GameObject>(assetBundleName);
39.    Instantiate(asset, contentHolder);
40.  }
41. }
```

In this example, there is a public method with a string parameter that generates an object by deserializing the JSON. Once data is collected, a Web request is initiated to download the asset from the cloud storage.

UnityWebRequestAssetBundle is used to download the Asset Bundle and once the process is complete, the *DownloadHandlerAssetBundle* class is used to get the Asset Bundle content loaded into the app storage. Once downloaded, the *LoadAsset* method in the *AssetBundle* class is used to find the prefab included in the bundle by name. The identified prefab is then instantiated and placed into a transform reference known as *contentHolder*. This will be the empty game object inside the cloud image target in the scene.

Add the script to any game object and assign the *ExecuteMetaData(string)* method as a listener to the *OnMetaDataReceived* custom event created in the cloud target data retriever component. Additionally, assign the transform of the game object inside the image target to the content holder to load content inside the AR marker, as shown in Figure 9.22:

FIGURE 9.22 Asset loading configuration for cloud targets.

Click *Play* and click the *Scan* button added before to see how it downloads and shows the object on the target. Now one can publish the app and dynamically update new markers, metadata, and Asset Bundles to build a dynamic AR app that does not require app updates.

CONCLUSION

This chapter covered the basics of building a dynamic AR app, and the supporting content to achieve that by building two projects. There was a discussion of JSONs as data holders and how serialization and deserialization can be made within Unity, along with *UnityWebRequest* to download text data as well as Asset Bundles. The high-level architectures of each project were explained as well as how data are transferred across platforms to build applications by connecting them together; however, both of the projects were far from being production-ready. They need polishing, proper error handling, and additional user interfaces integration to make them useful.

This chapter concludes further discussions of possibilities with Vuforia; however, Vuforia has more integrations such as area targets, barcode readers, model targets, and ground planes, all of which are outside the scope of this book. Access Vuforia documentation to get a wider knowledge of all the components discussed in the previous chapter as well as the current one.

The next chapter will be talking about ARCore and ARKit with AR Foundation to build marker-less applications.

KEY POINTS

- JSON is a method used to store data in textual structured formats.
- JSON can be serialized into objects and vice versa.
- VuMark is an image target system by Vuforia to encode data into an image.
- *UnityWebRequest* class is used in Unity to retrieve and send data through REST API.
- Vuforia Cloud markers can be used to retrieve marker information without storing them in the app.
- Asset Bundles are a way of bundling assets and loading them in runtime.

QUESTIONS

Use the concepts and knowledge about building dynamic apps acquired from this chapter and develop a simple AR-based weather application.

- Allow the user to scan pictures of different cities and locations.
- Based on the locations, use an API to request real-time weather information.
- Use 3D models, animations, and text to present effective weather information on the scanned picture in AR.

MARKER-LESS AR APPS WITH ARKIT AND ARCORE

INTRODUCTION

The fundamental concept behind augmented reality (AR) involves placing objects in front of the camera input plane to mimic the positioning of a 3D model in the actual world. This was explained in Chapter 2, "Visualizing the AR Environment and Components"; Chapter 8, "Building Marker-based AR Apps with Vuforia," and Chapter 9, "Developing Marker-based Dynamic AR Apps," as Vuforia was used to build marker-based AR applications that provide a local space to hold 3D models.

This chapter is going to use Unity's AR Foundation, a package that uses Apple ARKit and Android ARCore to build marker-less AR applications with Unity. As mentioned in Chapter 2, tracking a plane, a face, or a body will provide a reference point in the 3D space that can be used as a local space to manipulate 3D objects. This chapter will discuss how to import and configure AR Foundation with Unity, how to build simple AR projects, and how to interact with 3D objects using ray casting.

STRUCTURE

This chapter will discuss the following topics:

- Setting up AR Foundation (iOS/Android)
- Setting up a marker-less tracking scene
  - Simulating the scene in the editor

- Plane detection and tracking—building an AR object viewer (object placement and manipulation)
  - Placing an object in the AR space
  - Moving object on touch if the object is placed already
  - Scaling the object with two touches
  - Rotating the object with a single touch and drag
- Face tracking—creating an AR face filter with AR Foundation
  - Default face tracking setup
  - Adding custom objects around a face
  - Adding face interactions
- Device tracking—building an AR shooter
- Additional components of AR Foundation

OBJECTIVES

After completion of this chapter, readers will be able to use AR Foundation to build marker-less AR applications that can spawn 3D content without predefined markers. Users will be able to place objects on a scanned location, a face, or just around any physical environment and use different input interactions to manipulate content in AR.

SETTING UP AR FOUNDATION

At the time of writing this book, Unity 2022.3 is the LTS version and, by default, supports AR Foundation version 5.0.6; however, if one is using an older version of Unity and sees an older AR Foundation version other than 5.0.6, one can manually install the package using its updated version number. AR Foundation uses ARKit and ARCore, which require the app to be tested only on the device and not through the Unity editor. AR Foundation version 5 includes a new tool to visualize an AR environment without the need to build and run on an actual device.

Check the latest available AR Foundation package by visiting this link:

https://docs.unity3d.com/Packages/com.unity.xr.arfoundation@5.0/manual/ index.

To set up AR Foundation, follow these steps:

1. In a new project, open the package manager by going to *Window* menu | *Package Manager*.

2. For those using the latest version of Unity (2022.3) and seeing AR Foundation version 5.x, click `Install` in the package manager and skip to step 6.

3. Click the plus + button at the top left corner and choose `Add package by name`.

4. In the name text box, type `com.unity.xr.arfoundation`.

5. In the version text box, type `5.0.6` and click `Add`.

6. AR Foundation works only if ARKit and ARCore are available within the project. Therefore, make sure to install either of them alongside AR Foundation. If there is a different version of ARKit and ARCore in the package manager, install the *same* version as AR Foundation using the same method above.

   a. If building for Apple iOS, use `com.unity.xr.arkit` with version `5.0.6`.

   b. If building for Android, use `com.unity.xr.arcore` with version `5.0.6`.

7. Additionally, Unity requires `XR Plug-in Management` to be installed alongside the preceding packages in order to maintain platform support and plug-ins for extended reality (XR).

8. Now, go to `Edit` | `Project Settings` and select `XR Plugin Management`.

9. To the right side, there are tabs that show the installed platforms. Each tab lists available plug-in providers that must be activated to enable XR support from Unity, as shown in Figure 10.1:

   a. For Apple, click the `iOS` tab and tick `ARKit`.

   b. For Android, click the `Android` tab (with the robot icon) and tick `ARCore`.

   Refer to Figure 10.1:

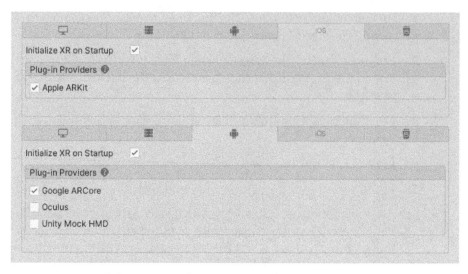

FIGURE 10.1 XR plug-in management for iOS and Android.

Those using *Universal Render Pipeline (URP)* in a project must have a URP asset and a renderer asset that contains the graphics settings. To render the camera background, add a setting to the URP renderer asset. Without this option, the background will be rendered black.

Find the URP renderer asset in the Assets folder. For those using the URP template offered by Unity, this asset is placed inside the *Settings* folder of their assets.

Click the renderer asset, and from the inspector window, click on *Add Renderer Feature*. From the drop-down, choose *AR Background Renderer Feature*.

SETTING UP A MARKER-LESS TRACKING SCENE

When it comes to marker-less tracking with AR Foundation, it can be either device tracking, plane tracking, or facial or body tracking now. The best way to test is through plane tracking, which is used to identify planes around a scan area.

Follow these steps:

1. In a new scene, remove the main camera. This procedure will be using a different setup provided by Unity.

2. From the `GameObject` menu (right-click the hierarchy or click the `GameObject` menu), choose *XR | XR Origin (Mobile AR)*. This will create an empty game object with a camera in it inside another empty game object known as the `Camera Offset`.

3. The XR Origin is the starting origin point of the AR world. By default, the starting point of the AR session will be the position of the AR Origin. The camera offset within the XR Origin will move the camera based on a given offset. When moving the device, the main camera will move, keeping the XR Origin in its place. This enables device tracking in an AR session that allows one to place any 3D model in the global space and visualize it in AR moving around one's device.

4. From the XR menu, add `AR Session`. The components in this game object control the life cycle of an AR session. Without an AR session, the camera will not load, and an AR session will never occur. There should always be only one AR session available in a scene.

This constitutes a basic marker-less tracking scene, but there are still no specified allowed targets. For this example, create a simple plane detection scene. Follow these steps:

1. Select the XR Origin and add the `AR Plane Manager` component. This component tracks the planes in an AR scene and generates planes by referring a `Plane Prefab` object.

2. From the `XR menu` add `AR Default Plane`. This is a GameObject with an AR plane component and an AR Plane mesh visualizer component. This will act as a 3D model placed on planes detected by the AR plane manager.

3. Drag and drop the `AR Default Plane` onto the `Plane prefab` parameter on the `AR Plane manager` added before.

4. If using URP, the default material added into the `AR Default Plane` may not render correctly. One can create a new material and swap it with the `DebugPlane` material in the mesh renderer component of the AR Default Plane. For better visualizations, change the material shader to URP/unlit, set the surface type to `Transparent`, and change the color with an alpha around 20%.

5. If building and running this application on an Apple or Android device, scanning the environment will show 2D polygons on top of the surroundings, as shown in Figure 10.2. This indicates the app and the plug-ins are working as expected:

FIGURE 10.2 AR plane visualization.

Simulating the Scene in the Editor

When building an app using AR Foundation, building and running iteratively on a device can be tiresome. With AR Foundation 5.0, there is a way to simulate an AR environment.

To set it up with one's project, follow these steps:

1. Go to *Edit | Project Settings* and select *XR Plugin Management*.

2. Under the first tab (Windows, Mac, and Linux), tick *XR Simulation*.

3. Go to *Window | XR | AR Foundation | XR Environment*. This will provide another window similar to a scene widow. This scene populates a sample environment to test the application. One can make one's own environment here or use a sample environment provided by Unity.

4. To install sample environments, click the *XR Environment* floating dropdown at the top of the window and choose *Install Sample Environments*.

This will import a package with a set of sample environments into the project. This may require one to choose environments and add what one requires—or import all if that is preferred.

5. Once the package is imported, it will be possible to select an environment from the same drop-down as before.

6. Click on the `Play` button and notice how the chosen environment is now visible within the game view. Use the *W*, *A*, *S*, and *D* keys while holding the mouse right click to look around, as shown in Figure 10.3:

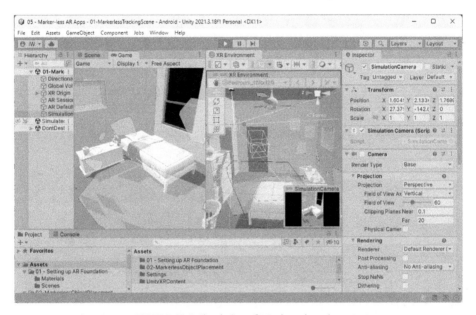

FIGURE 10.3 Simulation of AR plane detection.

PLANE DETECTION AND TRACKING: BUILDING AN AR OBJECT VIEWER

One of the major use cases of marker-less tracking is to place a virtual object in a physical space and visualize it by moving, rotating, and scaling it. This section of the chapter will show how to use ray casting and build a simple object viewer.

Placing the Object on a Scanned Plane

Now that it has been shown how to instantiate planes in the AR world, the next step is placing a 3D model on any of those planes. There are multiple ways of performing an object placement. One of the easiest ways is to get a position from a screen tap. Call this *TapToPlace*.

Create a new C# script and name it *ObjectPlacementManager.cs*. Add the following:

```
1.  using System.Collections;
2.  using System.Collections.Generic;
3.  using UnityEngine;
4.  using UnityEngine.XR.ARFoundation;
5.  using UnityEngine.XR.ARSubsystems;
6.
7.  public class ObjectPlacementManager : MonoBehaviour
8.  {
9.      [SerializeField] private GameObject placementPrefab;
10.     [SerializeField] private ARRaycastManager raycastManager;
11.
12.     private List<ARRaycastHit> hitList = new List<ARRaycas-
        tHit>();
13.     private GameObject lastPlacedObject;
14.
15.     void Update()
16.     {
17.         TapToPlace();
18.     }
19.
20.     private void TapToPlace()
21.     {
22.         if (placementPrefab != null)
23.         {
```

```
24.              if (Input.touchCount == 1 && Input.GetTouch(0).
phase.Equals(TouchPhase.Began))
25.              {
26.                  PlaceObject(Input.GetTouch(0).position);
27.              }
28.          }
29.      }
30.
31.    void PlaceObject(Vector2 screenPosition)
32.    {
33.        // If there is an object placed already
34.        if (lastPlacedObject != null)
35.            return;
36.
37.    if    (raycastManager.Raycast(
38.            screenPosition,
39.            hitList))
40.        {
41.        lastPlacedObject = Instantiate(
42.            placementPrefab,
43.            hitList[0].pose.position,
44.            Quaternion.identity);
45.        }
46. }
47. }
```

Here, there is a reference to a component known as *ARRaycastManager*. This component can cast a ray specifically for AR trackers such as the planes added before. Line 31 calls the *Raycast* method using the *ARRaycastManager*, which returns a *true* if it hits an object. The ray is cast from the touch position. As there can be many positions that the ray would hit, the method uses an existing list called *ARRaycastHit* and populates it with the positions that the ray hits in the 3D world.

Check if there has been an object placed already, and if not, place a new object and assign it to a temporary *Game* object known as *lastPlacedObject*.

Move Object on Touch If the Object Is Placed Already

When placing an object, one has a reference to the placed object. If there is only one touch point and that touch is being moved, move the object along the plane. To achieve this, modify the previous code.

Add the following method to the *ObjectPlacementManager.cs* script:

```
1.      void MoveObject()
2.      {
3.            if (Input.touchCount == 1 && Input.GetTouch(0).
phase.Equals(TouchPhase.Moved))
4.            {
5.                if (raycastManager.Raycast(
6.                    Input.GetTouch(0).position,
7.                    hitList))
8.                {
9.                    lastPlacedObject.transform.position = hit-
List[0].
pose.position;
10.               }
11.           }
12.
13.     }
```

Now, in the *Update* method, add this after *TapToPlace();*:

```
1.  if(lastPlacedObject != null) {
2.      MoveObject();
3.  }
```

Here, if there is an object placed already, the `MoveObject` method would check for a single touch and change the position of the object to wherever the ray cast hits the plane.

For those wanting to test this on their editors, note that `Input.GetTouch` or any touch-related methods and variables would not work directly. The easiest way is to use `Unity Remote 5`, with which one can cast a game window to an Android device and grab touch input from the screen. Get more information on Unity remote through the following link:

https://docs.unity3d.com/Manual/UnityRemote5.html

After building and running this, one can see how to move the object once placed on a plane and change its position.

Scaling the Object with Two Touches

Scaling the object while moving can be tricky. Here, use a single touch to move the object. If there is more than one touch on the screen, check for two touches and use a pinch move of two fingers to scale the object, as shown in Figure 10.4:

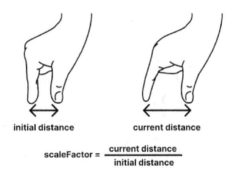

initial distance   current distance

$$scaleFactor = \frac{current\ distance}{initial\ distance}$$

FIGURE 10.4 Getting finger distance to calculate a scale factor.

As presented in Figure 10.4, when one gets two touches, it is possible to store the initial distance of the two touches and, every other time, store the distance of two fingers in another variable. This provides a scale factor with respect to the initial distance. This factor can be used to scale the object placed. The scale of the object should also be determined with respect to its scale at the time the initial distance is captured. In the script, add the following variables at the top:

```
1.      //Scale
2.      private float initialFingerDistance = 0;
3.      private Vector3 initialScale = Vector3.one;
4.      private float currentFingerDistance = 0;
5.      private float scaleFactor;
```

Now, create a new method called *ScaleObject()* and add the following:

```
1.      void ScaleObject()
2.      {
3.          if (Input.touchCount == 2)
4.          {
5.              if (Input.GetTouch(0).phase.Equals(TouchPhase.Began))
6.              {
7.                  initialFingerDistance = Vector2.Distance(Input.GetTouch(0).position, Input.GetTouch(1).position);
8.                  Debug.Log(initialFingerDistance.ToString());
9.                  initialScale = lastPlacedObject.transform.localScale;
10.             }
11.             else
12.             {
13.                 currentFingerDistance = Vector2.Distance(Input.GetTouch(0).position, Input.GetTouch(1).position);
14.                 scaleFactor = Mathf.Clamp(currentFingerDistance / initialFingerDistance, 0.01f, 10f);
15.                 lastPlacedObject.transform.localScale = initialScale * scaleFactor;
16.             }
17.         }
18.     }
```

As explained above, one captures the initial distance as well as the local scale of the object and then multiplies it with the scale factor calculated when moving one's fingers. In order for this to work, add the following in the update method after the *MoveObject()* method inside the conditional statement:

```
ScaleObject();
```

Rotating the Object with a Single Touch and Drag

Now, rotating the object can be tricky with a single touch since the same gesture is used to move the object. There must be a way to distinguish between a touch for movement and a touch for rotation. Different AR apps use different methods. In this example, use the following scenario to identify a touch to rotate or move:

- If there is no object, place the new object for any touch on the screen.
- If there is an object and the touch point is at the bottom of the screen, rotate the object based on the horizontal movement of the finger.
- Otherwise, move the object for all the touches that are not from the bottomof the screen.

To check if the touch point is at the bottom of the screen, do a proportional check. Unity's touch positions are calculated from the bottom. Therefore, the *y*-axis is closer to 0 when the touch point is at the bottom. Add the following method to the script:

```
1.     bool IsTouchingScreenBottom(float threshold)
2.     {
3.         if (Input.touchCount == 1)
4.         {
5.             return (Input.GetTouch(0).position.y / Screen.
height)
< threshold;
6.         }
7.
8.         return false;
9.     }
```

This method takes in a threshold value (between 0 and 1) and returns true if the touch position proportion with respect to the height of the screen is less than the threshold value.

The same principle can be used in scaling the object to rotate it. Here, one gets the first touch position and the current touch position and converts the difference of the *x* values of the two touch points to a rotation value. Add the following method to the script:

```
1.      void RotateObject()
2.      {
3.           if (Input.touchCount == 1)
4.           {
5.                if(Input.GetTouch(0).phase.Equals(TouchPhase.
Began))
6.                {
7.                     initialFingerPos = Input.GetTouch(0).
                     position.x;
8.                     initialRotation = lastPlacedObject.transform.
localRotation;
9.                }
10.               else
11.               {
12.                    currentFingerPos = Input.GetTouch(0).
                     position.x;
13.                    lastPlacedObject.transform.rotation =
initialRotation * Quaternion.Euler(0, initialFingerPos –
currentFingerPos , 0);
14.               }
15.          }
16.     }
```

In this method, one grabs the initial *x* position and the rotation of the object when touching the screen. By moving one's finger, the current *x* position is captured using *Quaternion.Euler* and then adding the rotation to the initial rotation of the object around the *y*-axis. Here use (*initialFingerPos–currentFingerPos*), which gives an opposite value to the direction one wants the object to rotate. Rotating clockwise requires the angle to be reduced. Hence, the finger movement should be toward the left.

Now, to get this to work, modify the complete update method as follows:

```
1.      void Update()
2.      {
3.          TapToPlace();
4.
5.          if(lastPlacedObject != null) {
6.              if (IsTouchingScreenBottom(0.15f))
7.              {
8.                  RotateObject();
9.              }
10.             else
11.             {
12.                 MoveObject();
13.                 ScaleObject();
14.             }
15.         }
16.     }
```

Here, 0.15f has been given as the threshold to check for the object rotation, which provides a 15% screen space at the bottom to rotate the object. As shown in Figure 10.5, build and run to test the object manipulation using finger gestures:

FIGURE 10.5 AR object placement and manipulation.

The prefab that visualizes the planes can be distracting and make the project unpolished. One can disable the `AR Plane Mesh Visualizer` component in the AR Default Plane object to remove the visualization. Also, add a simple shadow plane object at the bottom of the placement prefab to make it look realistic with the environment around. Do that by adding a simple shadow image attached to a quad.

FACE TRACKING—CREATING AN AR FACE FILTER WITH AR FOUNDATION

ARKit and ARCore support face recognition and tracking. This section of the chapter will describe using the face tracking components of the AR Foundation package to create a face filter. Follow the listed steps:

1. Create a new scene and remove the `Main Camera`. Add the following game objects:

   a. *XR | AR Session*

   b. *XR | XR Origin (Mobile AR)*

2. Now, select the `Main Camera` inside `XR Origin | Camera Offset`. Change the `Facing Direction` under the `AR Camera Manager` component to `User` instead of world. AR Foundation only supports face tracking with the front camera of the device.

3. For iOS devices, face tracking only works with devices that support face ID. Therefore, face tracking would not work for iPhone SE or any iPad without a face ID feature. Since AR Foundation 5.0 is being used here, the face tracking feature is integrated into the ARKit Unity package. Any earlier versions would require another package to be installed to support face tracking (`com.unity. xr.arkit-face-tracking`).

Default face tracking setup

To create a default face tracking setup, follow the listed steps:

1. Select the XR Origin and add the `AR Face Manager` component. Similar to what was done with the plane manager, add the game object `XR | AR Default Face`.

2. Create a new material and change the material under the mesh render component of the AR default face. One can also add a texture to this material.

3. Convert the AR default face to a prefab by dragging and dropping it into the project window.

4. Now, use this prefab as the `Face Prefab` under the `AR Face Manager` component added before.

5. Unfortunately, face tracking cannot be tested directly from the editor. Build and run the scene in a device and see how it generates the face, as shown in Figure 10.6:

FIGURE 10.6 AR default face with a custom material.

Adding custom objects around a face

What the default face prefab provides is a mesh that wraps around a face. By default, there is no way to simulate the face prefab within the editor. One can add a sample face object within the AR face prefab and use it as a reference to place other objects.

The Google ARCore software development kit (SDK) open-source project has provided a sample face 3D model to be used when making face applications. The same asset is provided within the asset package of this book (`Canonical_Face_Mesh.fbx`).

To add custom objects around a face, follow these steps:

1. Create a new `AR Default Face` object and disable the `AR Face Mesh Visualizer` component.

2. Drag and drop the face mesh 3D model inside the default face object and reset its position and rotation to 0 while keeping the scale to 1.

3. Now this face mesh can be used as a reference and any 3D model can be added around the face. The assets contain a 3D model of sunglasses that can be placed inside the face object, as shown in Figure 10.7.

4. Now, convert this to a prefab and assign it to the face prefab reference like before. Building and running the scene would provide an output as in Figure 10.7 (2):

FIGURE 10.7 Visualizing a custom AR face object.

Now, it is necessary to hide the face mesh that was added so that only the sunglasses will be visible. Do that by just deleting the face mesh; however, if that is done, the temple sides of the sunglasses will be visible when the face is turned. The 3D model is just an illusion that is placed in front of the face image. Therefore, it is necessary to mimic a 3D face within the app to hide the sunglasses but not the face, as shown in Figure 10.7 (2). This is known as *occlusion*, and it is similar to the occlusion object added for image targets in Chapter 8, "Building Marker-based AR Apps with Vuforia." Follow these steps:

1. Create a new material and change the shader to `VR / SpatialMapping / Occlusion`.

2. Now change the material of the face mesh object to this. It may look distorted within the editor, but when it is built and run on a device, it will look as shown in Figure 10.8. Remember to update the prefab every time a change is made on the face prefab:

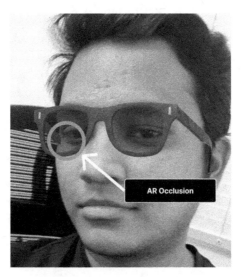

FIGURE 10.8 AR filter with occlusion.

Adding face interactions

Just as ray casting was used to place objects on a plane, touch interactions can be used to identify a face mesh and place objects. AR Foundation does not support ray casts against face meshes. Therefore, it will be necessary to use Unity's physics ray cast method to identify touch points on tracked faces. To add face interactions, follow these steps:

1. Create a new layer in Unity by clicking the `Layers` drop-down at the top right corner of Unity. Name the layer `Face`.

2. Create a duplicate of the previous face prefab. Change the layer of the parent game object only to `Face`.

3. Enable the AR mesh visualizer and use the occlusion material created earlier for the AR mesh.

4. Deactivate or remove the face mesh 3D model added before.

5. Apply the changes that were done to the prefab by clicking *Overrides* in the inspector window. Remove the prefab from the scene.

6. Now, create a new prefab to place on the face when it is tapped. In the *assets* folder may be found a 3D model of a flower, which will be used as a prefab to instantiate on the face with touch input.

Create a new C# script called *FaceEffectPlacementManager.cs* and add the following:

```
1.  using System.Collections;

2.  using System.Collections.Generic;

3.  using UnityEngine;

4.  using UnityEngine.XR.ARFoundation; 5.

6.  public class FaceEffectPlacementManager: MonoBehaviour {

7.      [SerializeField] private GameObject placementPrefab;

8.      [SerializeField] private Camera cam;

9.      [SerializeField] private LayerMask faceMask;

10.

11.     private Transform placementParent;

12.     private RaycastHit rayCastHit;

13.

14. GameObject tempPlacementObject;

15.

16.     void FindPlacementParent() {

17.         placementParent = FindObjectOfType < ARFace > ().
            transform;

18.         Logger.Log(placementParent.position.ToString());

19.  }
```

```
20.

21.    void Update() {

22.      if (Input.touchCount >= 0) {

23.        if (Physics.Raycast(cam.ScreenPointToRay(Input.
           GetTouch(0).
position), out rayCastHit, 10 f, faceMask.value)) {

24.          Logger.Log("Hit success! " + rayCastHit.point);

25.          FindPlacementParent();

26.

27.          if (placementParent != null) {

28.            tempPlacementObject = Instantiate
               (placementPrefab,
placementParent);

29.            tempPlacementObject.transform.position =
               rayCastHit.
point;

30.            tempPlacementObject.transform.up =
               rayCastHit.normal;

31.          }

32.        }

33.      }

34.  }

35. }
```

Here, it is necessary to identify the face object in runtime. Create a reference as *placementParent* and during a touch event, find and save the object using the *FindObjectOfType* method. A layer mask is used to identify touches against only the face. Once the object is instantiated within the parent, the position is set on the touch point of the face and rotated perpendicular to the face.

To cast a ray directly from the screen touch point, it will be necessary to use the camera as a reference, which allows the use of the *ScreenPointToRay()* method in the camera component.

Add the component to a game object within the scene and assign the placement game object (flower), the main camera (`XR Origin` | `Camera Offset` | `Main Camera`) and set the layer mask to Face.

Additionally, make sure to add the new face prefab (with the layer `Face`) to the AR face-manager component.

Now build and run the application. Once the face is detected and the face prefab is available, tap on the face and populate flowers, as shown in Figure 10.9. Please note that when one moves away from the camera, the face prefab will be destroyed, and all the objects placed during runtime will be lost:

FIGURE 10.9 Placing objects on the face using ray casts.

DEVICE TRACKING: BUILDING AN AR SHOOTER

Compared to plane and face tracking, device tracking does not require additional managers. Every AR application built with AR Foundation contains device tracking by default. When an AR session starts with the camera, the XR Origin creates a virtual origin point in the 3D space that makes the camera rotate and move with respect to the movement of one's device. Use device tracking for various applications such as GPS (location)-based AR navigation, spatial games, 360° video-based AR applications, and so on. In this section, use device tracking to build a simple game.

This will be a simple shooting game in which the players shoot objects coming toward them.

There will be enemies that spawn around the player regardless of the position and move toward the player. A button on the screen would cast a ray toward the enemies coming at the player that destroys the enemy while adding a point to the total score.

Create a new scene in Unity and add the XR Origin (mobile AR) and AR session. Believe it or not, the device tracking setup is now complete!

To see how device tracking works, add some 3D models around the origin point of the scene and see how it runs after clicking play. Make sure the objects are placed alongside the origin since the device position at the start is going to be the origin point in the physical space. To demonstrate an example, Figure 10.10 shows a simple setup of planets and how it is seen in the app, as follows:

FIGURE 10.10 Device tracking example.

Setting Up the Enemy

Remove the planet objects from the scene and add any 3D model that represents an enemy. For this example, use a *Space Invader* enemy 3D model from *sketchfab* (*Space Invader—https://skfb.ly/QoTL*, by *ZentoZekto*).

Create a new C# script called *Enemy.cs* and add the following:

```csharp
1.  using System.Collections;
2.  using System.Collections.Generic;
3.  using UnityEngine;
4.
5.  public class Enemy: MonoBehaviour {
6.      public float speed = 100;
7.
8.      private Transform player;
9.      private GameManager manager;
10.
11.
12.     public void SetPlayer(Transform _player, GameManager _manager) {
13.         //Setting the target for the enemy
14.         player = _player;
15.         manager = _manager;
16.     }
17.
18.     void Update() {
19.         // Check if the player is available, if, moves the enemy towards
the player
20.         if (player != null) {
21.             transform.LookAt(player);
22.             transform.position = Vector3.MoveTowards(transform.position, player.position, speed * Time.deltaTime);
23.         }
```

```
24.    }
25.
26.    private void OnCollisionEnter(Collision collision) {
27.      if (collision.transform.CompareTag("player")) {
28.        manager.GetDamage();
29.        Debug.Log("DIE!");
30.        Destroy(gameObject);
31.      }
32.    }
33. }
```

Based on the preceding code, as soon as the enemy object is placed in the scene, it will move toward the player at a given speed (*Vector3.MoveTowards*) while rotating itself toward the player (*transform.LookAt*). Using *OnCollisionEnter* and checking the player tag damages the player using a *GetDamage()* method from a game manager. Moreover, the enemy game object gets destroyed after the collision.

Setting Up the Game Manager

Since there is no Game Manager yet, this code will give errors. Create a new C# script called *GameManager.cs* and add the following:

```
1. using System.Collections;
2. using System.Collections.Generic;
3. using UnityEngine;
4.
5. public class GameManager: MonoBehaviour {
6.
7.    public BoxCollider spawnBoundBox;
8.    public GameObject enemyPrefab;
9.    public Transform shootPoint;
```

```
10.   public Transform player;

11.

12.   private int Score;

13.   private int Health;

14.   private bool isRunning;

15.

16. RaycastHit hit;

17.

18.   // Start is called before the first frame update

19.   void Start() {

20.     isRunning = false;

21. }

22.

23.   public void StartGame() {

24.     Score = 0;

25.     Health = 10;

26.     isRunning = true;

27.     StartCoroutine(spawnEnemy());

28. }

29.

30.   Ienumerator spawnEnemy() {

31.     while (isRunning) {

32.       // Get a random position using the bounds of the box col-
lider

33.       var randomPosition = new Vector3(Random.Range(spawn-
BoundBox.bounds.min.x, spawnBoundBox.bounds.max.x),

34.             Random.Range(spawnBoundBox.bounds.min.y, spawn-
BoundBox.bounds.max.y),
```

```
35.         Random.Range(spawnBoundBox.bounds.min.z, spawn-
BoundBox.bounds.max.z));

36.

37.     // Spawn a new enemy

38.     GameObject enemy = Instantiate(enemyPrefab, randomPosi-
tion,

Quaternion.identity);

39.      enemy.GetComponent<Enemy>().SetPlayer(player, this);

40.

41.     // Wait for some time before spawning again

42.      yield return new WaitForSeconds(2.0 f);

43.   }

44. }

45.

46.  public void ShootLasers() {

47.     if (Physics.Raycast(shootPoint.position, shootPoint.for-
ward,

out      hit)) {

48.     if (hit.collider.CompareTag("enemy"))   {

49.     Score++;

50.

51.     //Destroy the enemy

52.     Destroy(hit.collider.gameObject);

53.   }

54. }

55.}

56.

57.  public void GetDamage() {

58.     Health--;
```

```
59.      if (Health <= 0) {
60.          //Game Over
61.          isRunning = false;
62.          StopAllCoroutines();
63.      }
64.  }
65. }
```

The Game Manager has a public method *StartGame()* that resets all the values and starts a coroutine called *spawnEnemy()*.

The Ienumerator *spawnEnemy()* runs until the Boolean *isRunning* becomes false (at game over). It uses a box collider to generate a random position in a box area and spawn the enemy prefab inside of it. After spawning each enemy, Game Manager sets the current player transform (referred from a variable) as well as the Game Manager itself to call the *GetDamage()* method.

The *GetDamage()* method reduces the health of the player and if it reaches zero, the game stops and the coroutine will end.

There is a *ShootLasers()* method that takes a *shootpoint* (camera position) and casts a ray in the forward direction. This method destroys objects after filtering for enemies using the tagged *enemy*.

Go back to Unity and add the enemy object to the enemy 3D model. Add a box collider and a rigid body to the object. Additionally, add a new tag called *enemy* and assign it to the model. Choose a smaller value for the speed in the enemy component from the inspector window (around 3) and convert this to a prefab. It is now possible to remove the prefab from the scene.

Select the *Main Camera* inside the XR Origin and add a cube inside it. Rename the cube to *Spawner* and move it along the z-axis around 10 units.

Disable the *Mesh renderer* component of the box and enable the *Is Trigger* tick box inside the box collider component. One can scale the box toward its local *x* direction to expand the enemy spawn region.

Now, add a sphere inside the main camera and attach a rigid body component to it. Change the tag of the sphere to *player*. Disable *Is Kinematic* and *Use Gravity* of the rigid body component and disable its mesh renderer as well.

Now, add the Game Manager script to an empty game object and assign the following variables:

- *spawnBoundBox*: The box inside the main camera.
- *enemyPrefab*: Enemy prefab created with the enemy script earlier.
- *shootPoint*: Main camera transform.
- *Player*: Main camera.

Now, add two buttons in a canvas and label them as *Start* and *Shoot*. Assign the following methods to the *OnClick* event under the button component of the *Start* button:

- *Start* Button | *GameObject* | *SetActive()* | *Untick (false)*
- *GameManager* | *GameManager* | *StartGame()*
- *Shoot* Button | *GameObject* | *SetActive()* | *Tick (true)*

Refer to Figure 10.11:

FIGURE 10.11 Start button methods.

This will deactivate the *start* button, activate the *shoot* button, and start the game.

Assign the following method to the *OnClick* event under the button component of *shoot* button.

- *Game Manager* | *GameManager* | *ShootLaser()*

Refer to Figure 10.12:

On Click ()

| Runtime Only ▼ | GameManager.ShootLasers ▼ |

Game Manager (G ⊙)

+ –

FIGURE 10.12 Shoot button method.

Now, deactivate the *shoot* button from the scene, and build and run to test the game. Figure 10.13 is an enhanced version of the same game that uses text objects to show the score and the health. The project files are provided with the book:

FIGURE 10.13 AR shooter game with user interface (UI).

ADDITIONAL COMPONENTS OF AR FOUNDATION

AR Foundation is powerful since it uses both ARKit and ARCore and provides a unique codebase to build applications for both iOS and Android. The following are some of the components that are provided by the AR Foundation to build different AR projects.

AR Human Body Manager

This only works with iOS devices with an A12 chip or above running iOS 13. A human body manager can track a human body from the back camera of an iOS device. This can be used to create AR avatars, filters that use body tracking, and body gestures in applications.

Point Clouds

AR Point Cloud Manager uses prefabs with an AR Point Cloud component attached to generate a point cloud based on the objects it tracks in one's environment. A point cloud can be used to understand granular-level details of the points in a space. If one is developing a measurement application, getting point cloud data increases the accuracy of one's measurements since it is possible to capture the distances between each point.

Anchors

Anchors are specially tracked points in one's space. An AR Anchor can be spawned using the ARAnchor manager. An anchor is a specially tracked point in space. Anchors can be used for navigation-based AR applications since they can track a given point more accurately. Anchors are resource-intensive; therefore, it is recommended to use as few anchors in an application as possible.

Image tracking

AR Foundation can be used to track markers as well. Unlike Vuforia, this does not provide a cloud database to configure. Moreover, the AR Tracked Image Manager component uses a library of images (AR Reference Image library) and one prefab that instantiates during runtime. This is similar to how face objects are placed once a face is tracked.

CONCLUSION

This chapter discussed how to use AR Foundation to create markerless AR applications. As learned in Chapter 2, "Visualizing the AR Environment and Components," all the AR toolkits provide a local space that moves along with a tracked point in space. It can be a pretrained tracked marker or an anchor that was identified during runtime. This chapter discussed three different applications that use such a local space; however, once the marker was identified, the rest of the application did not require any AR development knowledge. What follows is one's ability to manipulate the game objects in the local space in a meaningful way; it could either be a game or any other interactive application.

The next chapter moves to another popular AR SDK with which it is possible to build world-scale AR applications.

KEY POINTS

- ARKit is used to build AR applications for Apple devices (iPhone, iPad).
- ARCore is used to build AR applications for Android devices.
- Both ARKit and ARCore run on specific devices only with hardware capabilities. Older devices may not work.
- AR Foundation is a Unity package that uses both ARKit and ARCore, and it allows developers to use just one codebase to build applications that run on both types of devices.
- AR Foundation supports plane tracking, face detection and tracking, body tracking (iOS only), point cloud tracking, anchoring, image tracking, and meshing.
- AR Foundation has *Manager* components that enable tracking of different trackers.
- The XR Origin (Mobile AR) is the physical world starting point of one's app, which matches the position of the XR Origin.
- The AR Session component manages the lifecycle of the AR tracking session.

QUESTION

1. Using the knowledge about AR Foundation obtained reading this chapter, build an AR game that allows players to build Lego-like structures using simple blocks. Use ray casts to place blocks on touched surfaces and different touch gestures to rotate and change their colors.

CHAPTER 11

WORLD-SCALE AR APP WITH NIANTIC LIGHTSHIP

INTRODUCTION

The previous chapters used Vuforia and AR Foundation to build marker-based and marker-less augmented reality (AR) applications. Vuforia's marker-based tracking is highly optimized to run on many Android and iOS devices. AR Foundation only runs on devices that support ARKit and ARCore. Niantic Lightship is another AR software development kit (SDK) that allows marker-less AR tracking. Apart from the basic plane detection, it has many features such as AR meshing (generates virtual boundaries on physical obstacles), occlusion, a visual positioning system, and semantic segmentation, as well as an integrated multiplayer capability system. Niantic Lightship runs on many Android and iOS devices and does not require any hardware capability, such as for ARCore and ARKit.

Niantic Lightship targets mainly world-based scans. The mesh recognition system allows detecting large-scale environments and generating virtual meshes that allow users to interact with the physical boundaries of the environment.

STRUCTURE

This chapter will discuss the following topics:

- Setting up Niantic Lightship with Unity
  - Downloading required tools and assets
  - Setting up a simple plane tracking scene

- Object placement in AR
  - Object occlusion
- Environment meshing
  - Setting up the scene to mesh the environment boundaries
  - Creating a simple physics simulation in AR
- Introduction to Niantic Lightship Visual Positioning System (VPS)
  - Scanning the environment for VPS
  - The flow of VPS scan recognition
  - Adding anchors using the VPS authoring tool
  - Updating anchor prefabs with proper visual elements
  - Using the Niantic application programming interface (API) to restore anchor data
  - Using Niantic VPS for scalable AR applications.

OBJECTIVES

After completion of this chapter, one will be able to learn the fundamentals of Niantic Lightship, object placement, and detecting and tracking large-scale environments. Users will also be able to improve the realism of AR content by integrating occlusion and meshing.

Additional C# scripting methods used in Niantic Lightship will also be explained and users will be able to subscribe to different events and perform actions based on subscribed events.

SETTING UP NIANTIC LIGHTSHIP WITH UNITY

Similar to Vuforia SDK, Niantic Lightship (ARDK) uses a license to authenticate the usage of the SDK. This license also is used to request world data for an application and also to establish multiuser connections across the network.

Niantic Lightship SDK is known as *Lightship ARDK*, and it can be downloaded by creating an account through the following link:

https://lightship.dev/

After creating the account, log in to the dashboard.

Downloading Required Tools And Assets

In the dashboard, click `Downloads` under the resources section.

For the examples explained in this book, it is necessary to download the following:

- Lightship ARDK (v2.5.x at the time of writing this edition of the book. For those seeing version 3.x or later, there have been some API changes that are noted in this chapter in addition to details of version 2.x)
- ARDK example scenes
- ARDK mock environments

All of these packages will be downloaded in `unitypackage` format. Now, it is possible to create a new Unity project and import all the downloaded packages. This project will be using the standard graphics pipeline (3D) for the base graphics pipeline as some of the assets within ARDK are not compatible with the *Universal Render Pipeline (URP)*.

Adding a New License Key and Authenticating an Application

Go back to the Lightship dashboard and click on the `Projects` tab. The moment one clicks on the `Create new project` button at the top, it will generate a new project with an `API Key`, as shown in Figure 11.1. One can now edit the name of the project and copy the API key:

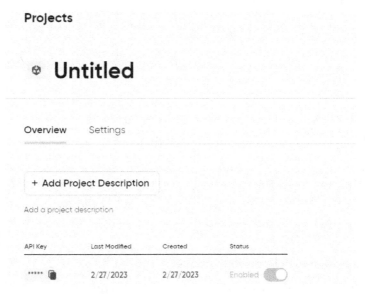

FIGURE 11.1 Creating a new API key in ARDK.

Once the license key has been copied, head over to the Unity project with all the ARDK assets imported. The method of adding the license key for ARDK is different. In the project, create a new `Resources` folder. Inside the `Resources` folder, add a new folder named `ARDK`.

Now, inside the ARDK folder, right-click and select `Create` | `ARDK` | `ArdkAuthConfig`.

This will create a Unity asset with the name `ArdkAuthConfig`, as shown in Figure 11.2. Now is the time to rename this.

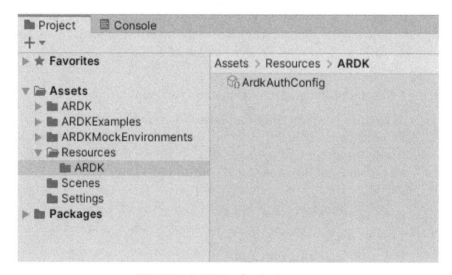

FIGURE 11.2 ARDK authentication setup.

Then select the asset, and in the inspector window, paste the API key inside the `API Key` parameter input.

NOTE *For those using Lightship version 3.0 or up, it is not necessary to create the ArdkAuthConfig file. Instead, open Lightship settings by selecting Lightship menu > Settings and pasting the API key in the inspector window into the appropriate field.*

Setting Up a Simple Plane Tracking Scene

Now the basic installation and authentication setup is complete. Niantic Lightship comes with in-built tools and examples to test the AR application without iteratively building on an Android or iOS device, similar to AR Foundation sample environments.

To setup a sample environment, follow these steps:

1. Go to the `Lightship` menu and click `ARDK | Virtual Studio`.

2. Make sure all three packages downloaded before have been installed to enable the new `Lightship` menu in the menu bar.

3. Once the virtual studio is open, select the `Mock` tab. Here, it will be possible to see different AR Mock Scenes with a drop-down.

4. From the drop-down, select `Living Room`.

Setting Up the Camera

NOTE   *For those using ARDK version 3.0 or up, install AR Foundation version 5.0+ and relevant OS SDK (ARKit or ARCore), as the latest versions of ARDK have handed over the AR session capabilities to AR Foundation. One must also install the XR plug-in management package from the package manager. Once done, skip to point 7.*

Now, in an empty scene, select the `Main Camera`, and perform the following:

1. In the `Camera` component, change the `Clear Flags` to `Solid Color`.

2. Change the color of the camera to `black`.

3. Add the following components to Main Camera:

   a. AR Camera Position Helper

   b. AR Rendering Manager

4. Make sure that the same Main Camera is referenced as `Main Camera` for both of the components.

5. Now, create an empty game object in the scene and add the following components. One can also rename the game object to `AR Session` and reset its transform to tidy up the scene.

   a. *AR Session Manager*: This will also add a `Capability Checker` component to the same game object, as shown in Figure 11.3.

   b. If are building for an Android device, add the `Android Permission Requester` component.

6. In the `Android Permission Requester` component, click the `Plus` button under `Permissions` and select `Camera` from the drop-down.

7. For those using ARDK version 3.0 or up, use the XR Origin and AR session provided by AR Foundation to set up the basic camera rig. Go back to Chapter 10, "Marker-less AR apps with ARKit and ARCore," to review the installation process. Now, the basic AR session setup is complete.

8. To enable plane tracking, add the `AR Plane Manager` component to the same game object (*ARDK Version 3: Add this to "Camera Offset" in the XROrigin*). Similar to AR Foundation, Niantic too can detect horizontal and vertical planes. Click the `Detected Plane Types` drop-down and choose `Horizontal` and `Vertical`. Refer to Figure 11.3:

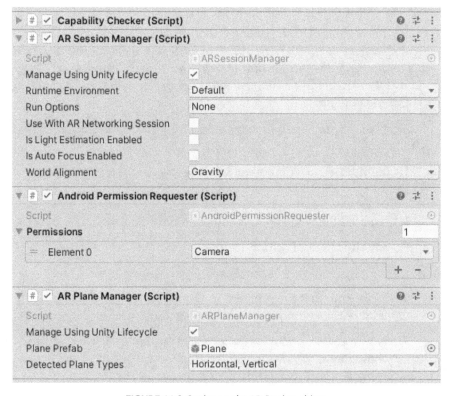

FIGURE 11.3 Setting up the AR Session object.

9. In order to visualize the planes that are tracked, one can add a `Plane Prefab`. Niantic has already provided a sample prefab to add here. Go to `ARDK | Extensions | Planefinding` and choose `PlanePrefab` prefab as the plane prefab of the AR Plane Manager, as shown in Figure 11.3.

10. Now, click the `Play` button and notice how the sample scene appears, as shown in Figure 11.4. Hold the right click and move around using the W, A, S, and D keys of the keyboard to identify horizontal and vertical planes. One can also build and run the application and scan the environment to view scanned planes. Refer to Figure 11.4:

FIGURE 11.4 ARDK Mock Scene with plane detection.

OBJECT PLACEMENT IN AR

In Lightship ARDK, many interactions use C# Actions, allowing developers to create methods and subscribe to different actions (events). Lightship contains several classes and interfaces that will be employed to use the current AR session that is running and subscribe to its current frame to identify touch hits. Lightship ARDK also has an in-built Input manager that can track both touch and mouse clicks with a single call. This can be a little complicated, but look at the following script to understand the algorithm:

```
1. using UnityEngine;
2.
3. using Niantic.ARDK.Utilities.Input.Legacy;
4.
5. using Niantic.ARDK.AR;
6. using Niantic.ARDK.Utilities;
7. using Niantic.ARDK.AR.ARSessionEventArgs;
8. using Niantic.ARDK.AR.HitTest;
```

```
9.
10. public class ARPlacement : MonoBehaviour
11. {
12.     [SerializeField] private GameObject placementObject;
13.     [SerializeField] private Camera cam;
14.
15.     Touch touch;
16.     IARSession session;
17.
18.     void Start()
19.     {
20.         ARSessionFactory.SessionInitialized +=
    OnSessionInitialized;
21.     }
22.
23.     private void OnSessionInitialized
    (AnyARSessionInitializedArgs args)
24.     {
25.         ARSessionFactory.SessionInitialized -=
    OnSessionInitialized;
26.         session = args.Session;
27.     }
28.
29.
30.     void Update()
31.     {
32.         if (PlatformAgnosticInput.touchCount <= 0)
33.         {
34.             return;
35.         }
36.
37.         touch = PlatformAgnosticInput.GetTouch(0);
38.         if (touch.phase == TouchPhase.Began)
39.         {
40.             TouchBegan(touch);
41.         }
42.     }
43.
```

```
44.    void TouchBegan(Touch touch)
45.    {
46.        // check a valid frame
47.        var currentFrame = session.CurrentFrame;
48.
49.        if (currentFrame == null) return;
50.
51.        if (cam == null) return;
52.
53.        var hit = currentFrame.HitTest(cam.pixelWidth,
    cam.pixelHeight, touch.position, ARHitTestResultType.
    ExistingPlaneUsingExtent | ARHitTestResultType.
    EstimatedHorizontalPlane);
54.
55.        if (hit.Count == 0) return;
56.
57.        // Move the object to the position
58.        placementObject.transform.position = hit[0].
    WorldTransform.ToPosition();
59.
60.        // lookat
61.        placementObject.transform.LookAt(new Vector3(
62.            currentFrame.Camera.Transform.GetPosition().x,
63.            placementObject.transform.position.y,
64.            currentFrame.Camera.Transform.GetPosition().z
65.            ));
66.
67.    }
68. }
```

This code subscribes a method *OnSessionInitialized(AnyARSession Initialized args)* to the *SessionInitialized* action of ARDK's *ARSession Factory*. In simple terms, when the SDK initializes the session, it passes data and executes the *OnSessionInitialized* method added in the preceding script.

Checking the *OnSessionInitialized* method, one can see an immediate unsubscribing from the action (line 25) and taking the session from the argument data that was passed by the AR session factory. This session is needed to access frame information from the screen later on.

Used here is a static class called `PlatformAgnosticInput` that works on both mobile and the editor (touch and mouse clicks) and checks for touches. If there is more than one touch, grab the position of the first touch and call the method `TouchBegan`. This is the method being used to cast a ray to get the hit position to instantiate an object.

The `TouchBegan` method, which runs in the update loop, checks the `CurrentFrame` of the session at the time of the touch to get frame information.

If there is valid frame information, the method `HitTest`, which is an integrated method of the `CurrentFrame` object, is used with camera information (`pixelWidth` and `pixelHeight`), `touchPosition`, and hit plane information. This method returns an array of hits, which allows one to choose the first element of the array and obtain its world position by calling the `WorldTransform`. `ToPosition()` method.

There has already been a simple snippet added to make the object rotate toward the camera when changing the position. As can be seen, this code does not instantiate an object for the first time. It uses an existing object in space. Now, head back to Unity to arrange the component.

Add the `ARPlacement` component to the game object that the the AR session is attached to. Reference the `MainCamera` to the `Cam` variable.

The `Placement Object` variable needs to have a model in the scene. ARDK examples contain an object useful for testing purposes (`Assets | ADRK Examples | Common | Prefabs | Yeti`).

Drag and drop the object to the scene and set its position to (1000,1000,1000). This is to make the object not visible when the camera is opened for the first time.

Now, assign it as the `Placement Object`.

Now, click play and touch on a tracked floor and notice how the object gets placed in the scene. Try building the same app on a mobile device.

Object Occlusion

Lightship ARDK has a very powerful AI-based mesh recognition system without the use of additional sensors. This system can generate occluding meshes in runtime and render them before the object, so the objects can be seen behind physical obstacles.

To enable occlusion for the preceding project, follow these steps:

1. Select the `Main Camera` (AR Camera) and attach the `AR Depth Manager` component.

2. To optimize the occlusion for an object already on the scene, add the `AR Depth Interpolation Adaptor` component to the main camera and add the `renderer` component of the `Yeti` object. This is optional, but it overrides the `Interpolation Preference` value in the `AR Depth Manager` component.

3. If one is using ARDK version 3.0, add the `AROcclusionManager` component from AR Foundation to the XR Origin component. Also, add the `OcclusionContentProvider` component in place of *AR Depth Interpolation Adaptor.*

Figure 11.5 shows how the object placement works with and without the AR Depth Manager:

FIGURE 11.5 Difference of using the AR Depth Manager/AR Occlusion Manager.

ENVIRONMENT MESHING

Niantic ARDK comes with in-built functionality to mesh the world obstacles without the need for a dedicated sensor such as the LiDAR sensor. The AR Depth Manager component is used to enable and track the mesh spaces, but currently, it does not have any physical properties included. As with the first exercise, add a mesh visualizer and see how the mesh is being recognized.

Setting Up the Scene to Mesh the Environment Boundaries

Create a new basic Niantic AR scene setup without the *AR Plane Manager*; however, make sure that the main camera has the *AR Depth Manager* component attached.

Follow these steps:

1. Open *Assets | Extensions | Meshing* and find the *ARMesh* prefab in the folder.

2. Drag and drop the prefab into the scene.

3. Click the prefab and notice the *ARMeshManager* component added to it. This component uses the AR Depth Manager information and the namespace *Niantic.ARDK.AR.Mesh* to generate a mesh in runtime.

4. Unfortunately, meshing cannot be tested in the editor. Therefore, build and run and scan the environment. Notice how it scans and draws a mesh on the environment as shown in Figure 11.6:

FIGURE 11.6 Visualizing the AR mesh (check the color image for better clarity).

Creating a Simple Physics Simulation in AR

The basic AR mesh prefab does not offer collisions, and the simulation is not realistic with visualization. This exercise describes how to create a simple ball throw with touch input to create and throw objects in the environment, making them collide with the physical objects in the environment.

Creating an Object to Throw

Follow these steps:

1. Create a new sphere and make the scale of the object (0.3,0.3,0.3)

2. Add a material to the sphere and rename it as `Ball`.

3. Select the ball and add a `Rigidbody` component.

4. There is also a need to create a *physic material*. In the assets folder, right-click inside a folder and select `Create | Physic Material`.

5. Rename the material as `Rubber` and select it. Set the `Dynamic friction` to `0.2`, `Static friction` to `0.3`, and `Bounciness` to `0.8`. Keep other drop-downs `Average`. The use of physical materials to provide collision effects, such as friction and bounciness, makes a realistic simulation.

6. Now add the physic material asset created as the `Material` of the `Sphere Collider` of the ball object.

7. Drag and drop the ball into the project window folder to convert it to a prefab.

Throwing the Ball at Runtime

Create a new C# script called `ThrowObject.cs` and add the following. This script simply uses touch input, instantiates a prefab instance, and applies a force toward the forward direction of the camera, destroying it after a given time:

```
1.  using UnityEngine;
2.  using Niantic.ARDK.Utilities.Input.Legacy;
3.
4.  public class ThrowObject: MonoBehaviour {
5.    public GameObject throwObjectPrefab;
```

```
6.    public float throwForce;

7.    public Camera cam;

8.    public float timeToDestroy = 10;

9.

10.   Touch touch;

11.   Vector3 throwPosition;

12.   GameObject throwObject;

13.

14.   void Update() {

15.     if (PlatformAgnosticInput.touchCount <= 0) return;

16.     if (cam == null || throwObjectPrefab == null) return;

17.

18.     touch = PlatformAgnosticInput.GetTouch(0);
19.

20.     if (touch.phase == TouchPhase.Began) {

21.         throwPosition = cam.transform.position + cam.
transform.forward;

22.

23.       throwObject = Instantiate(throwObjectPrefab,
throwPosition,Quaternion.identity);

24.
25.         throwObject.GetComponent < Rigidbody >
().AddForce(cam.transform.forward * throwForce);

26.

27.       Destroy(throwObject, timeToDestroy);

28.     }

29. }

30. }
```

Go back to Unity and add the script to any game object (the one with the AR session is preferred).

Add the Ball prefab as the *Throw Object Prefab*. Drag the Main Camera into the *Cam* property. Any values can be added to the *Throw Force* and *Time to Destroy*. With typical scales, 200 and 10, respectively, would be good values.

Now, select the `AR Mesh` prefab in the scene. Within the `ARMeshManager` component, click `Use Invisible Material` to replace the AR visualization with invisible material.

For the `Mesh Prefab`, add the prefab `MeshColliderChunk` from the `Assets | ARDK | Extensions | Meshing` folder. By selecting the prefab, it will be seen that it has a mesh collider as well as a mesh renderer. This mesh collider will be used to calculate the physics boundaries of the mesh it generates, allowing users to interact with physics-integrated objects in the scene.

Build and run the scene. Scan the environment and keep tapping on the screen to see how it throws balls from the screen toward the physical space and how they bounce off and interact with physical obstacles in the environment, as shown in Figure 11.7:

FIGURE 11.7 AR meshing with collisions.

INTRODUCTION TO NIANTIC LIGHTSHIP VPS

Niantic ARDK is able to identify and track world-scale environments. This can be an indoor location that is private to the developer, such as a private venue, or a public place, such as a city attraction or an exterior of a building. This allows developers to build AR applications that work on certain geolocations and track waypoints very accurately. Some of the use cases of world-scale AR applications include the following:

- Location-based AR games, such as Niantic's very own Pokémon GO, the Jurassic Park AR game, and Minecraft worlds
- AR wayfinding applications; an example use case would be a theme park app to guide people toward certain parts of the park
- AR billboards placed in the exteriors of buildings for marketing activations
- Large-scale training simulations in AR

People around the world contribute to scanning diffierent places and submitting that data to Niantic's VPS cloud. This allows anyone to create AR applications that involve tracking world places. Anyone can do that by using an app called *Niantic Wayfarer*.

Niantic Wayfarer partners with people around the world to add content to the Niantic *Geospatial* library. Check the current map of all the scanned places around the world by visiting the `Geospatial Browser` section of the Lightship developer console.

Individual developers can also scan their own environments and upload them to the cloud but make them private. This allows developers to build private environment-based AR applications limited to their private scans.

This section will demonstrate the scanning of a private space and using Lightship VPS to localize that space to spawn a custom 3D model. This model will activate on scanning the same environment previously scanned. Think of this use case as a *marker-based* scenario, but instead of an image or an object, this tracks a bigger environment.

Scanning an Environment for VPS

In order to scan an environment and upload to Lightship cloud, a Lightship account is necessary as well as the *Niantic Wayfarer* app installed on one's device. Currently, a beta version for iOS devices is available and a full Android version is accessible from the Google Play Store.

Download the *Niantic Wayfarer* app and install it. Log in with the same Lightship developer account to get access to the application page. It might be helpful to provide camera and precise location permissions since the app scans rely on camera and location data.

From the Niantic Wayfarer app, one can scan and upload environments as private or public. If the scans are public, they are processed and evaluated before being available to others. If private, it may take up to 4 hours for the scans to be processed and available for development use. This section discusses scanning an interior room and uploading the data to the private scan space.

Open the Wayfarer app, making sure one's location on the given map is precise, and click *Scan*, as shown in Figure 11.8. In a single scan, move the camera around while noticing how it generates the mesh of the environment. Scan at least 60 seconds and make sure to obtain as many details as possible into the mesh:

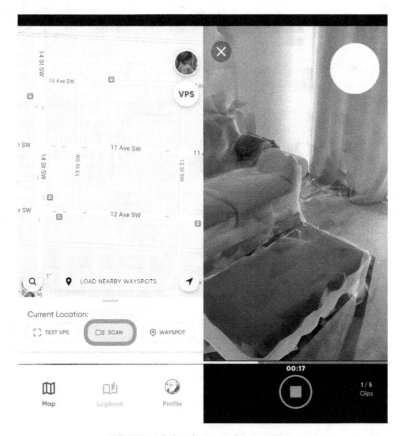

FIGURE 11.8 Starting an environment scan.

Once done with the scan, continue it to scan nearby places. A single scan allows the generation of meshes for five clips, thus allowing one to scan a large environment. In the preceding example, it was only necessary to scan the room. Therefore, only one clip was created.

Once the scan is completed, upload the scan as a private scan type. Make sure to immediately upload. If not, one can perform many scans together and upload only the selected scans, as shown in Figure 11.9:

FIGURE 11.9 Uploading the scanned environment.

The size of a single scan may depend on the size of the environment; however, as soon as the upload is started, it is possible to check the status of the upload by visiting the logbook, as shown in Figure 11.10. If the upload status is *complete*, the uploaded data will be shown as currently in *Processing*, under the *Private meshes* section of the developer dashboard:

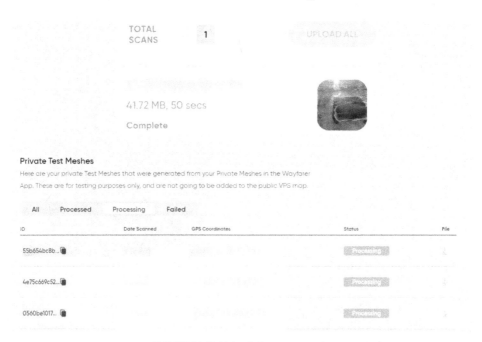

FIGURE 11.10 Uploaded scan test meshes.

After the process is complete (which takes from 10 minutes to 4 hours), it will be possible to download the processed scan. Click the `Download` button in the table, in the `File` column once the status is shown as `Processed`.

The Flow of VPS Scan Recognition

Before importing the scanned environment and making configurations, it is necessary to understand how Niantic VPS localization works.

There are two main interfaces provided by Niantic to save and load anchors within a scanned location:

- `WayspotAnchorService`: A high-level API where the cache is managed by the API.
- `WayspoitAnchorController`: A low-level API where the cache is managed by the developer.

For simplicity of implementation, the `WaypoitAnchorService` will be used to save and load position data.

When one scans an environment, it starts the localization process for a VPS activation location. `WayspotAnchorService` can be used to validate and establish anchors in the environment and generate `payloads` for anchors. There are two ways to store and retrieve these anchor data:

- *Store and retrieve anchors in runtime:* This allows anyone to scan an environment and store generated payload data within the device (or a remote database) and retrieve them back and show them in the environment. A use case for this would be a collaborative space where people can add spatial Post-It notes where others can see them.
- *Use the remote authoring tool to add anchors during development time and load them in play time:* This allows developers to import a prescanned environment and place anchors in the environment to generate payloads, which can then be hardcoded into the application. An example of this would be a game that generates an AR experience around the Eiffel tower in France or any other landmark.

In this section, import the scanned environment to the development project and predefine a location anchor with a prefab that can be loaded when the actual application is scanned.

Importing the Scanned Location

In the project, click the `Lightship` menu | `VPS Authoring Assistant` | `Add Location`.

This will open a select dialog to choose the ZIP file downloaded from the Niantic dashboard. Choosing the file will open another window to generate and save payload data in the editor. Create a new folder inside the assets folder (for example, `Private meshes`) and choose that folder. This will generate a prefab and an asset that can be imported into the scene.

Moreover, it will open a new `VPS Authoring` window, along with a new scene that has the scanned environment as a 3D object with a warning not to add or delete any objects to the scene, as shown in Figure 11.11:

FIGURE 11.11 VPS Authoring tool with a private scan.

Adding Anchors Using the Vps Authoring Tool

Close the VPS Authoring tool with `Lightship | ARDK | VPS Authoring assistant | Close`.

This will remove the additional scene with the environment added before.

Create a new empty game object with a scale of 1,1,1 and add a sphere as a child object.

Now change the scale of the sphere to (0.3, 0.3, 0.3). Rename the game object and convert it to a prefab.

Open the VPS Authoring tool again. Check Figure 11.12 for the step-by-step process:

1. Click the drop-down and select the ID of the private scan that was imported.

2. By default, there will be a single anchor attached to the environment; however, add one more by clicking the `Create New Anchor` button. This will generate a new empty game object in the new scene called `Anchor`.

3. Drag and drop the prefab created earlier into the `Associated Prefab` placeholder in the VPS Authoring tool. If wanted, also rename the anchor by clicking the pencil icon next to the name of the anchor in (2). In Figure 11.12, it is renamed to `Sofa`.

4. Select the anchor object in the editor and use transform tools to move, rotate and scale the prefab. It will not be possible to edit the prefab this time, but one can copy and transform the data of the anchor to do prefab modifications later. Copy the values individually in section (6) of Figure 11.12 and save them for later.

5. Now click the `Save All Anchors` button. This will update a manifest in the folder where one's private mesh was added. Also, a `Payload` will be generated uniquely for this anchor.

6. Click the `Payload` to copy the payload string. Save this for later.

Multiple anchors can be added to this. If one does so, copy the payloads and save them for the retrieval process later. Refer to Figure 11.12:

FIGURE 11.12 Adding and saving an anchor using the VPS Authoring tool.

Close the VPS Authoring tool to set up the prefab.

Updating the Prefab with Proper Visual Elements

Open the folder that the private mesh has been imported to, where a prefab will be visible as well as an asset that holds the anchor data. Drag and drop the prefab directly to the hierarchy. Make sure the position and rotation values are 0, and the scale is 1. This will add a 3D model of the scan of the environment.

Now, drag and drop the prefab associated with the anchor to the scene as well.

Select the prefab and paste the position data copied from step (4) earlier to the new prefab. Make sure that the prefab is placed correctly on the anchor placed before, as shown in Figure 11.13:

FIGURE 11.13 Placing an instance of the anchor prefab for modification.

Now, any object within the prefab that matches the environment 3D model can be added. In Figure 11.13, a sample living room is scanned and an anchor is placed on top of the sofa. This prefab can be used to instantiate once the scan is complete and the anchors are validated.

The example in Figure 11.14 shows how text objects and other elements are placed inside the prefab, which will be generated when the app localizes the area. Here, a quad and a text object are added to annotate the sofa, and a flowerpot is placed behind the tea table.

Now click the Sofa prefab and apply the changes. Delete both the prefab and the environment mesh from the scene. Refer to Figure 11.14:

FIGURE 11.14 Using the scanned model as a reference to modify the anchor-associated prefab.

Using Niantic API to Restore Anchor Data

This section discusses using the copied payload to load the wayspot anchors and position the prefab in the correct location once the environment is localized by the AR session.

Create a new C# script called *VPSLocalizer.cs* and add the following:

```
1.  using System.Collections;

2.  using System.Collections.Generic;

3.  using UnityEngine;

4.  using Niantic.ARDK.AR.WayspotAnchors;

5.  using Niantic.ARDK.LocationService;

6.  using Niantic.ARDK.AR;

7.  using Niantic.ARDK.AR.ARSessionEventArgs;

8.  using System;

9.

10. public class VPSLocalizer: MonoBehaviour {
```

```
11.    public GameObject anchorPrefab;

12.    [SerializeField] private float desiredAccuracyinMeters,
updateDistanceIn-
Meters;13.

14.    IARSession session;

15.    IWayspotAnchorsConfiguration wayspotAnchorsConfig;

16.    ILocationService locationService;

17.    IWayspotAnchor[] anchors;

18.

19.    WayspotAnchorService wayspotAnchorService;

20.

21.    Dictionary < System.Guid, GameObject > anchs =
new Dictionary <System.Guid, GameObject > ();

22.

23.    void Start() {

24.      ARSessionFactory.SessionInitialized += OnSessionInitialized;

25. }

26.

27.    private void OnSessionInitialized(AnyARSessionInitializedArgs
args) {

28.      ARSessionFactory.SessionInitialized -= OnSessionInitialized;

29.      session = args.Session;

30.

31.      wayspotAnchorsConfig = WayspotAnchorsConfigurationFactory.
Create();

32.      locationService = LocationServiceFactory.Create(session.
RuntimeEnvironment);

33.

34.      locationService.Start(desiredAccuracyinMeters,
updateDistanceInMeters);

35.      wayspotAnchorService = new WayspotAnchorService(session,
locationService, wayspotAnchorsConfig);

36.
```

```
37.    wayspotAnchorService.LocalizationStateUpdated +=
HandleLocalizationStateUpdated;
38. }
39.
40.  private void
HandleLocalizationStateUpdated(LocalizationStateUpdatedArgs args) {
41.    if (args.State == LocalizationState.Localized) {
42.      var payload = WayspotAnchorPayload.Deserialize("PASTE THE
PAYLOAD YOU COPIED FROM THE ANCHOR");
43.
44.      anchors = wayspotAnchorService.RestoreWayspotAnchors
(payload);
45.
46.      foreach(var item in anchors) {
47.        var go = Instantiate(anchorPrefab);
48.
49.        anchs.Add(item.ID, go);
50.
51.        item.TransformUpdated += OnTransformUpdated;
52.      }
53.    }
54.
55.    if (args.State == LocalizationState.Failed) {
56.      Debug.Log("Localization Failed!");
57.    }
58. }
59.
60.  private void OnTransformUpdated(WayspotAnchorResolvedArgs
args) {
61.    var anchor = anchs[args.ID].transform;
62.    anchor.position = args.Position;
63.    anchor.rotation = args.Rotation;
64.  }
65. }
```

Here, one will be calling the `OnSessionInitialized()` method when the AR session is started to initiate the localization. This is done by starting the location service, and then the wayspot anchor service. Once the anchor service is initialized, it keeps tracking its localization status.

Use the AR session, the location service that determines the location accuracy given in meters (as variables) and the wayspot anchor configuration object, in line 35.

Once the `WayspotAnchorService` is created, a `HandleLocalizationState Updated` method is subscribed along with arguments that explain the status of the localization process. This method will be executed every time there is an update to the localization.

The localization state updated method checks the status of the method. If it is the *Localized* state, then the anchors can be restored from the payload; however, the payload must be first deserialized, as shown in line 42. Here, it will be necessary to add the copied anchor that matches the prefab modified earlier.

Calling the method `RestoreWayspotAnchors()` from the wayspot service with the deserialized payload as input, as seen in line 44, will return an array of anchors. (Per payload, this will be one anchor.)

Now, iterate through all the anchors that were restored and instantiate the prefab associated for the anchor. At the same time, populate a dictionary using the ID of the anchor as the key and the `GameObject` as the value.

When a prefab is instantiated for the first time, it will be placed in the origin position instead of the actual position. Therefore, it is necessary to validate the anchor position with the wayspot anchor service, and it will pass the updated position data through an event call. This is implemented by subscribing to the `TransformUpdated` event with the `OnTransformUpdated` method, including `WayspotAnchorResolvedArgs` as parameters, as shown in line 51.

The `OnTransformUpdate` method will execute as soon as the anchor transform data are resolved, and the argument will contain position, rotation, and the ID of the anchor. Use the dictionary to find the `gameobject` associated with the ID and assign position and the rotation to the prefab. This will result in the prefab populating in the area in origin and setting its position to the correct place after a short period.

Now add this script as a component anywhere in the scene and assign the anchor prefab. For location accuracy data, add 0.1 for both variables.

Build and run the app. Scan the same environment and see how it populates the 3D prefab exactly on the anchor position placed inside the editor, as shown in Figure 11.15:

FIGURE 11.15 Localizing and loading anchor data in the private environment.

Using Niantic VPS for Scalable AR Applications

In the preceding example, only one anchor was added to a private mesh scan currently in the online database. Localization for private environments only works with one's app ID, and the meshes should be one's personal examples. Moreover, deleting the mesh would stop the localization from the app since one's app will match the scanned surface only with the meshes one has uploaded.

The payload was hardcoded and assigned only one associated prefab for this example. If there is more than one anchor and different prefabs for each anchor, save the prefab and payload data in a database (it can be internal persistence such as `playerpref` or a file or an external database using HTTP Rest API to retrieve data).

Wayspot anchors are only stored for 6 months. Therefore, it will be necessary to check for the time and recreate the anchor in runtime using the wayspot anchor controller.

One can also contribute to the Niantic public scan cloud by scanning and uploading data through the wayfarer app. Public meshes can be downloaded from the GeoSpatial Browser page on the Lightship dashboard and used to test public locations using the VPS Authoring tool.

More information on Niantic Lightship ARDK API, including examples, can be checked by logging into Lightship documentation:

https://lightship.dev/docs/ardk/

CONCLUSION

This chapter showed how to use the Niantic Lightship ARDK to develop environment and world-scale AR experiences. Lightship ARDK is a powerful tool for scanning and detecting physical boundaries effectively and has very efficient environment detection and localization technology. One can use the occlusion, meshing, and VPS technologies to build AR applications so that one can persist and restore data in AR more efficiently. This can be used to solve localization and tracking issues that many AR applications have. The next chapter looks into enhancing the experience of AR applications developed using Unity.

KEY POINTS

- Niantic ARDK requires a developer account and an app ID to enable AR features.
- ARDK natively supports meshing regardless of the hardware capabilities of the device.
- AR occlusion is provided by default, and meshing can be visualized using a simple material attached to the AR Depth Manager.

- Adding a collider to the mesh prefab integrated physical features to scanned boundaries.
- Niantic VPS can be used to scan, create, and persist anchor data as payloads and then retrieve data again after localization.
- The VPS Authoring tool can be used to create anchors in the development stage for prescanned environments.
- The generated payload contains information on the anchors and thus can be used to position the associated prefabs properly.

QUESTION

1. Using Niantic VPS and meshing-related components such as depth tracking and occlusion, build an AR exploration application that has a character which takes one around different wayspot anchors of a scanned environment. Utilize Unity components such as colliders, ray casts, and animations for a better user experience.

CHAPTER 12

BEST PRACTICES IN AUGMENTED REALITY APPLICATION DESIGN

INTRODUCTION

So far, different tools have been used with Unity to build different kinds of augmented reality (AR) applications; however, these tools only touch the surface of the capabilities that these software development kits (SDKs) offer. In order to build compelling AR applications, developers must also take design considerations into action. The AR app that one builds should not only display 3D content properly, but it should also be user-friendly.

This chapter will be going through some best practices in designing AR applications and also learning how these can be implemented in Unity.

STRUCTURE

This chapter will discuss the following topics:

- Safety is key.
  - Showing warnings at the beginning
  - Showing warnings while using the app
- Guide the user with interactions.
- Be mindful of the scale.
- Use audio and visual cues.

■ Free flow restrictions.
■ AR interactions.
■ User interface (UI) considerations.

OBJECTIVES

Completing this chapter will demonstrate how to polish an AR application with proper best design practices, making the AR application user-friendly and pleasant to interact with. Apart from teaching the best practices, it will also explain how to use Unity's integrated tools, other third-party tools, and C# to implement such best practices into each application, regardless of the type of application.

SAFETY IS KEY

One of the major considerations in AR app design is how developers implement safety warnings into their applications. Mobile app stores such as the Apple App Store and Google Play Store enforce the indication of safety within the application as a part of the compliance process.

People open their cameras on their phones when it comes to AR applications. Instead of focusing on what is in their surroundings, people would look at the world through another lens. This increases immersion in the AR application but, at the same time, creates a risk of an accident by the user's unawareness of the surroundings. Therefore, add components to applications that warn users at the beginning of the experience and, if needed, during the use of the app.

Showing Warnings at the Beginning

Before opening the camera, add another scene in Unity with UI components or a screen space overlay on the AR experience with a button prompt to provide a list of warnings to make the user aware of the surroundings. The UI scene will be the first to load in build settings. One can also use visual elements to demonstrate the warnings by using the image component in Unity. Refer to Figure 12.1:

FIGURE 12.1 The UI elements show a warning before opening the camera.

Some of the warnings that can be provided for the user are as follows:

- Please be aware of the surroundings when using this AR application.
- Do not use the app while driving, walking, or operating machinery that requires your attention.
- Do not use the app in public places where you may disturb or endanger others or violate their privacy.
- Do not use the app for prolonged periods; it may cause eye strain, fatigue, or nausea.
- Do not use the app if you have a history of epilepsy or other medical conditions that may be triggered by flashing lights or rapid movements.

An example of warnings across different AR mobile applications can be seen in Figure 12.2:

FIGURE 12.2 Pokémon GO, Mission to Mars AR, and Happy Baby Elephant AR apps show a warning before launching the app.

Showing Warnings While Using the AR App

The AR feature in Google Maps now alerts users to crossroads while looking at the phone. It also warns when the phone is held up for too long to focus on the surroundings. However, this design feature must be implemented in a way that does not break immersion. Moreover, showing warnings on top of an application causes a negative experience for the user. Therefore, it needs to be done carefully, depending on the AR application type. For example, an action game in AR cannot be interrupted with prompts while a player is playing the game. Therefore, only prewarnings will be necessary. An app such as Google Maps requires continuous attention to the surroundings and will not hinder the AR experience if the user looks away from the app.

In Unity, one can use the *Input.Gyro* to get access to the gyroscope sensor of the mobile device. The *attitude* variable of the Gyro object is a vector that matches the device's orientation. This can be used to check if the device is placed perpendicular to the floor surface for a long time, assuming that the device is being used for a longer period. Use a *coroutine* or a *timer* value to check the time that the device has been in use, and if it reaches a predetermined amount, show a simple UI prompt at the top of the view without hindering the experience of the user. Refer to Figure 12.3:

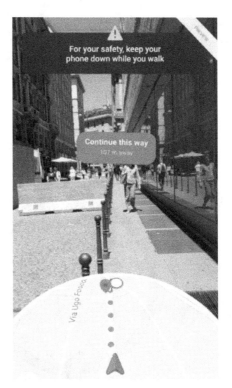

FIGURE 12.3 Google Maps AR app showing a warning.
Source: Photo by frequentmiler.

GUIDE THE USER WITH THE INTERACTIONS

AR-related interactions within an AR application can be novel to a user. Scanning an environment or a marker, tapping on the floor, or another inter-active point are not everyday interactions that a person would do with their mobile phones. Developers design apps based on their personal experiences, assuming that users would follow their thinking patterns. This is a false assumption, as any app development requires frequent user testing and feedback. Adding novel interaction methods into the mix makes people dislike the experience that the app provides.

Therefore, adding visual guidance for every interaction is a must-have in AR applications. This also validates some of the technical challenges in context recognition. As an example, in a marker-less AR application that uses simultaneous localization and mapping (SLAM) to track the planes in a physical environment, the camera should be moved to recognize the movement patterns and predict the planes. For this, a user must rotationally move the device. Many AR applications that use marker-less AR show an animation of a hand moving a phone to indicate how the device should be moved to enable tracking, as shown in Figure 12.4:

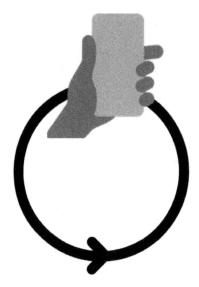

FIGURE 12.4 Animation of a hand holding a smartphone.

A similar interface can be used in Unity by showing a moving image placed on a canvas. Unity has an integration animation tool that can create a simple animation of the image moving in circles. The animation can be hidden once the app identifies at least one plane in the environment. This is possible in AR Foundation by accessing and subscribing to the *planesChanged* event in *AR Plane Manager*. This action will be invoked whenever a new plane is added, updated, or removed.

For a marker-based AR application, a UI with a translucent image of the marker that needs to be tracked can be placed, as shown in Figure 12.5. One can also add an info carousel for users to understand how to interact with the markers that need to be scanned. The user should always be aware of what is to be done next. App stores, such as the Apple App Store, do not allow developers to publish marker-based AR apps if the app does not indicate what and how to scan and if the proper interaction instructions are not given within the app. Therefore, it is a must to consider when publishing apps.

When the scanning has begun, and the objects are placed, the app should instruct what users can and cannot do with *coach marks* and interaction animations. This helps many users get used to new interactions, such as tapping on the floor, pinching, and other interactions.

Refer to Figure 12.5:

FIGURE 12.5 Initializing UI element prototypes for marker-based AR applications.

BE MINDFUL OF THE SCALE

An AR app can be experienced in different ways. It can be on a table, inside a room, or outside. When placing objects, the developers should scale the experience in a way that matches the surroundings in which it is placed. In Unity, scaling objects that are placed is not recommended. Components such as particle systems do not like scaling since the particles have to be scaled hierarchically. Moreover, movement and physics may not work as intended if the objects are scaled.

If an AR Foundation is being used for marker-less AR, one can scale the camera, which scales the view spectrum of the camera origin. When the camera origin is scaled, the objects that are not scaled will create the illusion of being scaled. Therefore, by measuring the distance from the camera to the floor or the tracked plane, one can decide whether it is a small or large space, such as outdoors.

The scale of the objects in the AR experience involves the ability for exploration. One of the main points of AR applications is the flexibility of movement. Therefore, use that to create room for exploration. Games such as Pokémon Go and Minecraft worlds provide better exploration capabilities by making the objects placed around and scaling them up so users do not have to look for the objects around them.

Refer to Figure 12.6:

FIGURE 12.6 The scale of the experience depends on the environment.
Source: Backgrounds by Freepik.

USE AUDIO AND VISUAL CUES

An AR application relies on media. It requires people to freely move their devices to engage; however, it is necessary to implement different audio-visual cues to get a better feeling for the interactive elements. This allows users to feel the interactions more naturally and helps them find their way around the application. Some audio-visual cues that can be added to one's AR app are discussed in the following subsections.

Indicating Objects That Are out of Camera View

Imagine AR content placed in a virtual space, but the camera is moved out of the 3D model view. Finding one's way back to where the 3D model could be assisted by showing a UI visual marker representing the direction of the object, as shown in Figure 12.7:

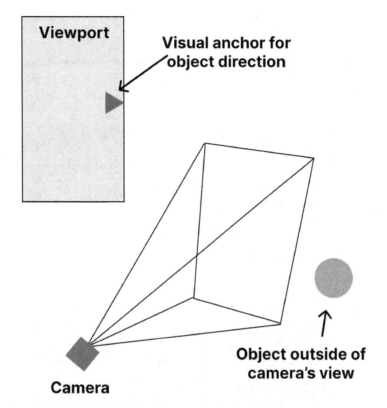

FIGURE 12.7 Showing a visual anchor for an AR object outside the viewport.

In Unity, this can be done by referencing the target object as *target*, the camera as *cam*, and the anchor on a screen space canvas as *arrow* with the following C# snippet within an update method:

```
1. var pos = cam.WorldToViewportPoint(target.position);
2. var xx = Mathf.Lerp(0, Screen.width, pos.x) - 1;
3. var yy = Mathf.Lerp(0, Screen.height, pos.y) - 1;
4. arrow.position = new Vector2(xx,yy);
```

Adding Visual Markers on Interactable Objects

When there are interactable objects in an AR app, because many are 3D models, it can be hard to distinguish between an interactable object and a noninteractable one. Therefore, the interactable objects must stand out from the other objects. As an example, imagine exploring a 3D art AR installation, with some elements that one is supposed to interact with. The tapped object can have a simple visual indicator to stand out:

- A simple glowing effect on the 3D model can be done using the particle system of Unity.
- With an outline using custom shaders URP, a shader graph can create and apply an outline shader.
- Using text annotations with interaction tooltips. Looking at a text from different angles can break immersion. Use the *Billboard* concept so that a text object is always rotated toward the camera. This way, the text will always be facing the camera.
- Simple animations such as growing and shrinking. Animations can be made easily using the animation tool within Unity.

An example of how an object can stand out, demonstrating the preceding examples, is shown in Figure 12.8:

FIGURE 12.8 Visual cues to stand out (glowing, outline, tooltip, and animations).

Using 3D Audio Cues

Adding audio is always an improvement to the feel of the application. Having a simple audio cue for taps and movement of objects that are similar to real sounds can enhance the experience. Apart from normal sound effects, Unity Audio Source supports 3D sound that can be heard based on proximity.

Imagine an AR app that requires one to get closer to an object that emits a sound effect. Make the sound effect realistic by setting up the audio source to emit sounds based on proximity, which increases its volume when the user is closer to the object. This can be done by setting up 3D audio settings in the `Audio Source` component, as shown in Figure 12.9:

FIGURE 12.9 Enable 3D spatial audio in the Audio Source component.

In any audio source attached to a game object in a scene, set the spatial blend to 3D. Change the volume roll-off to linear and set the min and max distances as required to have proper 3D spatial audio in AR.

Showing Physical Properties in Visual Cues

In some AR applications, there may be different objects representing different physical properties, such as weight, color, speed, and so on. Visual elements can easily represent some properties, while some cannot. For example, weight cannot be presented directly in a visual format. Imagine an interaction allowing users to pick and move physical objects in AR. A simple way to show the weight with a visual cue is to have a simple line that bends depending on the weight/mass of the object. This will provide the illusion that the object has a weight, and tweaking the bending of the curve can make the users feel the difference of each object that is being lifted. Figure 12.10 shows a simple example of how it can look in 3D:

FIGURE 12.10 Using a curved line to represent weight.

The following is a code snippet that can be used to tap (the code uses a mouse click) and move an object by lifting. It uses a spring joint to attach to the object with different masses and curves using linear interpolation:

```
1.  using Unity.VisualScripting;
2.  using UnityEngine;
3.
4.  public class LiftObject: MonoBehaviour {
5.    [SerializeField] private float curveHeight;
6.    [SerializeField] private Material lineMat;
7.    [SerializeField] private Gradient lineColor;
8.    [SerializeField] private int lineFrequency = 20;
9.
10.   private Camera cam;
11.   private SpringJoint joint;
12.   private LineRenderer line;
13.   private Rigidbody pointRB;
14.   private Rigidbody objectRB;
15.   private RaycastHit hit;
16.   private GameObject pointer;
17.   private Vector3 localHitpoint;
18.   private bool isConnected;
19.
20. Vector3 pointA, pointB, pointC, pointAB, pointBC;
21.
22.   void Start() {
```

```
23.     cam = Camera.main;
24.     isConnected = false;
25. }
26.
27.  private void Update() {
28.     if (Input.GetMouseButtonDown(0)) {
29.     if (!isConnected && Physics.Raycast(cam.
   ScreenPointToRay(Input.
mousePosition), out hit)) {
30.          if (!hit.transform.CompareTag("liftable"))
31.            return;
32.
33.          isConnected = true;
34.           localHitpoint = hit.transform.
   InverseTransformPoint(hit.
point);
35.
36.          pointer = new GameObject("pointer");
37.          pointer.transform.position = hit.point;
38.          pointer.transform.parent = cam.transform;
39.
40.          pointRB = pointer.AddComponent < Rigidbody > ();
41.          pointRB.isKinematic = true;
42.          objectRB = hit.transform.GetComponent < Rigidbody >
   ();
43.
44.          joint = objectRB.AddComponent < SpringJoint > ();
45.          joint.spring = 500;
46.          joint.damper = 1;
47.          joint.tolerance = 0.001 f;
48.          joint.connectedBody = pointRB;
49.
50.          line = gameObject.AddComponent < LineRenderer > ();
51.          line.material = lineMat;
52.          line.startWidth = 0.01 f;
53.          line.endWidth = 0.005 f;
54.          line.colorGradient = lineColor;
```

```
55.           line.positionCount = lineFrequency;
56.       } else {
57.         //clear line, rotate and drop object
58.         isConnected = false;
59.         isConnected = false;
60.         Destroy(pointer.gameObject);
61.         Destroy(line);
62.       }
63.
64.   }
65.
66.   if (isConnected && pointer != null) {
67.     if (line != null) {
68.         pointA = cam.ScreenToWorldPoint(new Vector3(Screen.
   width, 0, 1));
69.         pointC = hit.transform.TransformPoint(localHitpoint);
70.         pointB = pointA + (pointC - pointA) / 2 + Vector3.up
   * curveHeight * objectRB.mass;
71.
72.         for (int i = 0; i < lineFrequency; i++) {
73.             pointAB = Vector3.Lerp(pointA, pointB, i /
   (float) lineFrequency);
74.             pointBC = Vector3.Lerp(pointB, pointC, i /
   (float)
lineFrequency);
75.
76.             line.SetPosition(i, Vector3.Lerp(pointAB, pointBC,
   i / (float) lineFrequency));
77.         }
78.     }
79.   }
80. }
81. }
```

FREE FLOW RESTRICTIONS

One of the biggest use cases of AR applications is the ability to freely move the virtual camera, which moves with the physical device to explore. 3D applications use different methods to build interactions, which users can easily identify by moving the camera. For example, imagine an AR treasure hunt game that requests players to guess the content inside a 3D box in AR. Having the flexibility to move the camera around, users can peek inside the 3D model and see how it has been implemented. Sometimes, accidentally peeking into a 3D model can break the immersion of the experience.

In order to stop users from peeking inside 3D models, they can be configured to send an event to the UI to block the view by adding an overlay. The event can be triggered either using trigger colliders or checking the distance from the camera to the center of the object.

Figure 12.11 is an example overlay that can be used to inform users to move the device away if it collides with a 3D model in the scene.

This can sometimes create unnecessary performance issues due to unneeded collision requirements. Therefore, it is best to choose only the objects that could break immersion or be unfair to the rules of the AR application:

FIGURE 12.11 UI overlay to inform users not to clip objects.

AR INTERACTIONS

Interacting with elements in AR through a smartphone application can call for different types of touch input. Most of the touch inputs can be converted to realistic interactions in order to manipulate objects. Previous chapters discussed how different interactions allow users to move, scale, and rotate objects, using tap and place and sometimes autorecognizable implementations. When it comes to interacting with 3D elements in an AR world, there can be certain design considerations that one can integrate to make these interactions smooth. Some of them are discussed in the following subsections.

Using a Reticle to Interact with Smaller Objects

A *reticle* is a small UI point that can be placed as an overlay on the app screen. Instead of touching a smaller object that can be covered by a finger, one can use a button on the screen to point and select it. This will increase the precision of selecting an object in AR rather than tapping directly above the object. In Unity, this can be done by casting a ray from the screen midpoint toward the camera's forward direction.

Refer to Figure 12.12:

FIGURE 12.12 Using a reticle with a button instead of a direct tap.

Interacting with Objects Further from the Camera

AR allows users to move the camera freely. This can cause direct interactable objects to appear smaller when the camera moves further away. Suppose the app depends on touch-based interactions (touch to select an object or press a button in AR, and so on). In that case, the developer must either switch the interaction to a reticle or find another way to interact with the object. Moving back and forth between different interaction methods can confuse the user. Therefore, a simple way to allow interaction with objects that appear smaller is to change the size of the collision boundaries to match the size of a finger regardless of the object it is in. Figure 12.13 shows an example of how the *sphere collider* of an object changes the size of the collision boundary concerning the distance it has from the camera.

In the example, the distance between the camera with the object has been made indirectly proportional to the scale of the sphere collider, keeping a minimum and a maximum value it can take. On the left side, it shows the distance to the object from the camera when it is closer and away from the object. The right side shows how the object appears from the camera to the user. As it can be inspected, touching on the object in both scenarios can make it selectable due to the scale of the collider.

Refer to Figure 12.13:

FIGURE 12.13 Scaling the touch area for the distance of the object.

UI CONSIDERATIONS

Like ordinary smartphone applications, user interface and user experience design for AR applications can be similar to how users interact with non-AR elements such as buttons, pages, and screens; however, user interfaces for AR applications can either enhance or break the immersive experience for the user.

When in AR mode, keep the UI on the screen to a minimum. Users are in AR mode to move the device and explore the surroundings. Therefore, having different UI components, such as buttons, sliders, or toolbars from the side, can be highly distracting. Refer to the following:

▪ If UI elements require showing information, move them from the overlay canvas to a world space canvas that can be placed as an AR element in 3D space. This allows users to freely move their devices to focus on information that is relevant.

▪ Having UI pop-ups can be distracting. As an example, winning a reward in an AR game can be presented in a world space UI with additional 3D effects and sounds apart from the UI popup on the screen space of the device. Refer to Figure 12.14:

FIGURE 12.14 Using world space canvas instead of screen space pop-ups.

▪ Keep screen space user interface elements to a minimum. Have one or two buttons that open different toolbars or other UI elements but always hide them when the objective of the UI element is complete, as shown in Figure 12.15:

FIGURE 12.15 Less is better. Keep screen space UI to a minimum.

CONCLUSION

This chapter discussed some best practices for designing a handheld-based AR application. It mainly covered user experience considerations to enhance immersion. These best practices are not mandatory for a working AR app; however, having considered best to worst case scenarios and handling them while polishing the app for users to enjoy a smooth experience can make a big difference in the success of an AR app.

The next chapter will cover Unity-based optimization methods to smooth the 3D apps readers are developing.

KEY POINTS

- Safety is a key factor in building AR applications. Inform users of ways to be safe when using an AR app.
- Never leave users guessing. Inform them of all the interactions.
- Use visual and audio cues to convey AR object properties.
- Keep user interfaces for AR simple.
- Use world space user interfaces over screen space to enhance the AR experience.

QUESTION

1. What are some best practices that can be used when building an AR-based storytelling application? Explain with evaluations in terms of input methods and audio-visual user experiences.

AR App Performance Optimization

INTRODUCTION

Augmented reality (AR) applications running on mobile devices solve many challenges. AR renders 3D models and performs logic based on the codes written on top of the algorithms running for context recognition and camera input. Based on the software development kit (SDK) being used, the algorithm for context recognition can be different. Compared to a non-AR 3D interactive application, the number of resources an AR app requires from a mobile device is significantly larger.

Therefore, when building an AR app, there are resource limitations to adhere to. This involves reducing the rendering, processing, and memory required by an AR app. This chapter will describe some fundamental elements in Unity that AR application developers need to know to build a smooth AR application.

STRUCTURE

This chapter will discuss the following topics:

- Performance metrics
  - Frames per second
  - Tris and verts
  - Draw calls

- Optimization of a 3D app
  - Graphical processing unit (GPU) instancing
  - Static and dynamic batching
  - Occlusion culling and frustum culling
  - Textures and UV maps
  - Light baking
  - User interface (UI) optimizations
- Optimization considerations in coding

OBJECTIVES

After completion of this chapter, readers will be able to optimize an AR app to reduce the resource requirements needed. There will also be instructions on the key metrics for application performance and necessary actions to mitigate any performance-related challenges in an app.

PERFORMANCE METRICS

In any application, the performance of the application can be measured by looking at some metrics. The smoothness of the application and the time it takes to load are some of the visual metrics that can be inspected in many 3D applications. Just like running a high-end 3D game on a low-end computer makes the game crash and lag, AR apps can cause similar issues when running on devices with fewer resources, such as mobile devices. This section will explain some of the key performance metrics that can be used to determine the smoothness of the application.

Frames Per Second

In running any application, the device it runs allocates its power for calculations and renders everything on the screen. In order to animate objects and move from one screen to another, the processor clears and redraws everything at a high frequency.

If the device takes longer to process calculations, it takes longer pauses in between redraws on the screen. This makes the screen update at a lower frequency. Having low-frequency screen redraws becomes visually significant as it creates a graphical lag on the screen. This frequency of drawing the screen is known as *frames per second* (*FPS* or *fps*).

High FPS implies that the app takes little time to process, which validates an optimized application. If the logic of an app is expensive and if it does heavy calculations, the FPS count would drop, and the overall experience is hindered. Therefore, FPS can be considered a performance metric to validate whether an app is optimized enough.

Any app running at over 30 fps on a normal device can be optimized enough. High-end devices running highly optimized apps can go over 100 fps, or even 400 fps, based on how big the app is. Anything lower than 30 fps is visually significant and can be considered neither optimized nor running on a recommended device.

Figure 13.1 features the varying movement of an object with different FPS:

Frames Per Second (FPS)

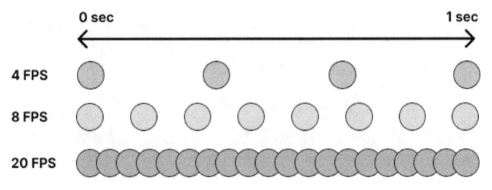

FIGURE 13.1 How the movement of an object can be represented with different FPS.

Many AR SDKs are optimized enough to render content that clips to higher fps, but with limitations. If the app runs 60 fps, it is 60 times per second that the SDK should calculate the context information, such as the knowledge of planes around the device. If it runs 30 fps, that means that the device can take a rest compared to 60 fps. For Apple iPhone, ARKit usually runs at 60 fps, while many Android devices that are compatible with ARCore have a maximum of 30 fps even though their logic is highly optimized. Only Google Pixel devices run ARCore with 60 fps.

The FPS of a Unity scene at runtime can be checked via the `Stats` section in the `Game` window, as shown in Figure 13.2:

FIGURE 13.2 FPS counter in game window—Stats.

There can be multiple factors that can hinder the FPS apart from the expensive calculations the scripts in it do. The number of objects in the scene, lighting, and UI elements can cause massive drops in fps, if not optimized properly. The second section of this chapter will explain different ways to improve fps.

Tris and Verts

Every object in a 3D scene is rendered in a 3D world. Objects rendered in a 3D world are made out of points (vertices) and lines connecting the points (edges). Combining edges creates triangles (tris). In order to have smooth 3D models, the models should have more vertices and triangles. All triangle information should be loaded into device memory, and they have to be rendered individually to be visible through the screen. Therefore, it requires higher processing and rendering power to draw an object with a greater number of triangles compared to a model with fewer triangles.

Figure 13.3 shows how the triangles of a scene can be viewed through the Wireframe view and how they are displayed in the stats:

FIGURE 13.3 How triangles of a scene can be viewed through the Wireframe view and how they are displayed in stats.

Having a higher number of 3D models or having 3D models with high poly counts (triangles) will cause the app to slow and hinder the user experience. Therefore, it is necessary to use 3D models that are low poly with lesser triangle counts. One can use a 3D model viewer or 3D modeling tools such as Blender to view the number of triangles and even use them to reduce the triangles as well; however, the lower the poly count, the less the object appears to be realistic in AR. Therefore, a balance is needed along with other 3D modeling tips, such as using *normal maps* and *height maps* to make visual illusions that provide details to low poly 3D models.

Draw Calls

In 3D applications, it takes numerous iterations to render a scene to be visible. For example, a drawing of an object with a light next to it requires the object vertices to be rendered, as well as the color, shadows, and any postprocessing effects, which accumulate into multiple draw calls. In Unity, different materials are rendered separately, and different objects are rendered separately. Figure 13.4 shows how a rendering of a single game object has taken multiple steps to render on the game view. It is also possible to check the number of batches that Unity has taken to render a simple scene:

FIGURE 13.4 Some steps of rendering a single frame (left) and the number of batches it has taken to render the frame (right).

This implies one conclusion: having a higher number of draw calls and large batch count leads to diminished performance of the application. Therefore, certain actions become necessary to reduce the number of draw calls and batches to render a frame quickly.

OPTIMIZATION OF A 3D APP

This section will go through some methods that are useful to improve the performance of a 3D application both graphically and programmatically. The focus of this section covers some basics to improve the performance metrics discussed in the previous section.

GPU Instancing

When Unity renders an object with a material, it takes one draw call per object per material. GPU instancing can be used to draw one material for all the objects in the scene in just one draw call. Figure 13.5 is an example of a Unity scene with 10,000 objects, using the same object and the same material without GPU instancing. This scene with the Unity project is provided along with the book.

Open the scene *02-GPU instancing* to test. The figure shows that it has taken over 19,000 draw calls to render the frame with a fps of 90, without GPU instancing. With GPU instancing, one gets 42 batches with a higher fps of around 150.

NOTE   *If one is using Universal Render Pipeline (URP), there is a batcher that comes with it, which supersedes the GPU instancing. One may not get the same result with URP unless the objects are batched (this will be covered in the next subsection).*

Refer to Figure 13.5:

FIGURE 13.5 Rendering thousands of objects without and with GPU instancing.

GPU instancing can be enabled by checking the `GPU Instancing` option in the material. Unity's standard lit and unlit shaders support GPU instancing by default. For those using a custom shader, that should support GPU instancing to work properly with Unity. Figure 13.6 shows a material that uses the Unity standard shader that allows enabling GPU instancing:

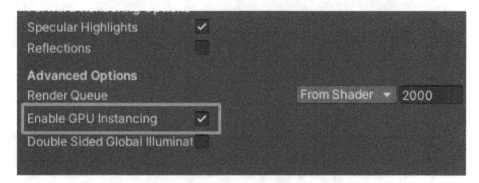

FIGURE 13.6 Enabling GPU instancing of a material.

Static and Dynamic Batching

Another way to reduce batching and draw calls is to define the objects that need to be batched together. This allows Unity to get objects with the same mesh and batch them into a single batch, and render is done in just one draw call. This is similar to GPU instancing, and depending on the application, developers must check what is best to use—batching or GPU instancing.

The 3D models in the app are not moving and thus are static; one can batch all those objects as *static*. This can be done by selecting all the static objects and enabling `Batching Static` from the static drop-down in the inspector window, as shown in Figure 13.7. If the objects are moving, the objects can be batched dynamically. Usually, static batching is more performant than dynamic batching since it does not transform object vertices in the CPU. Unity, by default, supports dynamic batching. Using URP, one can enable and disable the dynamic batcher in the URP settings.

Figure 13.7 shows the difference between the batches with and without static batching:

FIGURE 13.7 Difference of the batch count with static batching.

Refer to Figure 13.8:

FIGURE 13.8 Enabling static batching in Unity.

Occlusion Culling and Frustum Culling

In 3D applications, there is no need to render any 3D object that is out of the camera's view frustum. This is mainly because the user does not see the objects from the camera. This is known as *frustum culling*. In some scenarios, 3D objects can be occluded (covered) from other 3D objects. In this scenario, the camera does not need to render the covered objects. This is known as *occlusion culling*.

In Unity, both occlusion culling and frustum culling occur by default. This is usually dynamic and checks which are less performant compared to static methods. If any objects are static (not moving, such as buildings, trees, and so on), these objects can also contribute to static occlusion culling. Like static batching, one can choose which object must be statically occluded using the inspector window. Figure 13.9 shows a simple scene with frustum culling applied to objects only within the camera frustum.

In addition to rendering, one can manually activate different functions of game objects in one's code by checking `renderer.isVisible`, a variable of the object. For example, imagine an AR 3D object that calls an application programming interface (API) to retrieve data every second. This does not need to happen if the user is not looking at the object. Checking the `render.isVisible` variable, one can pause sending the API request if the value is false and resume it again if it is true.

Refer to Figure 13.9:

FIGURE 13.9 Frustrum culling in Unity.

Textures and UV Maps

In a previous subsection, it was learned that every material on every object contributes to one batch call. If a single object has x number of materials, Unity will take x number of iterations to render the complete model. Having a 3D model with multiple meshes (different 3D objects within one object) also increases the number of draw calls required to render the image.

Some 3D models have multiple materials, which define the colors of different faces of a 3D mesh. Figure 13.10 is an example of such a 3D model, which has different colors of the 3D model, and they are represented by different materials, via the mesh renderer. Having just one light and rendering a single color in background, the model has taken altogether 22 batches to render the scene:

FIGURE 13.10 3D model with multiple materials.

For an optimized 3D application, this is overkill. Having multiple materials to render a small portion of a 3D model can drastically increase the number of batch counts.

One can use textures to have multiple colors on a 3D model with just one material. Textures are 2D images that can be wrapped around a 3D model. There is another concept known as *UV maps*, where different faces of a 3D mesh can be placed on different position values of a texture to map colors. 3D modeling tools like Blender can use a single texture to map different faces of the 3D model to it.

Figure 13.11 is an example of how a color palette texture is mapped (UV mapped) to different parts of the 3D model (eyes, nose, ears, and so on) in Blender 3D modeling software:

FIGURE 13.11 Setting up a texture with a UV map to create a single material.

Once importing this 3D model to Unity, just with a texture on a single material, the batch count of the frame is reduced to 6 from 22, compared to before, as shown in Figure 13.12. Visually, both objects look alike:

FIGURE 13.12 The same object with a single material and texture.

Light Baking

The amount of lighting is another component that helps increase the number of draw calls of a frame. In Unity, there are different kinds of lights—for example, directional light, point light, spotlight, and area light, to name a few. These lights contribute to additional draw calls since every light, every object needs to be illuminated and rendered apart from its original rendering iterations. Therefore, more lights imply more processing power needed and, hence, the reduction of FPS and the increase of draw calls.

Consider a 3D model in AR that does not move over time. The shadows of the object may not move either. In this case, this 3D object can be marked as static. All the static objects can be attributed to a concept known as *light baking*. This means the lights of the scene, its color changes, and shadows can be *painted* onto one giant texture that can be placed over the scene. Light baking might not be useful for AR apps since objects can be dynamic and moved around in an experience; however, it is beneficial to include in 3D apps as needed.

In Unity, all the objects that are not moving should be marked as static. Lights that do not contribute to any dynamic objects but make shadows on static objects can be marked as *Baked* as their light mode from the light components. Baking lights require the use of a *light mapper*. Unity already contains a light mapper that can take all the bake lights and static objects to generate a light map texture. This can be viewed from `Window | Rendering | Lighting`. The lighting window has a `Generate Lighting` option under `Scene` tab, which initiates the light mapper that generates the baked content. Figure 13.13 shows the same scene with dynamic lights alongside baked lights, along with the number of batches it renders:

FIGURE 13.13 A scene with dynamic light and baked lights.

UI Optimizations

In Unity, Canvas objects are used to include user interfaces. Like 3D models, Unity renders any UI content over 2D meshes. Unity's *Canvas*, the object, holds the rendering of all the underlying components of the UI.

Many developers use a single canvas element to hold as many UI components as possible. While this option is not highly resource intensive for smaller UI elements, large games with highly refreshing UI can have a huge overhead in recalculating the rendering of UI elements. This is due to how the Unity canvas is built. When a single element updates within a canvas game object, the canvas refreshes its children to update the renderer. This is an iterative for all the elements within the canvas.

To overcome this, add as many canvases as needed to separate highly changing UI elements and static UI elements. In AR world space, canvases can contain canvases within canvases to omit updating unnecessary elements. Text that does not update can be added to a texture and be placed in a single material to be added to *quad* 3D planes.

Using a `texture atlas` instead of single images can render many UI elements with 2D sprites in one batch. To achieve this, one needs to install the *2D sprite* package from Unity's package manager. Figure 13.14 shows an arrangement of 2D assets in a UI which has taken 6 batches to render:

FIGURE 13.14 Rendering UI elements with different sprites.

One can use all the sprites and group them into a single *atlas* in Unity, which generates a single image of all the sprites combined. This can be created with the 2D sprites pack installed by right-clicking any folder area and clicking `Create | 2D | Sprite Atlas`.

Select the generated atlas asset and choose the folders containing all the sprites. Also enable `Sprite packing` from the Unity editor by going to `Edit | Project Settings | Editor`. As shown in Figure 13.15, picking the `Pack Preview` button in the sprite atlas generates a single image with all the sprites combined, reducing the batches to 3. For a smaller number of sprites, this is a 50% optimization that becomes increasingly optimized with more sprites/2D images in the scene:

FIGURE 13.15 Using the same UI elements with sprites packed.

OPTIMIZATION CONSIDERATIONS IN CODING

So far, the discussion has concerned tips for graphics-related objectives to optimize a 3D app in Unity. Another key objective to consider is how optimized the code is. Any code written in any language turns into machine readable code that performs instructions on the CPU. How much work one allocates to the CPU and how much memory one utilizes from the *random access memory (RAM)* determines how smooth an app can be if all graphical optimizations are achieved.

Following are some objectives that one can fulfill in developing any 3D application:

■ *Cache variables*: Creating variables takes up space in memory. If one is reusing variables such as a component reference, which uses the `Get-Component` method, calling the reference every frame within the update method can cause a massive performance hit since the method itself is a search method that must iterate through the components attached to a game object. Therefore, having a variable at the class level and assigning the component only during a single method call, such as the `Awake` or `Start` method, can cache the variable for later use.

■ *Reduce using Find methods:* Unity, by default has a series of `Find` methods that allows one to search for different objects and components by either name or type. This is a search method that could iterate over all the objects and all the components in a scene. This is very resource heavy, which can slow an application's performance if it runs at a high frequency. Instead, use static variables and design patterns such as *singleton* and dictionary data types to quickly get references to existing objects and components without `Find` methods.

■ *Avoid using iterations within iterations:* If there are any iterative code blocks, having more iterative code blocks within iterative code can cause code to run for longer periods. This is due to the exponential nature of how iterations work in code. For example, having a `for` loop with 10 iterations within another for loop with 10 iterations will have 100 iterations of code execution. Running this within the Unity update method will perform 100 iterations per frame. This can sometimes be unnecessary for the code. Therefore, look for ways to reduce the iterations by filtering different code parameters. One can also use recursive functions and other optimized algorithms to replace multiple iterations.

■ *Remove debug code in production:* When developing any code, using `Debug` methods can be very useful for understanding code values, whether the execution reaches the code, and even drawing debug elements in scene view; however, these codes do not reach the final application. Rather, they will still be executed within the app. More debug code, such as `Debug. Log` handles strings that can cause additional unnecessary processing power. Therefore, remove all the `debug.log` code from the code before building the app.

⬚ There are many different algorithms that can be used to solve different problems. Even if each algorithm achieves the same result, their execution can be different. Some algorithms perform well, while others do not. Developing apps continuously trains individuals to use the best and most optimized algorithm that suits their requirements.

CONCLUSION

This chapter went through some of the basic optimization techniques one can consider getting better outcomes for a 3D application. Developing a 3D application can be overwhelming, with different spectrums that have to be considered. Adding AR on top of that can increase the workload for building a polished AR application; however, keeping optimization in mind from the start can be highly beneficial in the long run, as it does not require additional effort at the end to redo one's methods.

This chapter ends the complete series of building AR applications. Throughout all the chapters, different methods of AR development were identified using different SDKs. These tools change frequently. They update with optimized algorithms, and the ways of implementing them can change rapidly; however, the principles of how things were done during the first chapters of this book remain the same. Developers must keep practicing by building different types of projects that force them to read documentation, follow best practices, and understand different ways of building AR applications.

KEY POINTS

⬚ Frames per second (FPS), triangle count in 3D models, and draw calls are some of the performance metrics that determine the performance of a 3D app.

⬚ GPU instancing can be used to group the rendering of objects with the same material and reduce draw calls.

⬚ Batching can reduce the batch count when rendering the same object. This can be static or dynamic.

⬚ Frustrum and occlusion culling can reduce the overhead of rendering objects not visible to the camera.

⬚ Reducing the number of materials and different meshes can improve an app's performance massively.

⬚ Combining textures into one atlas reduces the number of draw calls.

- Baking lights of static objects omit additional rendering passes to calculate light estimations. This reduces the draw calls on the screen.
- Processes of the app can be further optimized by following code optimization techniques.

QUESTIONS

1. What is the purpose of level of detail (LOD) systems in Unity, and how can they improve graphical performance?

2. How can Unity's occlusion culling feature enhance graphical performance in large scenes?

3. Explain the benefits of using a sprite atlas in Unity's 2D rendering and how it optimizes graphical performance.

   Answers appear in the appendix.

ANSWER KEY FOR CHAPTER QUESTIONS

CHAPTER 1

1. b.

2. b.

3. a.

4. a.

CHAPTER 2

1. b.

2. c.

3. a.

4. b.

5. d.

CHAPTER 3

1. Unity, HoloLens, Windows SDK.

2. Spark AR, Smartphones, no separate SDK.

3. Unity, Smartphones, Niantic Lightship.

4. Unity, Smartphones, Vuforia.

5. Web Development or 8th Wall, Web, Web XR, or 8th Wall.

CHAPTER 4

1. c.

2. a.

3. d.

4. b.

CHAPTER 5

1. c.

2. b.

3. d.

CHAPTER 6

1. a.

2. d.

3. c.

4. a.

5. c.

CHAPTER 7

1. Android SDK.

2. Developer options and USB Debugging.

3. Sign it with a certificate.

4. A breakpoint.

CHAPTER 8

Results will vary.

CHAPTER 9

Results will vary.

CHAPTER 10

Results will vary.

CHAPTER 11

Results will vary.

CHAPTER 12

Results will vary.

CHAPTER 13

1. Level of detail (LOD) systems in Unity are used to optimize graphical performance by reducing the complexity of 3D models as they move further away from the camera. This means that objects that are distant from the player will have lower-detail versions, reducing the number of polygons and textures being rendered. This optimization technique helps improve frame rates and reduces GPU and CPU workload, resulting in smoother gameplay and better performance.

2. Unity's occlusion culling is a technique that enhances graphical performance by determining which objects are not visible to the camera and therefore do not need to render. By identifying and excluding occluded objects from the rendering process, Unity reduces the number of draw calls and minimizes the overall workload on the GPU. This results in improved frame rates and allows developers to create larger and more detailed game environments without sacrificing performance.

3. A sprite atlas in Unity is a texture that contains multiple individual sprites packed into a single image. By using a sprite atlas, Unity reduces the number of texture swaps during rendering, which significantly improves graphical performance. When multiple sprites are combined into one atlas, there are fewer draw calls, and the GPU can efficiently render multiple sprites with a single pass. This optimization technique is particularly useful in 2D games with many different sprites on the screen at once, leading to smoother gameplay and better frame rates.

INDEX